# The Classics of Marxism

## Volume One

# The Classics of Marxism
## Volume One

*Manifesto of the Communist Party*
by Karl Marx and Frederick Engels

*Socialism: Utopian and Scientific*
by Frederick Engels

*The State and Revolution*
by V.I. Lenin

*The Transitional Program*
by Leon Trotsky

wellred
.books

London

# THE CLASSICS OF

# MARXISM
## Volume One

Published by Wellred Books, August 2013.
Copyright © Wellred Books. All rights reserved.

Editing and layout for this edition by
*Wellred Books*

Cover design by Mark Rahman.

**United States distribution:**
Wellred Books
PO Box 18302
Minneapolis, MN 55418

**United Kingdom distribution:**
Wellred Books
PO Box 50525
London
E14 6WG
England

Email: sales@marxistbooks.com
Wellred USA online sales:
www.marxistbooks.com

Email: books@wellredbooks.net
Wellred U.K. online sales:
www.wellredbooks.net

ISBN: 978 1 900 007 49 8

# CONTENTS

# INTRODUCTION

## Alan Woods

The publication by the US Workers' International League (WIL) in 2007 of the book *Four Marxist Classics* was an excellent initiative, and its republication for a British audience is very welcome, especially at this moment. The fact that it is to be turned into a series, and this is only the first volume, is even more welcome. At no time in history have the ideas of Marxism been more relevant and necessary than now.

The crisis of world capitalism, which began just over a year later with the financial crash of 2008 and is still continuing, has set in motion a revolutionary wave that is affecting one country after another. The dramatic events in Tunisia and Egypt were followed by the mass movement of the workers of Wisconsin in the USA, who chanted slogans like: "fight like an Egyptian" on their demonstrations.

The crisis of European capitalism has been reflected in the last twelve months by a wave of general strikes and mass demonstrations in France, Spain, Portugal, Italy and Greece. The mass movement that has broken out in cities and towns all over Spain, and led to the occupation of the central squares in Madrid and Barcelona, found an echo in Greece. In every major town the workers and youth have occupied the city centres, defying the police and the government. The revolutionary implications of these movements are obvious.

Britain has also been caught up in the general ferment, first with the sudden eruption of the youth towards the end of 2010, followed by the biggest demonstration called by the Trades Union Congress in history. On June 30 the public sector unions staged mass co-ordinated industrial action on a national scale involving up to 750,000 workers. In the autumn, millions of works are to be balloted for strike action over pensions, possibly fore-shadowing the biggest industrial movement since the General Strike of 1926. The class struggle is entering a new and higher stage.

## "Concentrated economics"

Lenin once wrote that politics is concentrated economics. It took an economic slump to upset the equilibrium of capitalism. Every government in the world has been striving ever since to restore the old equilibrium, with no sign of success. By bailing out the banks with vast sums of public money, the bourgeoisie has merely replaced bank defaults with the defaults of whole countries: first Iceland, then Greece, then Ireland, and Portugal have found themselves floundering like a man drowning on the high seas. Spain will be next, followed by Italy and Belgium. And Britain will not be far behind.

None of this was predicted by the bourgeois strategists. The economists obstinately denied that such a thing was possible. But the Marxists predicted it. In the preface to the US edition of *Four Marxist Classics*, I wrote the following:

"Like every other boom in history the present unstable boom will end in a slump. The only question is whether a crisis in China will topple the US economy into recession or whether a crisis in the USA will have the same effect in China. Either way the dominance of the world economy will assert itself. The illusion of the bourgeois that participation on the world market will solve all their problems will be exposed. All the factors that boosted the economic upswing in the last decade will turn into their opposite. Globalization will manifest itself as a global crisis of capitalism."

These lines were written in June 2007. One year later this prediction was confirmed by the biggest slump since the 1930s, the very thing that was not supposed to happen. All the "experts" of the bourgeoisie – the economists, politicians, bankers and university lecturers – repeatedly stated that such a crisis was no longer possible because they had learned the lessons of history. This confident assertion was answered long ago by Hegel who wrote in his introduction to The Philosophy of History: "What experience and history teach is this – that people and governments never have learned anything from history, or acted on principles deduced from it."

Now the bourgeois "experts" present a picture of perplexity. The bourgeois economists publicly proclaim the bankruptcy of their models and theories. Robert Solow, who won a Nobel Prize in 1987 for his work on economic growth, told *The Washington Post*: "I'm as puzzled as anyone else. I don't have any particular wisdom to sell."

*The Economist* (6 July, 2009) complained that Robert Lucas, hailed as "one of the greatest macroeconomists of his generation" and his followers are "making ancient and basic analytical errors all over the place". Harvard's Robert Barro, another towering figure in the discipline, is "making truly boneheaded arguments". And *The Economist* concludes that "the past 30 years of macroeconomics training at American and British universities" were a "costly waste of time".

Speaking at a conference in the London School of Economics, Paul Krugman of Princeton and the New York Times, and Willem Butler of the London School of Economics (LSE), respectively indicated that the world economic crisis is also a crisis of bourgeois economics. In the last of his Lionel Robbins lectures at the LSE on June 10, 2009, Krugman stated that most macroeconomics of the last 30 years was "spectacularly useless at best, and positively harmful at worst". And three years later they are no nearer to finding a solution.

## Tobogganing towards disaster

These prominent bourgeois economists admitted publicly in a kind of mea culpa that the economists did not grasp the origins of this crisis; failed to appreciate its worst symptoms; and cannot now agree about the cure. "In other words," wrote *The Economist*, "economists misread the economy on the way up, misread it on the way down and now mistake the right way out."

These words adequately express the current psychology of the bourgeoisie and its ideologists, who are unable to explain anything. To use a graphic expression in one of the works reproduced here, Trotsky's *Transitional Programme*, they are all "tobogganing towards disaster with their eyes closed."

Even worse was the plight of the leaders of New Labour, who had ditched any pretence of standing for socialism and swallowed the propaganda of the "free market economy" hook, line and sinker. Gordon Brown was the first to propose a giant handout to the banks, and actually boasted that he had set the agenda for the policy that was later followed by the EU and the USA.

Nowadays we no longer hear the argument repeated that the British government's bank bailout would solve the credit crunch. Instead its purpose was said to be "to avoid the collapse of the banking system." Yes, that is indeed the case. Without the massive injection of state aid the banks would have collapsed under the weight of colossal debts. But this argument leaves two things unsaid:

On a world scale the banking system continues to exist as a result of public money. This has not solved the crisis but only transforms a vast and unsustainable private debt into a vast and unsustainable public debt.

Three years and a general election later, this has been shown to be correct. Instead of banking insolvency we have state bankruptcy. We are entitled to ask what the politicians never ask: If the banks are able to survive by leaning on the crutches of the state, what is left of the "free market economy?" If the state underwrites the losses incurred by reckless speculation and bad investments, what is left of the argument that the bankers and capitalists deserve to be rewarded for risk taking?

If the bankers accept huge quantities of public money, by what right do they pay themselves huge bonuses, which are clearly rewarding incompetence and outright thievery? If the public is compelled to subsidise the bankers, does the public not have the right to take possession of the banks and run them according to the public interest?

In Britain, the prophets of New Labour, Brown and Darling, poured billions of pounds of public money into the pockets of the bankers in the form of loans and other guarantees. But there is a little problem here. The state does not have any money. It produces nothing but only takes a slice of the surplus value produced by the working class in the form of taxes. As I wrote in the *Socialist Appeal* on 14 October, 2008:

"This sum is far too large to come from taxes, so it will be borrowed. This increases the already high level of indebtedness of the British economy. It will impose a heavy burden on the taxpayer and impose severe restrictions on public spending for the foreseeable future."

The collapse of the finances of Iceland, Greece, Ireland and Portugal has forced one bailout after another on the more powerful economies of Europe, with Germany in first place. A collapse of Spain would be a far worse scenario. Germany would not be able to bail out an economy that is bigger than Greece, Ireland and Portugal put together. The implications for the European Union, and for Britain, are severe.

### Intensification of class struggle

Over a year before the slump I wrote in the 2007 Introduction to *Four Marxist Classics*:

"Everywhere the mood of the masses is changing. In Latin America there is a revolutionary ferment, which will intensify and spread to other continents. In Britain, the USA and other industrialised nations many people who previously did not question the existing social order are now asking questions. Ideas that previously were listened to by small numbers will find an echo among a far broader public. The ground is being prepared for an unprecedented upsurge of the class struggle on a world scale."

The outbreak of revolutions in Tunisia and Egypt and the mass upheavals in Spain and Greece are the clearest expression of this. The revolutionary awakening of the great Arab Nation is a development of world-historical significance. But it is only the most dramatic expression of a process that s beginning to unfold of a world scale, reflecting the fact that the crisis of capitalism is beginning to find its reflection in the consciousness of the masses.

Every attempt by the bourgeois and reformists to restore the economic equilibrium has the effect of destroying the social and political equilibrium. We see this very clearly in Greece and Spain. Now that the initial shock of mass unemployment has worn off, the workers of Europe are beginning to fight back. This poses a direct threat to the continued existence of capitalism.

These facts are a devastating answer to all those sceptics who argued that the workers would never fight. The working class will fight because it has no other alternative. But in order to fight effectively, courage and militancy are insufficient. It is necessary that the advanced guard of the class is armed with a clear perspective, a scientific method and a coherent programme and policy. This can only be provided by Marxism.

### The necessity of Marxism

Some have attempted to argue that the movements in Spain and Greece are proof that the revolution can succeed without any party, organisation and leadership. But such a line of argument is completely hollow. Many times in the history of warfare a big army composed of brave but untrained soldiers has been defeated by a smaller but disciplined and well trained army of professional troops led by skilled and experienced officers. To occupy the squares is a means of mobilising the masses in action. But in itself it is not enough. The ruling class may not be able to evict the protestors initially by force, but they can afford to wait until the movement begins to die down, and then act decisively to put an end to the "disturbances".

There are certain circumstances in which strikes and mass demonstrations can force the ruling class to make concessions. But this is not one of them. It goes without saying that Marxists will always be in the first line of any battle to improve the conditions of the working class. We will fight for any conquest, no matter how small, because the fight for socialism would be unthinkable without the day to day struggle for advance under capitalism. Only through a series of partial struggles, of a defensive and offensive character, can the masses discover their own strength and acquire the confidence necessary to fight to the end.

These movements are said to be purely spontaneous, like a stampede of startled antelopes on the plains of East Africa. To the degree that these movements may be said to be spontaneous, it is because the leaders of the existing mass organisations of the working class have provided no lead. On the contrary, the very organisations that were created by the working class to change society have become monstrous obstacles in the path of revolution. The bureaucratic apparatuses do not reflect the real angry mood that has been building up in society over a long period. It is no wonder, then, that the movement has come from below, outside these organisations and even directed against them.

The millions of people who have come out onto the streets and squares of Spain and Greece to oppose the policy of cuts and austerity do not trust the politicians and trade union leaders. And who can blame them? In both Greece and Spain the governments that are carrying out these attacks are supposed to be "socialist". The masses deposited their confidence in them, and find themselves betrayed. They conclude that in order to defend their interests they must not leave things to the politicians but must take action themselves.

This shows a correct revolutionary instinct. Those who sneer at the movement as "merely spontaneous" display their ignorance of the essence of a revolution, which is precisely the direct intervention of the masses in politics. This spontaneity is an enormous strength – but at the same time it will become a fatal weakness of the movement.

### The movement on a higher level

Of course, the mass movement will necessarily suffer from confusion in its initial stages. The masses can only overcome these shortcomings through their direct experience of the struggle. But it is absolutely necessary for the masses to pass beyond the initial confusion and naïveté, to grow and mature and the draw the correct conclusions.

Those "anarchist" leaders (yes, the anarchists also have leaders, or people who aspire to lead) who believe that confusion, organisational amorphousness and the absence of ideological definition are both positive and necessary play a pernicious role. It is like trying to maintain a child in a state of childishness, so that it is forever unable to talk, walk and think for itself.

In order to succeed it is necessary to take the movement to a higher level. This can only be done by linking it firmly to the movement of the workers in the factories and the trade unions. The slogan of the general strike comes to the fore. But even a general strike cannot solve the problems of society. It leads directly to the question of state power.

Confused and vacillating leaders are capable of producing only defeats and demoralisation. The struggle of the workers and youth would be infinitely easier if they were led by courageous and far-sighted people. In the course of struggle, the masses will put to the test every tendency and leader. They have weighed the leaders of the Pasok in the balance and found them wanting. They will soon discover the deficiencies of those accidental figures who appear in the early stages of the revolutionary movement like the foam that appears at the crest of the wave, and who will vanish just like the foam.

Through their experience, an increasing number of activists will come to see the need for a consistent revolutionary programme. This can only be provided by Marxism. Ideas which for decades were listened to by small groups will be eagerly sought out, first by hundreds, then by thousands and hundreds of thousands. What is required is, on the one hand, the patient preparatory work of the Marxist cadres, on the other hand, the concrete experience of the masses themselves.

### Marxism in Britain

Lenin once remarked that, for the masses, an ounce of practice is worth a ton of theory. That is quite true. Whether in Britain or in Greece, Egypt or the United States, the masses can only learn by experience. Yet Lenin and Trotsky, like Marx and Engels, devoted their entire lives to a careful study of theory and their works are a treasury of ideas that today are a vital part of the armoury of working class struggle. Here we have the accumulated wisdom of over 150 years of the class struggle, together with the most profound contributions to political economy, philosophy and sociology.

Historically Britain has played a most important role in the development of socialism and the working class movement. My Welsh compatriot, that mighty thinker Robert Owen, was one of the founding fathers of socialism. Together with the French utopian socialists, Saint Simon and Fourier, he exercised a powerful influence on the thinking of the youthful Marx and Engels. He not only proved that it was possible for the workers to run society without the aid of bankers and capitalists, but put forward the idea of a general strike (the Grand National Holiday). His writings on the future socialist society contain many brilliant insights.

The Chartists were the first workers' political party, and they succeeded in mobilising the working class independently of the bourgeoisie. The left wing Chartists (the 'Physical Force Men') advocated revolutionary tactics and politics that led to an armed uprising of the Welsh Chartists in Newport. Left wing Chartists like Ernest Jones were in contact with Marx and Engels, who worked in the British workers' movement for the better part of their lives.

Marx and Engels always paid tribute to the positive traits of the British workers; their organisational strength, their stubborn determination and deep-seated class instinct. But they were always aware of the weak side of British Labour: the tendency towards compromise and reformism, and above all the lack of theory, a narrow "practical" mentality and an aversion to abstract thinking and broad generalisations. The one man born in these islands with a serious claim to theoretical originality was James Connolly, the celebrated Irish Labour leader, revolutionary and martyr, who was in fact born in Edinburgh.

Historically, the British considered themselves superior to other Europeans in all things. They had bigger factories, better roads and trains, more inventions. And just as British exports proved the superiority of British manufacturing over cheap German imitations, what did British politics and philosophy have to learn from the Continent?

How times have changed! Though Britain emerged victorious from two World Wars, the last hundred years have been a history of one defeat after another on the world stage. The days of British glory are only a distant memory. The "Empire on which the sun never sets" has long vanished off the face of the earth. Britain's industry lies in ruins. Her exports have collapsed. Germany dominates Europe and the USA dominates the world. Britannia, who used to rule the waves, is now reduced to a second-rate island off the coast of Europe.

Despite the absurd illusions of Cameron and Clegg, Britain cannot remain aloof from the crisis that is sweeping through Europe. The future of Britain is one of heightened class struggle. An entirely new perspective opens up, one in which the old ideas will no longer be applicable. The changed situation demands new thinking. Today the marvellously profound ideas of Marxism are more relevant and necessary than ever. The new generation has rebelled against the old discredited formulas and is open to the revolutionary ideas of Marxism. It is to this generation that we dedicate this volume.

London, September, 2011

Frederick Engels in 1860

Karl Marx in 1861

# Manifesto of the Communist Party

## Karl Marx and Frederick Engels

*This pamphlet was commissioned by the Communist League in 1847
and was first published on February 21, 1848. It was co-written by
Karl Marx and Frederick Engels and is probably the most influential
political writing of all time. It outlines the basic perspectives of what
would subsequently be referred to as "Marxism." These ideas have
formed the basis for revolutionary struggles throughout the world up
to the present day.*

# Manifesto of the Communist Party

A spectre is haunting Europe—the spectre of communism. All the powers of old Europe have entered into a holy alliance to exorcise this spectre: pope and tsar, Metternich and Guizot, French Radicals and German police spies.

Where is the party in opposition that has not been decried as communistic by its opponents in power? Where is the opposition that has not hurled back the branding reproach of communism, against the more advanced opposition parties, as well as against its reactionary adversaries?

Two things result from this fact:

    I. Communism is already acknowledged by all European powers to be itself a power.

    II. It is high time that communists should openly, in the face of the whole world, publish their views, their aims, their tendencies, and meet this nursery tale of the spectre of communism with a manifesto of the party itself.

To this end, communists of various nationalities have assembled in London and sketched the following manifesto, to be published in the English, French, German, Italian, Flemish and Danish languages.

# I
# Bourgeois and Proletarians[1]

The history of all hitherto existing society[2] is the history of class struggles.

Freeman and slave, patrician and plebeian, lord and serf, guild-master[3] and journeyman, in a word, oppressor and oppressed, stood in constant opposition to one another, carried on an uninterrupted, now hidden, now open fight, a fight that each time ended, either in a revolutionary reconstitution of society at large, or in the common ruin of the contending classes.

In the earlier epochs of history, we find almost everywhere a complicated arrangement of society into various orders, a manifold gradation of social rank. In ancient Rome we have patricians, knights, plebeians, slaves; in the Middle Ages, feudal lords, vassals, guildmasters, journeymen, apprentices, serfs; in almost all of these classes, again, subordinate gradations.

---

1   By bourgeoisie is meant the class of modern capitalists, owners of the means of social production and employers of wage labor. By proletariat, the class of modern wage laborers who, having no means of production of their own, are reduced to selling their labor power in order to live. [Engels, 1888 English edition]

2   That is, all *written* history. In 1847, the prehistory of society, the social organization existing previous to recorded history, was all but unknown. Since then, August von Haxthausen (1792–1866) discovered common ownership of land in Russia, Georg Ludwig von Maurer proved it to be the social foundation from which all Teutonic races started in history, and, by and by, village communities were found to be, or to have been, the primitive form of society everywhere from India to Ireland. The inner organization of this primitive communistic society was laid bare, in its typical form, by Lewis Henry Morgan's (1818–61) crowning discovery of the true nature of the *gens* and its relation to the *tribe*. With the dissolution of the primeval communities, society begins to be differentiated into separate and finally antagonistic classes. I have attempted to retrace this dissolution in *The Origin of the Family, Private Property, and the State*, second edition, Stuttgart, 1886. [Engels, 1888 English Edition and 1890 German Edition (with the last sentence omitted)]

3   Guild-master, that is, a full member of a guild, a master within, not a head of a guild. [Engels, 1888 English Edition]

The modern bourgeois society that has sprouted from the ruins of feudal society has not done away with class antagonisms. It has but established new classes, new conditions of oppression, new forms of struggle in place of the old ones.

Our epoch, the epoch of the bourgeoisie, possesses, however, this distinct feature: it has simplified class antagonisms. Society as a whole is more and more splitting up into two great hostile camps, into two great classes directly facing each other—bourgeoisie and proletariat.

From the serfs of the Middle Ages sprang the chartered burghers of the earliest towns. From these burgesses the first elements of the bourgeoisie were developed.

The discovery of America, the rounding of the Cape, opened up fresh ground for the rising bourgeoisie. The East Indian and Chinese markets, the colonization of America, trade with the colonies, the increase in the means of exchange and in commodities generally, gave to commerce, to navigation, to industry, an impulse never before known, and thereby, to the revolutionary element in the tottering feudal society, a rapid development.

The feudal system of industry, in which industrial production was monopolized by closed guilds, now no longer sufficed for the growing wants of the new markets. The manufacturing system took its place. The guildmasters were pushed on one side by the manufacturing middle class; division of labor between the different corporate guilds vanished in the face of division of labor in each single workshop.

Meantime the markets kept ever growing, the demand ever rising. Even manufacture no longer sufficed. Thereupon, steam and machinery revolutionized industrial production. The place of manufacture was taken by the giant, modern industry; the place of the industrial middle class by industrial millionaires, the leaders of the whole industrial armies, the modern bourgeois.

Modern industry has established the world market, for which the discovery of America paved the way. This market has given an immense development to commerce, to navigation, to communication by land. This development has, in its turn, reacted on the extension of industry; and in proportion as industry, commerce, navigation, railways extended, in the same proportion the bourgeoisie developed, increased its capital, and pushed into the background every class handed down from the Middle Ages.

We see, therefore, how the modern bourgeoisie is itself the product of a long course of development, of a series of revolutions in the modes of production and of exchange.

Each step in the development of the bourgeoisie was accompanied by a corresponding political advance of that class. An oppressed class under the sway of the feudal nobility, an armed and self-governing association in the medieval commune[4]: here independent urban republic (as in Italy and Germany); there taxable "third estate" of the monarchy (as in France); afterwards, in the period of manufacturing proper, serving either the semifeudal or the absolute monarchy as a counterpoise against the nobility, and, in fact, cornerstone of the great monarchies in general, the bourgeoisie has at last, since the establishment of modern industry and of the world market, conquered for itself, in the modern representative state, exclusive political sway. The executive of the modern state is but a committee for managing the common affairs of the whole bourgeoisie.

The bourgeoisie, historically, has played a most revolutionary part.

The bourgeoisie, wherever it has got the upper hand, has put an end to all feudal, patriarchal, idyllic relations. It has pitilessly torn asunder the motley feudal ties that bound man to his "natural superiors," and has left remaining no other nexus between man and man than naked self-interest, than callous "cash payment." It has drowned the most heavenly ecstasies of religious fervor, of chivalrous enthusiasm, of philistine sentimentalism, in the icy water of egotistical calculation. It has resolved personal worth into exchange value, and in place of the numberless indefeasible chartered freedoms, has set up that single, unconscionable freedom—free trade. In one word, for exploitation, veiled by religious and political illusions, it has substituted naked, shameless, direct, brutal exploitation.

The bourgeoisie has stripped of its halo every occupation hitherto honored and looked up to with reverent awe. It has converted the physician, the lawyer, the priest, the poet, the man of science, into its

---

4    This was the name given their urban communities by the townsmen of Italy and France, after they had purchased or conquered their initial rights of self-government from their feudal lords. [Engels, 1890 German edition]

"Commune" was the name taken, in France, by the nascent towns even before they had wrested from their feudal lords and masters local self-government and political rights as the "Third Estate." Generally speaking, for the economical development of the bourgeoisie, England is here taken as the typical country; for its political development, France. [Engels, 1888 English Edition]

paid wage laborers.

The bourgeoisie has torn away from the family its sentimental veil, and has reduced the family relation to a mere money relation.

The bourgeoisie has disclosed how it came to pass that the brutal display of vigor in the Middle Ages, which reactionaries so much admire, found its fitting complement in the most slothful indolence. It has been the first to show what man's activity can bring about. It has accomplished wonders far surpassing Egyptian pyramids, Roman aqueducts, and Gothic cathedrals; it has conducted expeditions that put in the shade all former exoduses of nations and crusades.

The bourgeoisie cannot exist without constantly revolutionizing the instruments of production, and thereby the relations of production, and with them the whole relations of society. Conservation of the old modes of production in unaltered form was, on the contrary, the first condition of existence for all earlier industrial classes. Constant revolutionizing of production, uninterrupted disturbance of all social conditions, everlasting uncertainty and agitation distinguish the bourgeois epoch from all earlier ones. All fixed, fast-frozen relations, with their train of ancient and venerable prejudices and opinions, are swept away, all new-formed ones become antiquated before they can ossify. All that is solid melts into air, all that is holy is profaned, and man is at last compelled to face with sober senses his real conditions of life, and his relations with his kind.

The need of a constantly expanding market for its products chases the bourgeoisie over the entire surface of the globe. It must nestle everywhere, settle everywhere, establish connections everywhere.

The bourgeoisie has through its exploitation of the world market given a cosmopolitan character to production and consumption in every country. To the great chagrin of Reactionists, it has drawn from under the feet of industry the national ground on which it stood. All old-established national industries have been destroyed or are daily being destroyed. They are dislodged by new industries, whose introduction becomes a life-and-death question for all civilized nations, by industries that no longer work up indigenous raw material, but raw material drawn from the remotest zones; industries whose products are consumed, not only at home, but in every quarter of the globe. In place of the old wants, satisfied by the production of the country, we find new wants, requiring for their satisfaction the products of distant lands and climes. In place of the old local and national seclusion and self-sufficiency, we have intercourse in every direction, universal interdependence of nations. And as in material, so also in intellectual production. The intellectual creations of individual nations become common property. National one-sidedness and narrow-mindedness become more and more impossible, and from the numerous national and local literatures, there arises a world literature.

The bourgeoisie, by the rapid improvement of all instruments of production, by the immensely facilitated means of communication, draws all, even the most barbarian, nations into civilization. The cheap prices of commodities are the heavy artillery with which it batters down all Chinese walls, with which it forces the barbarians' intensely obstinate hatred of foreigners to capitulate. It compels all nations, on pain of extinction, to adopt the bourgeois mode of production; it compels them to introduce what it calls civilization into their midst, i.e., to become bourgeois themselves. In one word, it creates a world after its own image.

The bourgeoisie has subjected the country to the rule of the towns. It has created enormous cities, has greatly increased the urban population as compared with the rural, and has thus rescued a considerable part of the population from the idiocy of rural life. Just as it has made the country dependent on the towns, so it has made barbarian and semibarbarian countries dependent on the civilized ones, nations of peasants on nations of bourgeois, the East on the West.

The bourgeoisie keeps more and more doing away with the scattered state of the population, of the means of production, and of property. It has agglomerated population, centralized the means of production, and has concentrated property in a few hands. The necessary consequence of this was political centralization. Independent, or but loosely connected provinces, with separate interests, laws, governments, and systems of taxation, became lumped together into one nation, with one government, one code of laws, one national class-interest, one frontier, and one customs tariff.

The bourgeoisie, during its rule of scarce one hundred years, has created more massive and more colossal productive forces than have all preceding generations together. Subjection of nature's forces to man, machinery, application of chemistry to industry and agriculture, steam-navigation, railways, electric telegraphs, clearing of whole continents for cultivation, canalization of rivers, whole populations conjured out of the ground—what earlier century had even a presentiment that such productive forces slumbered in the lap of social labor?

We see then: the means of production and of exchange, on whose foundation the bourgeoisie built itself up, were generated in feudal society. At a certain stage in the development of these means of production and of exchange, the conditions under which feudal society produced and exchanged, the feudal organization of agriculture and manufacturing industry, in one word, the feudal relations of property became no longer compatible with the already developed productive forces; they became so many fetters. They had to be burst asunder; they were burst asunder.

Into their place stepped free competition, accompanied by a social and political constitution adapted in it, and the economic and political sway of the bourgeois class.

A similar movement is going on before our own eyes. Modern bourgeois society, with its relations of production, of exchange and of property, a society that has conjured up such gigantic means of production and of exchange, is like the sorcerer who is no longer able to control the powers of the nether world whom he has called up by his spells. For many a decade past the history of industry and commerce is but the history of the revolt of modern productive forces against modern conditions of production, against the property relations that are the conditions for the existence of the bourgeois and of its rule. It is enough to mention the commercial crises that by their periodical return put the existence of the entire bourgeois society on its trial, each time more threateningly. In these crises, a great part not only of the existing products, but also of the previously created productive forces, are periodically destroyed. In these crises, there breaks out an epidemic that, in all earlier epochs, would have seemed an absurdity— the epidemic of overproduction. Society suddenly finds itself put back into a state of momentary barbarism; it appears as if a famine, a universal war of devastation, had cut off the supply of every means of subsistence; industry and commerce seem to be destroyed; and why? Because there is too much civilization, too much means of subsistence, too much industry, too much commerce. The productive forces at the disposal of society no longer tend to further the development of the conditions of bourgeois property; on the contrary, they have become too powerful for these conditions, by which they are fettered, and so soon as they overcome these fetters, they bring disorder into the whole of bourgeois society, endanger the existence of bourgeois property. The conditions of bourgeois society are too narrow to comprise the wealth created by them. And how does the bourgeoisie get over these crises? On the one hand by enforced destruction of a mass of productive forces; on the other, by the conquest of new markets, and by the more thorough exploitation of the old ones. That is to say, by paving the way for more extensive and more destructive crises, and by diminishing the means whereby crises are prevented.

The weapons with which the bourgeoisie felled feudalism to the ground are now turned against the bourgeoisie itself.

But not only has the bourgeoisie forged the weapons that bring death to itself; it has also called into existence the men who are to wield those weapons—the modern working class—the proletarians.

In proportion as the bourgeoisie, i.e., capital, is developed, in the same proportion is the proletariat, the modern working class, developed—a class of laborers, who live only so long as they find work, and who find work only so long as their labor increases capital. These laborers, who must sell themselves piecemeal, are a commodity, like every other article of commerce, and are consequently exposed to all the vicissitudes of competition, to all the fluctuations of the market.

Owing to the extensive use of machinery, and to the division of labor, the work of the proletarians has lost all individual character, and, consequently, all charm for the workman. He becomes an appendage of the machine, and it is only the most simple, most monotonous, and most easily acquired knack, that is required of him. Hence, the cost of production of a workman is restricted, almost entirely, to the means of subsistence that he requires for maintenance, and for the propagation of his race. But the price of a commodity, and therefore also of labor, is equal to its cost of production. In proportion, therefore, as the repulsiveness of the work increases, the wage decreases. Nay more, in proportion as the use of machinery and division of labor increases, in the same proportion the burden of toil also increases, whether by prolongation of the working hours, by the increase of the work exacted in a given time or by increased speed of machinery, etc.

Modern industry has converted the little workshop of the patriarchal master into the great factory of the industrial capitalist. Masses of laborers, crowded into the factory, are organized like soldiers. As privates of the industrial army they are placed under the command of a perfect hierarchy of officers and sergeants. Not only are they slaves of the bourgeois class, and of the bourgeois state; they are daily and hourly enslaved by the machine, by the overlooker, and, above all, by the individual bourgeois manufacturer himself. The more openly this despotism proclaims gain to be its end and aim, the more petty, the more hateful and the more embittering it is.

The less the skill and exertion of strength implied in manual labor, in other words, the more modern industry becomes developed, the more is the labor of men superseded by that of women. Differences of age and sex have no longer any distinctive social validity for the working class. All are instruments of labor, more or less expensive to use, according to their age and sex.

No sooner is the exploitation of the laborer by the manufacturer, so far at an end, that he receives his wages in cash, than he is set upon by the other portions of the bourgeoisie, the landlord, the shopkeeper, the pawnbroker, etc.

The lower strata of the middle class—the small tradespeople, shopkeepers, and retired tradesmen generally, the handicraftsmen and peasants—all these sink gradually into the proletariat, partly because their diminutive capital does not suffice for the scale on which modern industry is carried on, and is swamped in the competition with the large capitalists, partly because their specialized skill is rendered worthless by new methods of production. Thus the proletariat is recruited from all classes of the population.

The proletariat goes through various stages of development. With its birth begins its struggle with the bourgeoisie. At first the contest is carried on by individual laborers, then by the workpeople of a factory, then by the operative of one trade, in one locality, against the individual bourgeois who directly exploits them. They direct their attacks not against the bourgeois conditions of production, but against the instruments of production themselves; they destroy imported wares that compete with their labor, they smash to pieces machinery, they set factories ablaze, they seek to restore by force the vanished status of the workman of the Middle Ages.

At this stage, the laborers still form an incoherent mass scattered over the whole country, and broken up by their mutual competition. If anywhere they unite to form more compact bodies, this is not yet the consequence of their own active union, but of the union of the bourgeoisie, which class, in order to attain its own political ends, is compelled to set the whole proletariat in motion, and is moreover yet, for a time, able to do so. At this stage, therefore, the proletarians do not fight their enemies, but the enemies of their enemies, the remnants of absolute monarchy, the landowners, the nonindustrial bourgeois, the petty bourgeois. Thus, the whole historical movement is concentrated in the hands of the bourgeoisie; every victory so obtained is a victory for the bourgeoisie.

But with the development of industry, the proletariat not only increases in number; it becomes concentrated in greater masses, its strength grows, and it feels that strength more. The various interests and conditions of life within the ranks of the proletariat are more and more equalized, in proportion as machinery obliterates all distinctions of labor, and nearly everywhere reduces wages to the same low level. The growing competition among the bourgeois, and the resulting commercial crises, make the wages of the workers ever more fluctuating. The increasing improvement of machinery, ever more rapidly developing, makes their livelihood more and more precarious; the collisions between individual workmen and individual bourgeois take more and more the character of collisions between two classes. Thereupon, the workers begin to form combinations (trade unions) against the bourgeois; they club together in order to keep up the rate of wages; they found permanent associations in order to make provision beforehand for these occasional revolts. Here and there, the contest breaks out into riots.

Now and then the workers are victorious, but only for a time. The real fruit of their battles lies, not in the immediate result, but in the ever expanding union of the workers. This union is helped on by the improved means of communication that are created by modern industry, and that place the workers of different localities in contact with one another. It was just this contact that was needed to centralize the numerous local struggles, all of the same character, into one national struggle between classes. But every class struggle is a political struggle. And that union, to attain which the burghers of the Middle Ages, with their miserable highways, required centuries, the modern proletarian, thanks to railways, achieve in a few years.

This organization of the proletarians into a class, and, consequently into a political party, is continually being upset again by the competition between the workers themselves. But it ever rises up again, stronger, firmer, mightier. It compels legislative recognition of particular interests of the workers, by taking advantage of the divisions among the bourgeoisie itself. Thus, the Ten Hours Bill in England was carried.

Altogether, collisions between the classes of the old society further, in many ways, the course of development of the proletariat. The bourgeoisie finds itself involved in a constant battle. At first with the aristocracy; later on, with those portions of the bourgeoisie itself, whose interests have become antagonistic to the progress of industry; at all times with the bourgeoisie of foreign countries. In all these battles, it sees itself compelled to appeal to the proletariat, to ask for its help, and thus, to drag it into the political arena. The bourgeoisie itself, therefore, supplies the proletariat with its own elements of political and general education, in other words, it furnishes the proletariat with weapons for fighting the bourgeoisie.

Further, as we have already seen, entire sections of the ruling class are, by the advance of industry, precipitated into the proletariat, or are at least threatened in their conditions of existence. These also supply the proletariat with fresh elements of enlightenment and progress.

Finally, in times when the class struggle nears the decisive hour, the progress of dissolution going on within the ruling class, in fact within the whole range of old society, assumes such a violent, glaring character, that a small section of the ruling class cuts itself adrift, and joins the revolutionary class, the class that holds the future in its hands. Just as, therefore, at an earlier period, a section of the nobility went over to the bourgeoisie, so now a portion of the bourgeoisie goes over to the proletariat, and in particular, a portion of the bourgeois ideologists, who have raised themselves to the level of comprehending theoretically the historical movement as a whole.

Of all the classes that stand face to face with the bourgeoisie today, the proletariat alone is a really revolutionary class. The other classes decay and finally disappear in the face of modern industry; the proletariat is its special and essential product.

The lower middle class, the small manufacturer, the shopkeeper, the artisan, the peasant, all these fight against the bourgeoisie, to save from extinction their existence as fractions of the middle class. They are therefore not revolutionary, but conservative. Nay more, they are reactionary, for they try to roll back the wheel of history. If by chance, they are revolutionary, they are only so in view of their impending transfer into the proletariat; they thus defend not their present, but their future interests, they desert their own standpoint to place themselves at that of the proletariat.

The "dangerous class," [lumpenproletariat] the social scum, that passively rotting mass thrown off by the lowest layers of the old society, may, here and there, be swept into the movement by a proletarian revolution; its conditions of life, however, prepare it far more for the part of a bribed tool of reactionary intrigue.

In the condition of the proletariat, those of old society at large are already virtually swamped. The proletarian is without property; his relation to his wife and children has no longer anything in common with the bourgeois family relations; modern industry labor, modern subjection to capital, the same in England as in France, in America as in Germany, has stripped him of every trace of national character. Law, morality, religion, are to him so many bourgeois prejudices, behind which lurk in ambush just as many bourgeois interests.

All the preceding classes that got the upper hand sought to fortify their already acquired status by subjecting society at large to their conditions of appropriation. The proletarians cannot become masters of the productive forces of society, except by abolishing their own previous mode of appropriation, and thereby also every other previous mode of appropriation. They have nothing of their own to secure and to fortify; their mission is to destroy all previous securities for, and insurances of, individual property.

All previous historical movements were movements of minorities, or in the interest of minorities. The proletarian movement is the self-conscious, independent movement of the immense majority, in the interest of the immense majority. The proletariat, the lowest stratum of our present society, cannot stir, cannot raise itself up, without the whole superincumbent strata of official society being sprung into the air.

Though not in substance, yet in form, the struggle of the proletariat with the bourgeoisie is at first a national struggle. The proletariat of each country must, of course, first of all settle matters with its own bourgeoisie.

In depicting the most general phases of the development of the proletariat, we traced the more or less veiled civil war, raging within existing society, up to the point where that war breaks out into open revolution, and where the violent overthrow of the bourgeoisie lays the foundation for the sway of the proletariat.

Hitherto, every form of society has been based, as we have already seen, on the antagonism of oppressing and oppressed classes. But in order to oppress a class, certain conditions must be assured to it under which it can, at least, continue its slavish existence. The serf, in the period of serfdom, raised himself to membership in the commune, just as the petty bourgeois, under the yoke of the feudal absolutism, managed to develop into a bourgeois. The modern laborer, on the contrary, instead of rising with the process of industry, sinks deeper and deeper below the conditions of existence of his own class. He becomes a pauper, and pauperism develops more rapidly than population and wealth. And here it becomes evident, that the bourgeoisie is unfit any longer to be the ruling class in society, and to impose its conditions of existence upon society as an overriding law. It is unfit to rule because it is incompetent to assure an existence to its slave within his slavery, because it cannot help letting him sink into such a state, that it has to feed him, instead of being fed by him. Society can no longer live under this bourgeoisie, in other words, its existence is no longer compatible with society.

The essential conditions for the existence and for the sway of the bourgeois class is the formation and augmentation of capital; the condition for capital is wage labor. Wage labor rests exclusively on competition between the laborers. The advance of industry, whose involuntary promoter is the bourgeoisie, replaces the isolation of the laborers, due to competition, by their revolutionary combination, due to association. The development of modern industry, therefore, cuts from under its feet the very foundation on which the bourgeoisie produces and appropriates products. What the bourgeoisie therefore produces, above all, are its own grave diggers. Its fall and the victory of the proletariat are equally inevitable.

# II
# Proletarians and Communists

In what relation do the communists stand to the proletarians as a whole? The communists do not form a separate party opposed to other working-class parties.

They have no interests separate and apart from those of the proletariat as a whole.

They do not set up any sectarian principles of their own, by which to shape and mould the proletarian movement.

The communists are distinguished from the other working-class parties by this only:

> (1) In the national struggles of the proletarians of the different countries, they point out and bring to the front the common interests of the entire proletariat, independently of all nationality.
>
> (2) In the various stages of development which the struggle of the working class against the bourgeoisie has to pass through, they always and everywhere represent the interests of the movement as a whole.

The communists, therefore, are on the one hand, practically, the most advanced and resolute section of the working-class parties of every country, that section which pushes forward all others; on the other hand, theoretically, they have over the great mass of the proletariat the advantage of clearly understanding the line of march, the conditions, and the ultimate general results of the proletarian movement.

The immediate aim of the communists is the same as that of all other proletarian parties: formation of the proletariat into a class, overthrow of the bourgeois supremacy, conquest of political power by the proletariat.

The theoretical conclusions of the communists are in no way based on ideas or principles that have been invented, or discovered, by this or that would-be universal reformer.

They merely express, in general terms, actual relations springing from an existing class struggle, from a historical movement going on under our very eyes. The abolition of existing property relations is not at all a distinctive feature of communism.

All property relations in the past have continually been subject to historical change consequent upon the change in historical conditions.

The French Revolution, for example, abolished feudal property in favor of bourgeois property.

The distinguishing feature of communism is not the abolition of property generally, but the abolition of bourgeois property. But modern bourgeois private property is the final and most complete expression of the system of producing and appropriating products, that is based on class antagonisms, on the exploitation of the many by the few.

In this sense, the theory of the communists may be summed up in the single sentence: Abolition of private property.

We communists have been reproached with the desire of abolishing the right of personally acquiring property as the fruit of a man's own labor, which property is alleged to be the groundwork of all personal freedom, activity and independence.

Hard-won, self-acquired, self-earned property! Do you mean the property of petty artisan and of the small peasant, a form of property that preceded the bourgeois form? There is no need to abolish that; the development of industry has to a great extent already destroyed it, and is still destroying it daily.

Or do you mean the modern bourgeois private property?

But does wage labor create any property for the laborer? Not a bit. It creates capital, i.e., that kind of property which exploits wage labor, and which cannot increase except upon condition of begetting a new supply of wage labor for fresh exploitation. Property, in its present form, is based on the antagonism of capital and wage labor. Let us examine both sides of this antagonism.

To be a capitalist, is to have not only a purely personal, but a social *status* in production. Capital is a collective product, and only by the united action of many members, nay, in the last resort, only by the united action of all members of society, can it be set in motion.

Capital is therefore not only personal; it is a social power.

When, therefore, capital is converted into common property, into the property of all members of society, personal property is not thereby transformed into social property. It is only the social character of the property that is changed. It loses its class character.

Let us now take wage labor.

The average price of wage labor is the minimum wage, i.e., that quantum of the means of subsistence which is absolutely requisite to keep the laborer in bare existence as a laborer. What, therefore, the wage laborer appropriates by means of his labor merely suffices to prolong and reproduce a bare existence. We by no means intend to abolish this personal appropriation of the products of labor, an appropriation that is made for the maintenance and reproduction of human life, and that leaves no surplus wherewith to command the labor of others. All that we want to do away with is the miserable character of this appropriation, under which the laborer lives merely to increase capital, and is allowed to live only in so far as the interest of the ruling class requires it.

In bourgeois society, living labor is but a means to increase accumulated labor. In communist society, accumulated labor is but a means to widen, to enrich, to promote the existence of the laborer.

In bourgeois society, therefore, the past dominates the present; in communist society, the present dominates the past. In bourgeois society capital is independent and has individuality, while the living person is dependent and has no individuality.

And the abolition of this state of things is called by the bourgeois, abolition of individuality and freedom! And rightly so. The abolition of bourgeois individuality, bourgeois independence, and bourgeois freedom is undoubtedly aimed at.

By freedom is meant, under the present bourgeois conditions of production, free trade, free selling and buying.

But if selling and buying disappears, free selling and buying disappears also. This talk about free selling and buying, and all the other "brave words" of our bourgeois about freedom in general, have a meaning, if any, only in contrast with restricted selling and buying, with the fettered traders of the Middle Ages, but have no meaning when opposed to the communistic abolition of buying and selling, of the bourgeois conditions of production, and of the bourgeoisie itself.

You are horrified at our intending to do away with private property. But in your existing society, private property is already done away with for nine-tenths of the population; its existence for the few is solely due to its nonexistence in the hands of those nine-tenths. You reproach us, therefore, with intending to do away with a form of property, the necessary condition for whose existence is the nonexistence of any property for the immense majority of society.

In one word, you reproach us with intending to do away with your property. Precisely so; that is just what we intend.

From the moment when labor can no longer be converted into capital, money, or rent, into a social power capable of being monopolized, i.e., from the moment when individual property can no longer be transformed into bourgeois property, into capital, from that moment, you say, individuality vanishes.

You must, therefore, confess that by "individual" you mean no other person than the bourgeois, than the middle-class owner of property. This person must, indeed, be swept out of the way, and made impossible.

Communism deprives no man of the power to appropriate the products of society; all that it does is to deprive him of the power to subjugate the labor of others by means of such appropriations.

It has been objected that upon the abolition of private property, all work will cease, and universal laziness will overtake us.

According to this, bourgeois society ought long ago to have gone to the dogs through sheer idleness; for those of its members who work, acquire nothing, and those who acquire anything do not work. The whole of this objection is but another expression of the tautology: that there can no longer be any wage labor when there is no longer any capital.

All objections urged against the communistic mode of producing and appropriating material products, have, in the same way, been urged against the communistic mode of producing and appropriating intellectual products. Just as, to the bourgeois, the disappearance of class property is the disappearance of production itself, so the disappearance of class culture is to him identical with the disappearance of all culture.

That culture, the loss of which he laments, is, for the enormous majority, a mere training to act as a machine.

But don't wrangle with us so long as you apply, to our intended abolition of bourgeois property, the standard of your bourgeois notions of freedom, culture, law, etc. Your very ideas are but the outgrowth of the conditions of your bourgeois production and bourgeois property, just as your jurisprudence is but the will of your class made into a law for all, a will whose essential character and direction are determined by the economical conditions of existence of your class.

The selfish misconception that induces you to transform into eternal laws of nature and of reason, the social forms springing from your present mode of production and form of property—historical relations that rise and disappear in the progress of production—this misconception you share with every ruling class that has preceded you. What you see clearly in the case of ancient property, what you admit in the case of feudal property, you are of course forbidden to admit in the case of your own bourgeois form of property.

Abolition [*Aufhebung*] of the family! Even the most radical flare up at this infamous proposal of the communists.

On what foundation is the present family, the bourgeois family, based? On capital, on private gain. In its completely developed form, this family exists only among the bourgeoisie. But this state of things finds its complement in the practical absence of the family among the proletarians, and in public prostitution.

The bourgeois family will vanish as a matter of course when its complement vanishes, and both will vanish with the vanishing of capital.

Do you charge us with wanting to stop the exploitation of children by their parents? To this crime we plead guilty.

But, you say, we destroy the most hallowed of relations, when we replace home education by social.

And your education! Is not that also social, and determined by the social conditions under which you educate, by the intervention direct or indirect, of society, by means of schools, etc.? The Communists have not invented the intervention of society in education; they do but seek to alter the character of that intervention, and to rescue education from the influence of the ruling class.

The bourgeois claptrap about the family and education, about the hallowed co-relation of parents and child, becomes all the more disgusting, the more, by the action of modern industry, all the family ties among the proletarians are torn asunder, and their children transformed into simple articles of commerce and instruments of labor.

But you communists would introduce community of women, screams the bourgeoisie in chorus.

The bourgeois sees in his wife a mere instrument of production. He hears that the instruments of production are to be exploited in common, and, naturally, can come to no other conclusion than that the lot of being common to all will likewise fall to the women.

He has not even a suspicion that the real point aimed at is to do away with the status of women as mere instruments of production.

For the rest, nothing is more ridiculous than the virtuous indignation of our bourgeois at the community of women which, they pretend, is to be openly and officially established by the communists. The communists have no need to introduce community of women; it has existed almost from time immemorial.

Our bourgeois, not content with having wives and daughters of their proletarians at their disposal, not to speak of common prostitutes, take the greatest pleasure in seducing each other's wives.

Bourgeois marriage is, in reality, a system of wives in common and thus, at the most, what the communists might possibly be reproached with is that they desire to introduce, in substitution for a hypocritically concealed, an openly legalized community of women. For the rest, it is self-evident that the abolition of the present system of production must bring with it the abolition of the community of women springing from that system, i.e., of prostitution both public and private.

The communists are further reproached with desiring to abolish countries and nationality.

The working men have no country. We cannot take from them what they have not got. Since the proletariat must first of all acquire political supremacy, must rise to be the leading class of the nation, must constitute itself *the* nation, it is so far, itself national, though not in the bourgeois sense of the word.

National differences and antagonism between peoples are daily more and more vanishing, owing to the development of the bourgeoisie, to freedom of commerce, to the world market, to uniformity in the mode of production and in the conditions of life corresponding thereto.

The supremacy of the proletariat will cause them to vanish still faster. United action, of the leading civilized countries at least, is one of the first conditions for the emancipation of the proletariat.

In proportion as the exploitation of one individual by another will also be put an end to, the exploitation of one nation by another will also be put an end to. In proportion as the antagonism between classes within the nation vanishes, the hostility of one nation to another will come to an end.

The charges against communism made from a religious, a philosophical and, generally, from an ideological standpoint, are not deserving of serious examination.

Does it require deep intuition to comprehend that man's ideas, views, and conceptions, in one word, man's consciousness, changes with every change in the conditions of his material existence, in his social relations and in his social life?

What else does the history of ideas prove, than that intellectual production changes its character in proportion as material production is changed? The ruling ideas of each age have ever been the ideas of its ruling class.

When people speak of the ideas that revolutionize society, they do but express that fact that within the old society the elements of a new one have been created, and that the dissolution of the old ideas keeps even pace with the dissolution of the old conditions of existence.

When the ancient world was in its last throes, the ancient religions were overcome by Christianity. When Christian ideas succumbed in the eighteenth century to rationalist ideas, feudal society fought its death battle with the then-revolutionary bourgeoisie. The ideas of religious liberty and freedom of conscience merely gave expression to the sway of free competition within the domain of knowledge.

"Undoubtedly," it will be said, "religious, moral, philosophical, and juridical ideas have been modified in the course of historical development. But religion, morality, philosophy, political science, and law, constantly survived this change."

"There are, besides, eternal truths, such as Freedom, Justice, etc., that are common to all states of society. But communism abolishes eternal truths, it abolishes all religion, and all morality, instead of constituting them on a new basis; it therefore acts in contradiction to all past historical experience."

What does this accusation reduce itself to? The history of all past society has consisted in the development of class antagonisms, antagonisms that assumed different forms at different epochs.

But whatever form they may have taken, one fact is common to all past ages, *viz.*, the exploitation of one part of society by the other. No wonder, then, that the social consciousness of past ages, despite all the multiplicity and variety it displays, moves within certain common forms, or general ideas, which cannot completely vanish except with the total disappearance of class antagonisms.

The communist revolution is the most radical rupture with traditional relations; no wonder that its development involved the most radical rupture with traditional ideas.

But let us have done with the bourgeois objections to communism.

We have seen above, that the first step in the revolution by the working class is to raise the proletariat to the position of ruling class to win the battle of democracy.

The proletariat will use its political supremacy to wrest, by degrees, all capital from the bourgeoisie, to centralize all instruments of production in the hands of the state, i.e., of the proletariat organized as the ruling class; and to increase the total of productive forces as rapidly as possible.

Of course, in the beginning, this cannot be effected except by means of despotic inroads on the rights of property, and on the conditions of bourgeois production; by means of measures, therefore, which appear economically insufficient and untenable, but which, in the course of the movement, outstrip themselves, necessitate further inroads upon the old social order, and are unavoidable as a means of entirely revolutionizing the mode of production.

These measures will, of course, be different in different countries.

Nevertheless, in most advanced countries, the following will be pretty generally applicable:

1. Abolition of property in land and application of all rents of land to public purposes.
2. A heavy progressive or graduated income tax.
3. Abolition of all rights of inheritance.
4. Confiscation of the property of all emigrants and rebels.
5. Centralization of credit in the hands of the state, by means of a national bank with state capital and an exclusive monopoly.
6. Centralization of the means of communication and transport in the hands of the state.
7. Extension of factories and instruments of production owned by the state; the bringing into cultivation of wastelands, and the improvement of the soil generally in accordance with a common plan.
8. Equal liability of all to work. Establishment of industrial armies, especially for agriculture.
9. Combination of agriculture with manufacturing industries; gradual abolition of the distinction between town and country by a more equable distribution of the populace over the country.
10. Free education for all children in public schools. Abolition of children's factory labor in its present form. Combination of education with industrial production, etc, etc.

When, in the course of development, class distinctions have disappeared, and all production has been concentrated in the hands of a vast association of the whole nation, the public power will lose its political character. Political power, properly so called, is merely the organized power of one class for oppressing another. If the proletariat during its contest with the bourgeoisie is compelled, by the force of circumstances, to organize itself as a class, if, by means of a revolution, it makes itself the ruling class, and, as such, sweeps away by force the old conditions of production, then it will, along with these conditions, have swept away the conditions for the existence of class antagonisms and of classes generally, and will thereby have abolished its own supremacy as a class.

In place of the old bourgeois society, with its classes and class antagonisms, we shall have an association, in which the free development of each is the condition for the free development of all.

# III
# Socialist and Communist Literature

## 1. Reactionary Socialism

### A. Feudal Socialism

Owing to their historical position, it became the vocation of the aristocracies of France and England to write pamphlets against modern bourgeois society. In the French Revolution of July 1830, and in the English reform agitation,[5] these aristocracies again succumbed to the hateful upstart. Thenceforth, a serious political struggle was altogether out of the question. A literary battle alone remained possible. But even in the domain of literature the old cries of the restoration period had become impossible.[6]

In order to arouse sympathy, the aristocracy was obliged to lose sight, apparently, of their own interests, and to formulate their indictment against the bourgeoisie in the interest of the exploited working class alone. Thus, the aristocracy took their revenge by singing lampoons on their new master and whispering in his ears sinister prophesies of coming catastrophe.

In this way arose feudal socialism: half lamentation, half lampoon; half an echo of the past, half menace of the future; at times, by its bitter, witty and incisive criticism, striking the bourgeoisie to the very heart's core; but always ludicrous in its effect, through total incapacity to comprehend the march of modern history.

The aristocracy, in order to rally the people to them, waved the

---

5   A reference to the movement for a reform of the electoral law which, under the pressure of the working class, was passed by the British House of Commons in 1831 and finally endorsed by the House of Lords in June, 1832. The reform was directed against monopoly rule of the landed and finance aristocracy and opened the way to Parliament for the representatives of the industrial bourgeoisie. Neither workers nor the petty-bourgeois were allowed electoral rights, despite assurances they would. [Editor's note]

6   Not the English Restoration (1660–89), but the French Restoration (1814–30). [Engels, 1888 German edition]

proletarian alms-bag in front for a banner. But the people, so often as it joined them, saw on their hindquarters the old feudal coats of arms, and deserted with loud and irreverent laughter.

One section of the French Legitimists and "Young England" exhibited this spectacle.

In pointing out that their mode of exploitation was different to that of the bourgeoisie, the feudalists forget that they exploited under circumstances and conditions that were quite different and that are now antiquated. In showing that, under their rule, the modern proletariat never existed, they forget that the modern bourgeoisie is the necessary offspring of their own form of society.

For the rest, so little do they conceal the reactionary character of their criticism that their chief accusation against the bourgeois amounts to this, that under the bourgeois régime a class is being developed which is destined to cut up root and branch the old order of society.

What they upbraid the bourgeoisie with is not so much that it creates a proletariat as that it creates a *revolutionary* proletariat.

In political practice, therefore, they join in all coercive measures against the working class; and in ordinary life, despite their highfalutin phrases, they stoop to pick up the golden apples dropped from the tree of industry, and to barter truth, love, and honor, for traffic in wool, beetroot-sugar, and potato spirits.[7]

As the parson has ever gone hand in hand with the landlord, so has clerical socialism with feudal socialism.

Nothing is easier than to give Christian asceticism a socialist tinge. Has not Christianity declaimed against private property, against marriage, against the state? Has it not preached in the place of these, charity and poverty, celibacy and mortification of the flesh, monastic life and Mother Church? Christian socialism is but the holy water with which the priest consecrates the heart-burnings of the aristocrat.

---

7    This applies chiefly to Germany, where the landed aristocracy and squirearchy have large portions of their estates cultivated for their own account by stewards, and are, moreover, extensive beetroot-sugar manufacturers and distillers of potato spirits. The wealthier British aristocracy are, as yet, rather above that; but they, too, know how to make up for declining rents by lending their names to floaters or more or less shady joint-stock companies. [Engels, 1888 German edition]

## B. Petty-bourgeois Socialism

The feudal aristocracy was not the only class that was ruined by the bourgeoisie, not the only class whose conditions of existence pined and perished in the atmosphere of modern bourgeois society. The medieval burgesses and the small peasant proprietors were the precursors of the modern bourgeoisie. In those countries which are but little developed, industrially and commercially, these two classes still vegetate side by side with the rising bourgeoisie.

In countries where modern civilization has become fully developed, a new class of petty bourgeois has been formed, fluctuating between proletariat and bourgeoisie, and ever renewing itself as a supplementary part of bourgeois society. The individual members of this class, however, are being constantly hurled down into the proletariat by the action of competition, and, as modern industry develops, they even see the moment approaching when they will completely disappear as an independent section of modern society, to be replaced in manufactures, agriculture and commerce, by overlookers, bailiffs and shopmen.

In countries like France, where the peasants constitute far more than half of the population, it was natural that writers who sided with the proletariat against the bourgeoisie should use, in their criticism of the bourgeois régime, the standard of the peasant and petty bourgeois, and from the standpoint of these intermediate classes, should take up the cudgels for the working class. Thus arose petty-bourgeois socialism. Sismondi was the head of this school, not only in France but also in England.

This school of socialism dissected with great acuteness the contradictions in the conditions of modern production. It laid bare the hypocritical apologies of economists. It proved, incontrovertibly, the disastrous effects of machinery and division of labor; the concentration of capital and land in a few hands; overproduction and crises; it pointed out the inevitable ruin of the petty bourgeois and peasant, the misery of the proletariat, the anarchy in production, the crying inequalities in the distribution of wealth, the industrial war of extermination between nations, the dissolution of old moral bonds, of the old family relations, of the old nationalities.

In its positive aims, however, this form of socialism aspires either to restoring the old means of production and of exchange, and with them the old property relations, and the old society, or to cramping the modern means of production and of exchange within the framework of the old property relations that have been, and were bound to be, exploded by those means. In either case, it is both reactionary and utopian.

Its last words are: corporate guilds for manufacture; patriarchal relations in agriculture.

Ultimately, when stubborn historical facts had dispersed all intoxicating effects of self-deception, this form of socialism ended in a miserable hangover.

## C. German, or "True," Socialism

The socialist and communist literature of France, a literature that originated under the pressure of a bourgeoisie in power, and that was the expression of the struggle against this power, was introduced into Germany at a time when the bourgeoisie, in that country, had just begun its contest with feudal absolutism.

German philosophers, would-be philosophers, and *beaux esprits* (men of letters), eagerly seized on this literature, only forgetting, that when these writings immigrated from France into Germany, French social conditions had not immigrated along with them. In contact with German social conditions, this French literature lost all its immediate practical significance and assumed a purely literary aspect. Thus, to the German philosophers of the eighteenth century, the demands of the first French Revolution were nothing more than the demands of "Practical Reason" in general, and the utterance of the will of the revolutionary French bourgeoisie signified, in their eyes, the laws of pure Will, of Will as it was bound to be, of true human Will generally.

The work of the German *literati* consisted solely in bringing the new French ideas into harmony with their ancient philosophical conscience, or rather, in annexing the French ideas without deserting their own philosophic point of view.

This annexation took place in the same way in which a foreign language is appropriated, namely, by translation.

It is well known how the monks wrote silly lives of Catholic saints *over* the manuscripts on which the classical works of ancient heathendom had been written. The German *literati* reversed this process with the profane French literature. They wrote their philosophical nonsense beneath the French original. For instance, beneath the French criticism of the economic functions of money, they wrote "Alienation of Humanity," and beneath the French criticism of the bourgeois state

---

they wrote "Dethronement of the Category of the General," and so forth.

The introduction of these philosophical phrases at the back of the French historical criticisms, they dubbed "Philosophy of Action," "True Socialism," "German Science of Socialism," "Philosophical Foundation of Socialism," and so on.

The French socialist and communist literature was thus completely emasculated. And, since it ceased in the hands of the German to express the struggle of one class with the other, he felt conscious of having overcome "French one-sidedness" and of representing, not true requirements, but the requirements of truth; not the interests of the proletariat, but the interests of human nature, of man in general, who belongs to no class, has no reality, who exists only in the misty realm of philosophical fantasy.

This German socialism, which took its schoolboy task so seriously and solemnly, and extolled its poor stock-in-trade in such a mountebank fashion, meanwhile gradually lost its pedantic innocence.

The fight of the Germans, and especially of the Prussian bourgeoisie, against feudal aristocracy and absolute monarchy, in other words, the liberal movement, became more earnest.

By this, the long-wished for opportunity was offered to "True" socialism of confronting the political movement with the socialist demands, of hurling the traditional anathemas against liberalism, against representative government, against bourgeois competition, bourgeois freedom of the press, bourgeois legislation, bourgeois liberty and equality, and of preaching to the masses that they had nothing to gain, and everything to lose, by this bourgeois movement. German socialism forgot, in the nick of time, that the French criticism, whose silly echo it was, presupposed the existence of modern bourgeois society, with its corresponding economic conditions of existence, and the political constitution adapted thereto, the very things whose attainment was the object of the pending struggle in Germany.

To the absolute governments, with their following of parsons, professors, country squires, and officials, it served as a welcome scarecrow against the threatening bourgeoisie.

It was a sweet finish, after the bitter pills of flogging and bullets, with which these same governments, just at that time, dosed the German working-class risings.

While this "True" socialism thus served the government as a weapon for fighting the German bourgeoisie, it, at the same time, directly represented a reactionary interest, the interest of German philistines. In Germany, the *petty-bourgeois* class, a relic of the sixteenth century, and since then constantly cropping up again under various forms, is the real social basis of the existing state of things.

To preserve this class is to preserve the existing state of things in Germany. The industrial and political supremacy of the bourgeoisie threatens it with certain destruction—on the one hand, from the concentration of capital; on the other, from the rise of a revolutionary proletariat. "True" socialism appeared to kill these two birds with one stone. It spread like an epidemic.

The robe of speculative cobwebs, embroidered with flowers of rhetoric, steeped in the dew of sickly sentiment, this transcendental robe in which the German socialists wrapped their sorry "eternal truths," all skin and bone, served to wonderfully increase the sale of their goods amongst such a public.

And on its part German socialism recognized, more and more, its own calling as the bombastic representative of the petty-bourgeois philistine.

It proclaimed the German nation to be the model nation, and the German petty philistine to be the typical man. To every villainous meanness of this model man, it gave a hidden, higher, socialistic interpretation, the exact contrary of its real character. It went to the extreme length of directly opposing the "brutally destructive" tendency of communism, and of proclaiming its supreme and impartial contempt of all class struggles. With very few exceptions, all the so-called socialist and communist publications that now (1847) circulate in Germany belong to the domain of this foul and enervating literature.[8]

## 2. Conservative, or Bourgeois, Socialism

A part of the bourgeoisie is desirous of redressing social grievances in order to secure the continued existence of bourgeois society.

To this section belong economists, philanthropists, humanitarians, improvers of the condition of the working class, organizers of charity, members of societies for the prevention of cruelty to animals, temper-

---

8 The revolutionary storm of 1848 swept away this whole shabby tendency and cured its protagonists of the desire to dabble in socialism. The chief representative and classical type of this tendency is Mr. Karl Grün. [Engels, 1888 German edition]

ance fanatics, hole-and-corner reformers of every imaginable kind. This form of socialism has, moreover, been worked out into complete systems.

We may cite Proudhon's *Philosophie de la Misère* as an example of this form.

The socialistic bourgeois want all the advantages of modern social conditions without the struggles and dangers necessarily resulting therefrom. They desire the existing state of society, minus its revolutionary and disintegrating elements. They wish for a bourgeoisie without a proletariat. The bourgeoisie naturally conceives the world in which it is supreme to be the best; and bourgeois socialism develops this comfortable conception into various more or less complete systems. In requiring the proletariat to carry out such a system, and thereby to march straightway into the social New Jerusalem, it but requires in reality, that the proletariat should remain within the bounds of existing society, but should cast away all its hateful ideas concerning the bourgeoisie.

A second and more practical, but less systematic, form of this socialism sought to depreciate every revolutionary movement in the eyes of the working class by showing that no mere political reform, but only a change in the material conditions of existence, in economical relations, could be of any advantage to them. By changes in the material conditions of existence, this form of socialism, however, by no means understands abolition of the bourgeois relations of production, an abolition that can be affected only by a revolution, but administrative reforms, based on the continued existence of these relations; reforms, therefore, that in no respect affect the relations between capital and labor, but, at the best, lessen the cost, and simplify the administrative work, of bourgeois government.

Bourgeois socialism attains adequate expression when, and only when, it becomes a mere figure of speech.

Free trade: for the benefit of the working class. Protective duties: for the benefit of the working class. Prison reform: for the benefit of the working class. This is the last word and the only seriously meant word of bourgeois socialism.

It is summed up in the phrase: the bourgeois is a bourgeois—for the benefit of the working class.

## 3. Critical-Utopian Socialism and Communism

We do not here refer to that literature which, in every great modern revolution, has always given voice to the demands of the proletariat, such as the writings of Babeuf and others.

The first direct attempts of the proletariat to attain its own ends, made in times of universal excitement, when feudal society was being overthrown, necessarily failed, owing to the then undeveloped state of the proletariat, as well as to the absence of the economic conditions for its emancipation, conditions that had yet to be produced, and could be produced by the impending bourgeois epoch alone. The revolutionary literature that accompanied these first movements of the proletariat had necessarily a reactionary character. It inculcated universal asceticism and social leveling in its crudest form.

The socialist and communist systems properly so called, those of Saint-Simon, Fourier, Owen, and others, spring into existence in the early undeveloped period, described above, of the struggle between proletariat and bourgeoisie (see Section I. Bourgeois and Proletarians).

The founders of these systems see, indeed, the class antagonisms, as well as the action of the decomposing elements in the prevailing form of society. But the proletariat, as yet in its infancy, offers to them the spectacle of a class without any historical initiative or any independent political movement.

Since the development of class antagonism keeps even pace with the development of industry, the economic situation, as they find it, does not as yet offer to them the material conditions for the emancipation of the proletariat. They therefore search after a new social science, after new social laws, that are to create these conditions.

Historical action is to yield to their personal inventive action; historically created conditions of emancipation to fantastic ones; and the gradual, spontaneous class organization of the proletariat to an organization of society especially contrived by these inventors. Future history resolves itself, in their eyes, into the propaganda and the practical carrying out of their social plans.

In the formation of their plans, they are conscious of caring chiefly for the interests of the working class, as being the most suffering class. Only from the point of view of being the most suffering class does the proletariat exist for them.

The undeveloped state of the class struggle, as well as their own surroundings, causes socialists of this kind to consider themselves far

superior to all class antagonisms. They want to improve the condition
of every member of society, even that of the most favored. Hence, they
habitually appeal to society at large, without the distinction of class;
nay, by preference, to the ruling class. For how can people, when once
they understand their system, fail to see in it the best possible plan of
the best possible state of society?

Hence, they reject all political, and especially all revolutionary,
action; they wish to attain their ends by peaceful means, necessarily
doomed to failure, and by the force of example, to pave the way for
the new social gospel.

Such fantastic pictures of future society, painted at a time when the
proletariat is still in a very undeveloped state and has but a fantastic
conception of its own position, correspond with the first instinctive
yearnings of that class for a general reconstruction of society.

But these socialist and communist publications contain also a
critical element. They attack every principle of existing society. Hence,
they are full of the most valuable materials for the enlightenment of
the working class. The practical measures proposed in them—such as
the abolition of the distinction between town and country, of the family, of the carrying on of industries for the account of private individuals, and of the wage system, the proclamation of social harmony, the
conversion of the function of the state into a more superintendence of
production—all these proposals point solely to the disappearance of
class antagonisms which were, at that time, only just cropping up, and
which, in these publications, are recognized in their earliest indistinct
and undefined forms only. These proposals, therefore, are of a purely
utopian character.

The significance of critical-utopian socialism and communism
bears an inverse relation to historical development. In proportion as
the modern class struggle develops and takes definite shape, this fantastic standing apart from the contest, these fantastic attacks on it, lose
all practical value and all theoretical justification. Therefore, although
the originators of these systems were, in many respects, revolutionary,
their disciples have, in every case, formed mere reactionary sects. They
hold fast by the original views of their masters, in opposition to the
progressive historical development of the proletariat. They, therefore,
endeavor, and that consistently, to deaden the class struggle and to
reconcile the class antagonisms. They still dream of experimental realization of their social utopias, of founding isolated "*phalanstères*," of

establishing "Home Colonies," or setting up a "Little Icaria"9—duo-decimo editions of the New Jerusalem—and to realize all these castles in the air, they are compelled to appeal to the feelings and purses of the bourgeois. By degrees, they sink into the category of the reaction-ary conservative socialists depicted above, differing from these only by more systematic pedantry, and by their fanatical and superstitious belief in the miraculous effects of their social science.

They, therefore, violently oppose all political action on the part of the working class; such action, according to them, can only result from blind unbelief in the new gospel.

The Owenites in England, and the Fourierists in France, respec-tively, oppose the Chartists and the *Réformistes*.

---

9 *Phalanstères* were socialist colonies on the plan of Charles Fourier; *Icaria* was the name given by Cabet to his utopia and, later on, to his American communist colony. [Engels, 1888 English Edition]

"Home Colonies" were what Owen called his communist model societies. *Phalanstères* was the name of the public palaces planned by Fourier. *Icaria* was the name given to the utopian land of fancy, whose communist institutions Cabet portrayed. [Engels, 1890 German Edition]

# IV
# Position of the Communists in Relation to the Various Existing Opposition Parties

Section II has made clear the relations of the communists to the existing working-class parties, such as the Chartists in England and the Agrarian Reformers in America.

The communists fight for the attainment of the immediate aims, for the enforcement of the momentary interests of the working class; but in the movement of the present, they also represent and take care of the future of that movement. In France, the communists ally with the Social-Democrats,[10] against the conservative and radical bourgeoisie, reserving, however, the right to take up a critical position in regard to phases and illusions traditionally handed down from the great Revolution.

In Switzerland, they support the Radicals, without losing sight of the fact that this party consists of antagonistic elements, partly of democratic socialists, in the French sense, partly of radical bourgeois.

In Poland, they support the party that insists on an agrarian revolution as the prime condition for national emancipation, that party which fomented the insurrection of Kraków in 1846.

In Germany, they fight with the bourgeoisie whenever it acts in a revolutionary way, against the absolute monarchy, the feudal squirearchy, and the petty bourgeoisie.

But they never cease, for a single instant, to instill into the working class the clearest possible recognition of the hostile antagonism between bourgeoisie and proletariat, in order that the German workers may straightway use, as so many weapons against the bourgeoisie, the social and political conditions that the bourgeoisie must necessarily introduce along with its supremacy, and in order that, after the fall of the reactionary classes in Germany, the fight against the bourgeoisie itself may immediately begin.

---

10   The party then represented in Parliament by Ledru-Rollin, in literature by Louis Blanc, in the daily press by the *Réforme*. The name of Social-Democracy signified, with these its inventors, a section of the democratic or republican party more or less tinged with socialism. [Engels, English Edition 1888]

The communists turn their attention chiefly to Germany, because that country is on the eve of a bourgeois revolution that is bound to be carried out under more advanced conditions of European civilization and with a much more developed proletariat than that of England was in the seventeenth, and of France in the eighteenth century, and because the bourgeois revolution in Germany will be but the prelude to an immediately following proletarian revolution.

In short, the communists everywhere support every revolutionary movement against the existing social and political order of things.

In all these movements, they bring to the front, as the leading question in each, the property question, no matter what its degree of development at the time.

Finally, they labor everywhere for the union and agreement of the democratic parties of all countries.

The communists disdain to conceal their views and aims. They openly declare that their ends can be attained only by the forcible overthrow of all existing social conditions. Let the ruling classes tremble at a communistic revolution. The proletarians have nothing to lose but their chains. They have a world to win.

### *WORKERS OF ALL COUNTRIES, UNITE!*

Frederick Engels in 1877

# Socialism:
# Utopian and Scientific

**Frederick Engels**

*This work was originally the first three chapters of a larger work, a polemic against Eugen Dühring entitled* Anti-Dühring, *which was first published in 1878. This selection, in pamphlet form, first appeared in English in 1892, and along with the* Manifesto of the Communist Party, *quickly became one of the most popular works of Marxist theory.*

# I
# The Development of Utopian Socialism

**M**odern socialism is, in its essence, the direct product of the recognition, on the one hand, of the class antagonisms existing in the society of today between proprietors and non-proprietors, between capitalists and wageworkers; on the other hand, of the anarchy existing in production. But, in its theoretical form, modern socialism originally appears ostensibly as a more logical extension of the principles laid down by the great French philosophers of the eighteenth century. Like every new theory, modern socialism had, at first, to connect itself with the intellectual stock-in-trade ready to its hand, however deeply its roots lay in material economic facts.

The great men, who in France prepared men's minds for the coming revolution, were themselves extreme revolutionists. They recognized no external authority of any kind whatever. Religion, natural science, society, political institutions—everything was subjected to the most unsparing criticism: everything must justify its existence before the judgment seat of reason or give up existence. Reason became the sole measure of everything. It was the time when, as Hegel says, the world stood upon its head;[1] first in the sense that the human head, and

---

1   This is the passage on the French Revolution:
    "Thought, the concept of law, *all at once* made itself felt, and against this the old scaffolding of wrong could make no stand. In this conception of law, therefore, a constitution has now been established, and henceforth everything must be cased upon this. Since the sun had been in the firmament, and the planets circled around him, the sight had never been seen of man standing upon his head—i.e., on the Idea—and building reality after this image. Anaxagoras first said that the Nous, reason, rules the world; but now, for the first time, had men come to recognize that the Idea must rule the mental reality. And this was a *magnificent sunrise. All thinking Beings have participated in celebrating this holy day. A sublime emotion swayed men at that time, an enthusiasm of reason pervaded the world, as if now had come the reconciliation of the Divine Principle with the world.*" [Hegel, *The Philosophy of History,* 1840, p.535.]
    Is it not high time to set the Anti-Socialist Law in action against such teachings, subversive and to the common danger, by the late Professor Hegel? [Engels.]

the principles arrived at by its thought, claimed to be the basis of all human action and association; but by and by, also, in the wider sense that the reality which was in contradiction to these principles had, in fact, to be turned upside down. Every form of society and government then existing, every old traditional notion, was flung into the lumber room as irrational; the world had hitherto allowed itself to be led solely by prejudices; everything in the past deserved only pity and contempt. Now, for the first time, appeared the light of day, the kingdom of reason; henceforth superstition, injustice, privilege, oppression, were to be superseded by eternal truth, eternal right, equality based on nature and the inalienable rights of man.

We know today that this kingdom of reason was nothing more than the idealized kingdom of the bourgeoisie; that this eternal right found its realization in bourgeois justice; that this equality reduced itself to bourgeois equality before the law; that bourgeois property was proclaimed as one of the essential rights of man; and that the government of reason, the *contrat social* of Rousseau, came into being, and only could come into being, as a democratic bourgeois republic. The great thinkers of the eighteenth century could, no more than their predecessors, go beyond the limits imposed upon them by their epoch.

But, side by side with the antagonisms of the feudal nobility and the burghers, who claimed to represent all the rest of society, was the general antagonism of exploiters and exploited, of rich idlers and poor workers. It was this very circumstance that made it possible for the representatives of the bourgeoisie to put themselves forward as representing not one special class, but the whole of suffering humanity. Still further. From its origin the bourgeoisie was saddled with its antithesis: capitalists cannot exist without wageworkers, and, in the same proportion as the mediaeval burgher of the guild developed into the modern bourgeois, the guild journeyman and the day laborer, outside the guilds, developed into the proletarian. And although, upon the whole, the bourgeoisie, in their struggle with the nobility, could claim to represent at the same time the interests of the different working-classes of that period, yet in every great bourgeois movement there were independent outbursts of that class which was the forerunner, more or less developed, of the modern proletariat. For example, at the time of the German Reformation and the Peasants' War, the Anabaptists and Thomas Müntzer; in the great English Revolution, the Levellers; in the great French Revolution, Babeuf.

There were theoretical enunciations, corresponding with these revolutionary uprisings of a class not yet developed; in the sixteenth and seventeenth centuries, utopian pictures of ideal social conditions;[2] in the eighteenth century, actual communistic theories (Morelly and Mably). The demand for equality was no longer limited to political rights; it was extended also to the social conditions of individuals. It was not simply class privileges that were to be abolished, but class distinctions themselves. A communism, ascetic, denouncing all the pleasures of life, Spartan, was the first form of the new teaching. Then came the three great utopians: Saint-Simon, to whom the middle-class movement, side by side with the proletarian, still had a certain significance; Fourier and Owen, who in the country where capitalist production was most developed, and under the influence of the antagonisms begotten of this, worked out his proposals for the removal of class distinctions systematically and in direct relation to French materialism.

One thing is common to all three. Not one of them appears as a representative of the interests of that proletariat which historical development had, in the meantime, produced. Like the French philosophers, they do not claim to emancipate a particular class to begin with, but all humanity at once. Like them, they wish to bring in the kingdom of reason and eternal justice, but this kingdom, as they see it, is as far as heaven from earth, from that of the French philosophers.

For, to our three social reformers, the bourgeois world, based upon the principles of these philosophers, is quite as irrational and unjust, and, therefore, finds its way to the dust hole quite as readily as feudalism and all the earlier stages of society. If pure reason and justice have not, hitherto, ruled the world, this has been the case only because men have not rightly understood them. What was wanted was the individual man of genius, who has now arisen and who understands the truth. That he has now arisen, that the truth has now been clearly understood, is not an inevitable event, following of necessity in the chains of historical development, but a mere happy accident. He might just as well have been born 500 years earlier, and might then have spared humanity 500 years of error, strife, and suffering.

We saw how the French philosophers of the eighteenth century, the forerunners of the Revolution, appealed to reason as the sole judge of all that is. A rational government, rational society, were to be founded;

---

2   Engels refers here to the works of the utopian socialists Thomas More (16th century) and Tommaso Campanella (17th century)

everything that ran counter to eternal reasons was to be remorselessly done away with. We saw also that this eternal reason was in reality nothing but the idealized understanding of the eighteenth century citizen, just then evolving into the bourgeois. The French Revolution had realized this rational society and government.

But the new order of things, rational enough as compared with earlier conditions, turned out to be by no means absolutely rational. The state based upon reason completely collapsed. Rousseau's *contrat social* had found its realization in the Reign of Terror, from which the bourgeoisie, who had lost confidence in their own political capacity, had taken refuge first in the corruption of the Directorate, and, finally, under the wing of the Napoleonic despotism. The promised eternal peace was turned into an endless war of conquest. The society based upon reason had fared no better. The antagonism between rich and poor, instead of dissolving into general prosperity, had become intensified by the removal of the guild and other privileges, which had to some extent bridged it over, and by the removal of the charitable institutions of the Church. The "freedom of property" from feudal fetters, now veritably accomplished, turned out to be, for the small capitalists and small proprietors, the freedom to sell their small property, crushed under the overmastering competition of the large capitalists and landlords, to these great lords, and thus, as far as the small capitalists and peasant proprietors were concerned, became "freedom *from* property." The development of industry upon a capitalistic basis made poverty and misery of the working masses conditions of existence of society. Cash payment became more and more, in Carlyle's phrase, the sole nexus between man and man. The number of crimes increased from year to year. Formerly, the feudal vices had openly stalked about in broad daylight; though not eradicated, they were now at any rate thrust into the background. In their stead, the bourgeois vices, hitherto practiced in secret, began to blossom all the more luxuriantly. Trade became to a greater and greater extent cheating. The "fraternity" of the revolutionary motto was realized in the chicanery and rivalries of the battle of competition. Oppression by force was replaced by corruption; the sword, as the first social lever, by gold. The right of the first night was transferred from the feudal lords to the bourgeois manufacturers. Prostitution increased to an extent never heard of. Marriage itself remained, as before, the legally recognized form, the official cloak of prostitution, and, moreover, was supplemented by rich crops of adultery.

In a word, compared with the splendid promises of the philosophers, the social and political institutions born of the "triumph of reason" were bitterly disappointing caricatures. All that was wanting was the men to formulate this disappointment, and they came with the turn of the century. In 1802, Saint-Simon's Geneva letters appeared; in 1808 appeared Fourier's first work, although the groundwork of his theory dated from 1799; on January 1, 1800, Robert Owen undertook the direction of New Lanark.

At this time, however, the capitalist mode of production, and with it the antagonism between the bourgeoisie and the proletariat, was still very incompletely developed. Modern industry, which had just arisen in England, was still unknown in France. But modern industry develops, on the one hand, the conflicts which make absolutely necessary a revolution in the mode of production, and the doing away with its capitalistic character—conflicts not only between the classes begotten of it, but also between the very productive forces and the forms of exchange created by it. And, on the other hand, it develops, in these very gigantic productive forces, the means of ending these conflicts. If, therefore, about the year 1800, the conflicts arising from the new social order were only just beginning to take shape, this holds still more fully as to the means of ending them. The "have nothing" masses of Paris, during the Reign of Terror, were able for a moment to gain the mastery, and thus to lead the bourgeois revolution to victory in spite of the bourgeoisie themselves. But, in doing so, they only proved how impossible it was for their domination to last under the conditions then obtaining. The proletariat, which then for the first time evolved itself from these "have-nothing" masses as the nucleus of a new class, as yet quite incapable of independent political action, appeared as an oppressed, suffering order, to whom, in its incapacity to help itself, help could, at best, be brought in from without or down from above.

This historical situation also dominated the founders of socialism. To the crude conditions of capitalistic production and the crude class conditions correspond crude theories. The solution of the social problems, which as yet lay hidden in undeveloped economic conditions, the utopians attempted to evolve out of the human brain. Society presented nothing but wrongs; to remove these was the task of reason. It was necessary, then, to discover a new and more perfect system of social order and to impose this upon society from without by propaganda, and, wherever it was possible, by the example of model experiments. These new social systems were foredoomed as utopian; the more completely they were worked out in detail, the more they could not avoid drifting off into pure fantasies.

These facts once established, we need not dwell a moment longer upon this side of the question, now wholly belonging to the past. We can leave it to the literary small fry to solemnly quibble over these fantasies, which today only make us smile, and to crow over the superiority of their own bald reasoning, as compared with such "insanity." For ourselves, we delight in the stupendously grand thoughts and germs of thought that everywhere break out through their fantastic covering, and to which these philistines are blind.

Saint-Simon was a son of the great French Revolution, at the outbreak of which he was not yet thirty. The Revolution was the victory of the third estate, i.e., of the great masses of the nation, *working* in production and in trade, over the privileged *idle* classes, the nobles and the priests. But the victory of the third estate soon revealed itself as exclusively the victory of a smaller part of this "estate," as the conquest of political power by the socially privileged section of it, i.e., the propertied bourgeoisie. And the bourgeoisie had certainly developed rapidly during the Revolution, partly by speculation in the lands of the nobility and of the Church, confiscated and afterwards put up for sale, and partly by frauds upon the nation by means of army contracts. It was the domination of these swindlers that, under the Directorate, brought France to the verge of ruin, and thus gave Napoleon the pretext for his *coup d'etat*.

Hence, to Saint-Simon the antagonism between the third estate and the privileged classes took the form of an antagonism between "workers" and "idlers." The idlers were not merely the old privileged classes, but also all who, without taking any part in production or distribution, lived on their incomes. And the workers were not only the wageworkers, but also the manufacturers, the merchants, the bankers. That the idlers had lost the capacity for intellectual leadership and political supremacy had been proved, and was by the Revolution finally settled. That the nonpossessing classes had not this capacity seemed to Saint-Simon proved by the experiences of the Reign of Terror. Then, who was to lead and command? According to Saint-Simon, science and industry, both united by a new religious bond,

destined to restore that unity of religious ideas which had been lost
since the time of the Reformation—a necessarily mystic and rigidly
hierarchic "new Christianity." But science, that was the scholars; and
industry, that was, in the first place, the working bourgeois, manufacturers, merchants, bankers. These bourgeois were, certainly, intended
by Saint-Simon to transform themselves into a kind of public officials,
of social trustees; but they were still to hold, *vis-à-vis* of the workers, a
commanding and economically privileged position. The bankers especially were to be called upon to direct the whole of social production
by the regulation of credit. This conception was in exact keeping with
a time in which modern industry in France and, with it, the chasm
between bourgeoisie and proletariat was only just coming into existence. But what Saint-Simon especially lays stress upon is this: what
interests him first, and above all other things, is the lot of the class that
is the most numerous and the most poor (*"la classe la plus nombreuse
et la plus pauvre"*).

Already in his Geneva letters, Saint-Simon lays down the proposition that "all men ought to work." In the same work he recognizes also
that the Reign of Terror was the reign of the nonpossessing masses.

"See," says he to them, "what happened in France at the time when
your comrades held sway there: they brought about a famine."

But to recognize the French Revolution as a class war, and not simply one between nobility and bourgeoisie, but between nobility, bourgeoisie, and the nonpossessors, was, in the year 1802, a most pregnant
discovery. In 1816, he declares that politics is the science of production, and foretells the complete absorption of politics by economics.
The knowledge that economic conditions are the basis of political
institutions appears here only in embryo. Yet what is here already very
plainly expressed is the idea of the future conversion of political rule
over men into an administration of things and a direction of processes
of production—that is to say, the "abolition of the state," about which
recently there has been so much noise.

Saint-Simon shows the same superiority over his contemporaries,
when in 1814, immediately after the entry of the allies into Paris, and
again in 1815, during the Hundred Days' War, he proclaims the alliance of France and England, and then of both of these countries, with
Germany, as the only guarantee for the prosperous development and
peace of Europe. To preach to the French in 1815 an alliance with the
victors of Waterloo required as much courage as historical foresight.

If in Saint-Simon we find a comprehensive breadth of view, by virtue of which almost all the ideas of later socialists that are not strictly economic are found in him in embryo, we find in Fourier a criticism of the existing conditions of society, genuinely French and witty, but not upon that account any the less thorough. Fourier takes the bourgeoisie, their inspired prophets before the Revolution, and their interested eulogists after it, at their own word. He lays bare remorselessly the material and moral misery of the bourgeois world. He confronts it with the earlier philosophers' dazzling promises of a society in which reason alone should reign, of a civilization in which happiness should be universal, of an illimitable human perfectibility, and with the rose-colored phraseology of the bourgeois ideologists of his time. He points out how everywhere the most pitiful reality corresponds with the most high-sounding phrases, and he overwhelms this hopeless fiasco of phrases with his mordant sarcasm.

Fourier is not only a critic; his imperturbably serene nature makes him a satirist, and assuredly one of the greatest satirists of all time. He depicts, with equal power and charm, the swindling speculations that blossomed out upon the downfall of the Revolution, and the shop-keeping spirit prevalent in, and characteristic of, French commerce at that time. Still more masterly is his criticism of the bourgeois form of the relations between sexes, and the position of woman in bourgeois society. He was the first to declare that in any given society the degree of woman's emancipation is the natural measure of the general emancipation.

But Fourier is at his greatest in his conception of the history of society. He divides its whole course, thus far, into four stages of evolution—savagery, barbarism, the patriarchate, civilization. This last is identical with the so-called civil, or bourgeois, society of today—i.e., with the social order that came in with the sixteenth century. He proves "that the civilized stage raises every vice practiced by barbarism in a simple fashion into a form of existence, complex, ambiguous, equivocal, hypocritical"—that civilization moves "in a vicious circle," in contradictions which it constantly reproduces without being able to solve them; hence it constantly arrives at the very opposite to that which it wants to attain, or pretends to want to attain, so that, e.g., "under civilization poverty is born of superabundance itself."

Fourier, as we see, uses the dialectic method in the same masterly way as his contemporary, Hegel. Using these same dialectics, he argues against talk about illimitable human perfectibility, that every historical phase has its period of ascent and also its period of descent, and he applies this observation to the future of the whole human race. As Kant introduced into natural science the idea of the ultimate destruction of the earth, Fourier introduced into historical science that of the ultimate destruction of the human race.

While in France the hurricane of the Revolution swept over the land, in England a quieter, but not on that account less tremendous, revolution was going on. Steam and the new tool-making machinery were transforming manufacture into modern industry, and thus revolutionizing the whole foundation of bourgeois society. The sluggish march of development of the manufacturing period changed into a veritable storm and stress period of production. With constantly increasing swiftness the splitting-up into large capitalists and non-possessing proletarians went on. Between these, instead of the former stable middle class, an unstable mass of artisans and small shopkeepers, the most fluctuating portion of the population, now led a precarious existence.

The new mode of production was, as yet, only at the beginning of its period of ascent; as yet it was the normal, regular method of production—the only one possible under existing conditions. Nevertheless, even then it was producing crying social abuses—the herding together of a homeless population in the worst quarters of the large towns; the loosening of all traditional moral bonds, of patriarchal subordination, of family relations; overwork, especially of women and children, to a frightful extent; complete demoralization of the working class, suddenly flung into altogether new conditions, from the country into the town, from agriculture into modern industry, from stable conditions of existence into insecure ones that change from day to day.

At this juncture, there came forward as a reformer a manufacturer twenty-nine years old—a man of almost sublime, childlike simplicity of character, and at the same time one of the few born leaders of men. Robert Owen had adopted the teaching of the materialistic philosophers: that man's character is the product, on the one hand, of heredity; on the other, of the environment of the individual during his lifetime, and especially during his period of development. In the industrial revolution most of his class saw only chaos and confusion, and the opportunity of fishing in these troubled waters and making large fortunes quickly. He saw in it the opportunity of putting into practice his favorite theory, and so of bringing order out of chaos. He had already tried it with success, as superintendent of more than five hundred men in a Manchester factory. From 1800 to 1829, he directed the great cotton mill at New Lanark, in Scotland, as managing partner, along the same lines, but with greater freedom of action and with a success that made him a European reputation. A population, originally consisting of the most diverse and, for the most part, very demoralized elements, a population that gradually grew to 2,500, he turned into a model colony, in which drunkenness, police, magistrates, lawsuits, poor laws, charity, were unknown. And all this simply by placing the people in conditions worthy of human beings, and especially by carefully bringing up the rising generation. He was the founder of infant schools, and introduced them first at New Lanark. At the age of two, the children came to school, where they enjoyed themselves so much that they could scarely be got home again. While his competitors worked their people thirteen or fourteen hours a day, in New Lanark the working day was only ten-and-a-half hours. When a crisis in cotton stopped work for four months, his workers received their full wages all the time. And with all this the business more than doubled in value, and to the last yielded large profits to its proprietors.

In spite of all this, Owen was not content. The existence which he secured for his workers was, in his eyes, still far from being worthy of human beings. "The people were slaves at my mercy." The relatively favorable conditions in which he had placed them were still far from allowing a rational development of the character and of the intellect in all directions, much less of the free exercise of all their faculties.

> And yet, the working part of this population of 2,500 persons was daily producing as much real wealth for society as, less than half a century before, it would have required the working part of a population of 600,000 to create. I asked myself, what became of the difference between the wealth consumed by 2,500 persons and that which would have been consumed by 600,000?[3]

The answer was clear. It had been used to pay the proprietors of the establishment 5 per cent on the capital they had laid out, in addition to over 300,000 pounds clear profit. And that which held for New

3   From *The Revolution in Mind and Practice*, p.21, a memorial addressed to all the "red Republicans, Communists and Socialists of Europe," and sent to the provisional government of France, 1848, and also "to Queen Victoria and her responsible advisers."

Lanark held to a still greater extent for all the factories in England.

> If this new wealth had not been created by machinery, imperfectly as it
> has been applied, the wars of Europe, in opposition to Napoleon, and
> to support the aristocratic principles of society, could not have been
> maintained. And yet this new power was the creation of the working-
> classes. (Note, *l. c.*, p.22.)

To them, therefore, the fruits of this new power belonged. The
newly created gigantic productive forces, hitherto used only to enrich
individuals and to enslave the masses, offered to Owen the foundations for a reconstruction of society; they were destined, as the common property of all, to be worked for the common good of all.

Owen's communism was based upon this purely business foundation, the outcome, so to say, of commercial calculation. Throughout, it
maintained this practical character. Thus, in 1823, Owen proposed the
relief of the distress in Ireland by communist colonies, and drew up
complete estimates of costs of founding them, yearly expenditure, and
probably revenue. And in his definite plan for the future, the technical
working out of details is managed with such practical knowledge—
ground plan, front and side and bird's-eye views all included—that
the Owen method of social reform once accepted, there is from the
practical point of view little to be said against the actual arrangement
of details.

His advance in the direction of communism was the turning point
in Owen's life. As long as he was simply a philanthropist, he was
rewarded with nothing but wealth, applause, honor, and glory. He was
the most popular man in Europe. Not only men of his own class, but
statesmen and princes listened to him approvingly. But when he came
out with his communist theories that was quite another thing. Three
great obstacles seemed to him especially to block the path to social
reform: private property, religion, the present form of marriage.

He knew what confronted him if he attacked these—outlawry,
excommunication from official society, the loss of his whole social
position. But nothing of this prevented him from attacking them
without fear of consequences, and what he had foreseen happened.
Banished from official society, with a conspiracy of silence against
him in the press, ruined by his unsuccessful communist experiments
in America, in which he sacrificed all his fortune, he turned directly
to the working class and continued working in their midst for thirty
years. Every social movement, every real advance in England on behalf
of the workers links itself on to the name of Robert Owen. He forced
through in 1819, after five years' fighting, the first law limiting the

hours of labor of women and children in factories. He was president of the first congress at which all the trade unions of England united in a single great trade association. He introduced as transition measures to the complete communistic organization of society, on the one hand, cooperative societies for retail trade and production. These have since that time, at least, given practical proof that the merchant and the manufacturer are socially quite unnecessary. On the other hand, he introduced labor bazaars for the exchange of the products of labor through the medium of labor notes, whose unit was a single hour of work; institutions necessarily doomed to failure, but completely anticipating Proudhon's bank of exchange of a much later period, and differing entirely from this in that it did not claim to be the panacea for all social ills, but only a first step towards a much more radical revolution of society.

The utopians' mode of thought has for a long time governed the socialist ideas of the nineteenth century, and still governs some of them. Until very recently, all French and English socialists did homage to it. The earlier German communism, including that of Weitling, was of the same school. To all these, socialism is the expression of absolute truth, reason and justice, and has only to be discovered to conquer all the world by virtue of its own power. And as an absolute truth is independent of time, space, and of the historical development of man, it is a mere accident when and where it is discovered. With all this, absolute truth, reason, and justice are different with the founder of each different school. And as each one's special kind of absolute truth, reason, and justice is again conditioned by his subjective understanding, his conditions of existence, the measure of his knowledge and his intellectual training, there is no other ending possible in this conflict of absolute truths than that they shall be mutually exclusive of one another. Hence, from this nothing could come but a kind of eclectic, average socialism, which, as a matter of fact, has up to the present time dominated the minds of most of the socialist workers in France and England. Hence, a mishmash allowing of the most manifold shades of opinion: a mishmash of such critical statements, economic theories, pictures of future society by the founders of different sects, as excite a minimum of opposition; a mishmash which is the more easily brewed the more definite sharp edges of the individual constituents are rubbed down in the stream of debate, like rounded pebbles in a brook.

To make a science of socialism, it had first to be placed upon a real basis.

# II
# Dialectics

In the meantime, along with and after the French philosophy of the eighteenth century, had arisen the new German philosophy, culminating in Hegel.

Its greatest merit was the taking up again of dialectics as the highest form of reasoning. The old Greek philosophers were all born natural dialecticians, and Aristotle, the most encyclopedic of them, had already analyzed the most essential forms of dialectic thought. The newer philosophy, on the other hand, although in it also dialectics had brilliant exponents (e.g. Descartes and Spinoza), had, especially through English influence, become more and more rigidly fixed in the so-called metaphysical mode of reasoning, by which also the French of the eighteenth century were almost wholly dominated, at all events in their special philosophical work. Outside philosophy in the restricted sense, the French nevertheless produced masterpieces of dialectic. We need only call to mind Diderot's *Le Neveu de Rameau*, and Rousseau's *Discours sur l'origine et les fondements de l'inégalité parmi less hommes*. We give here, in brief, the essential character of these two modes of thought.

When we consider and reflect upon nature at large, or the history of mankind, or our own intellectual activity, at first we see the picture of an endless entanglement of relations and reactions, permutations and combinations, in which nothing remains what, where and as it was, but everything moves, changes, comes into being and passes away. We see, therefore, at first the picture as a whole, with its individual parts still more or less kept in the background; we observe the movements, transitions, connections, rather than the things that move, combine, and are connected. This primitive, naive but intrinsically correct conception of the world is that of ancient Greek philosophy, and was first clearly formulated by Heraclitus: everything is and is not, for everything is fluid, is constantly changing, constantly coming into being and passing away.[4]

---

4    Unknown to the Western world until the twentieth century, the Chinese philosopher Lao Tzu was a predecessor of, or possibly contemporary to, Heraclitus. Lao Tzu wrote the renowned *Tao Te Ching* in which he also espouses the fundamental principles of dialectics.

But this conception, correctly as it expresses the general character of the picture of appearances as a whole, does not suffice to explain the details of which this picture is made up, and so long as we do not understand these, we have not a clear idea of the whole picture. In order to understand these details, we must detach them from their natural, special causes, effects, etc. This is, primarily, the task of natural science and historical research: branches of science which the Greeks of classical times, on very good grounds, relegated to a subordinate position, because they had first of all to collect materials for these sciences to work upon. A certain amount of natural and historical material must be collected before there can be any critical analysis, comparison, and arrangement in classes, orders, and species. The foundations of the exact natural sciences were, therefore, first worked out by the Greeks of the Alexandrian period,[5] and later on, in the Middle Ages, by the Arabs. Real natural science dates from the second half of the fifteenth century, and thence onward it had advanced with constantly increasing rapidity. The analysis of nature into its individual parts, the grouping of the different natural processes and objects in definite classes, the study of the internal anatomy of organized bodies in their manifold forms—these were the fundamental conditions of the gigantic strides in our knowledge of Nature that have been made during the last four hundred years. But this method of work has also left us as legacy the habit of observing natural objects and processes in isolation, apart from their connection with the vast whole; of observing them in repose, not in motion; as constraints, not as essentially variables; in their death, not in their life. And when this way of looking at things was transferred by Bacon and Locke from natural science to philosophy, it begot the narrow, metaphysical mode of thought peculiar to the last century.

To the metaphysician, things and their mental reflexes, ideas, are isolated, are to be considered one after the other and apart from each

5   The Alexandrian period of the development of science comprises the period extending from the 3rd century B.C.E. to the seventeenth century A.D. It derives its name from the town of Alexandria in Egypt, which was one of the most important centers of international economic intercourses at that time. In the Alexandrian period, mathematics (Euclid and Archimedes), geography, astronomy, anatomy, physiology, etc., attained considerable development.

China also began development in natural sciences in the third century B.C.E.

other, are objects of investigation fixed, rigid, given once for all. He thinks in absolutely irreconcilable antitheses. "His communication is 'yea, yea; nay, nay'; for whatsoever is more than these cometh of evil." For him, a thing either exists or does not exist; a thing cannot at the same time be itself and something else. Positive and negative absolutely exclude one another; cause and effect stand in a rigid antithesis, one to the other.

At first sight, this mode of thinking seems to us very luminous, because it is that of so-called sound common sense. Only sound common sense, respectable fellow that he is, in the homely realm of his own four walls, has very wonderful adventures directly he ventures out into the wide world of research. And the metaphysical mode of thought, justifiable and necessary as it is in a number of domains whose extent varies according to the nature of the particular object of investigation, sooner or later reaches a limit, beyond which it becomes one-sided, restricted, abstract, lost in insoluble contradictions. In the contemplation of individual things, it forgets the connection between them; in the contemplation of their existence, it forgets the beginning and end of that existence; of their repose, it forgets their motion. It cannot see the woods for the trees.

For everyday purposes, we know and can say, e.g., whether an animal is alive or not. But, upon closer inquiry, we find that this is, in many cases, a very complex question, as the jurists know very well. They have cudgeled their brains in vain to discover a rational limit beyond which the killing of the child in its mother's womb is murder. It is just as impossible to determine absolutely the moment of death, for physiology proves that death is not an instantaneous, momentary phenomenon, but a very protracted process.

In like manner, every organized being is every moment the same and not the same; every moment, it assimilates matter supplied from without, and gets rid of other matter; every moment, some cells of its body die and others build themselves anew; in a longer or shorter time, the matter of its body is completely renewed, and is replaced by other molecules of matter, so that every organized being is always itself, and yet something other than itself.

Further, we find upon closer investigation that the two poles of an antithesis, positive and negative, e.g., are as inseparable as they are opposed, and that despite all their opposition, they mutually interpenetrate. And we find, in like manner, that cause and effect are conceptions which only hold good in their application to individual cases; but as soon as we consider the individual cases in their general connection with the universe as a whole, they run into each other, and they become confounded when we contemplate that universal action and reaction in which causes and effects are eternally changing places, so that what is effect here and now will be cause there and then, and vice versa.

None of these processes and modes of thought enters into the framework of metaphysical reasoning. Dialectics, on the other hand, comprehends things and their representations, ideas, in their essential connection, concatenation, motion, origin and ending. Such processes as those mentioned above are, therefore, so many corroborations of its own method of procedure.

Nature is the proof of dialectics, and it must be said for modern science that it has furnished this proof with very rich materials increasing daily, and thus has shown that, in the last resort, Nature works dialectically and not metaphysically; that it does not move in the eternal oneness of a perpetually recurring circle, but goes through a real historical evolution. In this connection, Darwin must be named before all others. He dealt the metaphysical conception of nature the heaviest blow by his proof that all organic beings, plants, animals, and man himself, are the products of a process of evolution going on through millions of years. But the naturalists who have learned to think dialectically are few and far between, and this conflict of the results of discovery with preconceived modes of thinking explains the endless confusion now reigning in theoretical natural science, the despair of teachers as well as learners, of authors and readers alike.

An exact representation of the universe, of its evolution, of the development of mankind, and of the reflection of this evolution in the minds of men, can therefore only be obtained by the methods of dialectics with its constant regard to the innumerable actions and reactions of life and death, of progressive or retrogressive changes. And in this spirit, the new German philosophy has worked. Kant began his career by resolving the stable solar system of Newton and its eternal duration, after the famous initial impulse had once been given, into the result of a historical process, the formation of the sun and all the planets out of a rotating, nebulous mass. From this, he at the same time drew the conclusion that, given this origin of the solar system, its future death followed of necessity. His theory, half a century later, was established mathematically by Laplace, and half a century after that, the spectroscope proved the existence in space of such incandescent masses of gas in various stages of condensation.

This new German philosophy culminated in the Hegelian system. In this system—and herein is its great merit—for the first time the whole world, natural, historical, intellectual, is represented as a process, i.e., as in constant motion, change, transformation, development; and the attempt is made to trace out the internal connection that makes a continuous whole of all this movement and development. From this point of view, the history of mankind no longer appeared as a wild whirl of senseless deeds of violence, all equally condemnable at the judgment seat of mature philosophic reason and which are best forgotten as quickly as possible, but as the process of evolution of man himself. It was now the task of the intellect to follow the gradual march of this process through all its devious ways, and to trace out the inner law running through all its apparently accidental phenomena.

That the Hegelian system did not solve the problem it propounded is here immaterial. Its epoch-making merit was that it propounded the problem. This problem is one that no single individual will ever be able to solve. Although Hegel was—with Saint-Simon—the most encyclopedic mind of his time, yet he was limited, first, by the necessary limited extent of his own knowledge and, second, by the limited extent and depth of the knowledge and conceptions of his age. To these limits, a third must be added. Hegel was an idealist. To him, the thoughts within his brain were not the more or less abstract pictures of actual things and processes, but, conversely, things and their evolution were only the realized pictures of the "Idea," existing somewhere from eternity before the world was. This way of thinking turned everything upside down, and completely reversed the actual connection of things in the world. Correctly and ingeniously as many groups of facts were grasped by Hegel, yet, for the reasons just given, there is much that is botched, artificial, labored, in a word, wrong in point of detail. The Hegelian system, in itself, was a colossal miscarriage—but it was also the last of its kind.

It was suffering, in fact, from an internal and incurable contradiction. Upon the one hand, its essential proposition was the conception that human history is a process of evolution, which, by its very nature, cannot find its intellectual final term in the discovery of any so-called absolute truth. But, on the other hand, it laid claim to being the very essence of this absolute truth. A system of natural and historical knowledge, embracing everything, and final for all time, is a contradiction to the fundamental law of dialectic reasoning.

This law, indeed, by no means excludes, but, on the contrary, includes the idea that the systematic knowledge of the external universe can make giant strides from age to age.

The perception of the fundamental contradiction in German idealism led necessarily back to materialism, but, *nota bene*, not to the simply metaphysical, exclusively mechanical materialism of the eighteenth century. Old materialism looked upon all previous history as a crude heap of irrationality and violence; modern materialism sees in it the process of evolution of humanity, and aims at discovering the laws thereof. With the French of the eighteenth century, and even with Hegel, the conception obtained of nature as a whole, moving in narrow circles, and forever immutable, with its eternal celestial bodies, as Newton, and unalterable organic species, as Linnaeus, taught. Modern materialism embraces the more recent discoveries of natural science, according to which nature also has its history in time, the celestial bodies, like the organic species that, under favorable conditions, people them, being born and perishing. And even if nature, as a whole, must still be said to move in recurrent cycles, these cycles assume infinitely larger dimensions. In both aspects, modern materialism is essentially dialectic, and no longer requires the assistance of that sort of philosophy which, queenlike, pretended to rule the remaining mob of sciences. As soon as each special science is bound to make clear its position in the great totality of things and of our knowledge of things, a special science dealing with this totality is superfluous or unnecessary. That which still survives of all earlier philosophy is the science of thought and its laws—formal logic and dialectics. Everything else is subsumed in the positive science of nature and history.

While, however, the revolution in the conception of nature could only be made in proportion to the corresponding positive materials furnished by research, already much earlier certain historical facts had occurred which led to a decisive change in the conception of history. In 1831, the first working-class rising took place in Lyons; between 1838 and 1842, the first national working-class movement, that of the English Chartists, reached its height. The class struggle between proletariat and bourgeoisie came to the front in the history of the most advanced countries in Europe, in proportion to the development, upon the one hand, of modern industry, upon the other, of the newly-acquired political supremacy of the bourgeoisie. Facts more and more strenuously gave the lie to the teachings of bourgeois economy as to the identity of the interests of capital and labor, as to the universal harmony and universal prosperity that would be the consequence of unbridled competition. All these things could no longer be ignored, any more than the French and English socialism, which was their theoretical, though very imperfect, expression. But the old idealist conception of history, which was not yet dislodged, knew nothing of class struggles based upon economic interests, knew nothing of economic interests; production and all economic relations appeared in it only as incidental, subordinate elements in the "history of civilization."

The new facts made imperative a new examination of all past history. Then it was seen that *all* past history, with the exception of its primitive stages, was the history of class struggles; that these warring classes of society are always the products of the modes of production and of exchange—in a word, of the *economic* conditions of their time; that the economic structure of society always furnishes the real basis, starting from which we can alone work out the ultimate explanation of the whole superstructure of juridical and political institutions as well as of the religious, philosophical, and other ideas of a given historical period. Hegel has freed history from metaphysics—he had made it dialectic; but his conception of history was essentially idealistic. But now idealism was driven from its last refuge, the philosophy of history; now a materialistic treatment of history was propounded, and a method found of explaining man's "knowing" by his "being," instead of, as heretofore, his "being" by his "knowing."

From that time forward, socialism was no longer an accidental discovery of this or that ingenious brain, but the necessary outcome of the struggle between two historically developed classes—the proletariat and the bourgeoisie. Its task was no longer to manufacture a system of society as perfect as possible, but to examine the historico-economic succession of events from which these classes and their antagonism had of necessity sprung, and to discover in the economic conditions thus created the means of ending the conflict. But the socialism of earlier days was as incompatible with this materialist conception as the conception of nature of the French materialists was with dialectics and modern natural science. The socialism of earlier days certainly criticized the existing capitalistic mode of production and its consequences. But it could not explain them, and, therefore, could not get the mastery of them. It could only simply reject them as bad. The more strongly this earlier socialism denounced the exploitation of the working class, inevitable under capitalism, the less able was it clearly to show in what this exploitation consisted and how it arose. But for this it was necessary—

1. to present the capitalistic method of production in its historical connection and its inevitableness during a particular historical period, and therefore, also, to present its inevitable downfall; and
2. to lay bare its essential character, which was still a secret. This was done by the discovery of *surplus value*.

It was shown that the appropriation of unpaid labor is the basis of the capitalist mode of production and of the exploitation of the worker that occurs under it; that even if the capitalist buys the labor power of his laborer at its full value as a commodity on the market, he yet extracts more value from it than he paid for; and that in the ultimate analysis, this surplus value forms those sums of value from which are heaped up constantly increasing masses of capital in the hands of the possessing classes. The genesis of capitalist production and the production of capital were both explained.

These two great discoveries, the materialistic conception of history and the revelation of the secret of capitalistic production through surplus value, we owe to Marx. With these discoveries, socialism became a science. The next thing was to work out all its details and relations.

# III
# Historical Materialism

The materialist conception of history starts from the proposition that the production of the means to support human life and, next to production, the exchange of things produced, is the basis of all social structure; that in every society that has appeared in history, the manner in which wealth is distributed and society divided into classes or orders is dependent upon what is produced, how it is produced, and how the products are exchanged. From this point of view, the final causes of all social changes and political revolutions are to be sought, not in men's brains, not in men's better insights into eternal truth and justice, but in changes in the modes of production and exchange. They are to be sought, not in the *philosophy*, but in the *economics* of each particular epoch. The growing perception that existing social institutions are unreasonable and unjust, that reason has become unreason, and right wrong,[6] is only proof that in the modes of production and exchange changes have silently taken place with which the social order, adapted to earlier economic conditions, is no longer in keeping. From this it also follows that the means of getting rid of the incongruities that have been brought to light must also be present, in a more or less developed condition, within the changed modes of production themselves. These means are not to be invented by deduction from fundamental principles, but are to be discovered in the stubborn facts of the existing system of production.

What is, then, the position of modern socialism in this connection?

The present situation of society—this is now pretty generally conceded—is the creation of the ruling class of today, of the bourgeoisie. The mode of production peculiar to the bourgeoisie, known, since Marx, as the capitalist mode of production, was incompatible with the feudal system, with the privileges it conferred upon individuals, entire social ranks and local corporations, as well as with the hereditary ties of subordination which constituted the framework of its social organization. The bourgeoisie broke up the feudal system and built upon its ruins the capitalist order of society, the kingdom of free competition, of personal liberty, of the equality, before the law, of all commodity

---

6   Mephistopheles in Goethe's *Faust*, Part I, Scene 4.

owners, of all the rest of the capitalist blessings. Thenceforward, the capitalist mode of production could develop in freedom. Since steam, machinery, and the making of machines by machinery transformed the older manufacture into modern industry, the productive forces, evolved under the guidance of the bourgeoisie, developed with a rapidity and in a degree unheard of before. But just as the older manufacture, in its time, and handicraft, becoming more developed under its influence, had come into collision with the feudal trammels of the guilds, so now modern industry, in its complete development, comes into collision with the bounds within which the capitalist mode of production holds it confined. The new productive forces have already outgrown the capitalistic mode of using them. And this conflict between productive forces and modes of production is not a conflict engendered in the mind of man, like that between original sin and divine justice. It exists, in fact, objectively, outside us, independently of the will and actions even of the men that have brought it on. Modern socialism is nothing but the reflex, in thought, of this conflict in fact; its ideal reflection in the minds, first, of the class directly suffering under it, the working class.

Now, in what does this conflict consist?

Before capitalist production, i.e., in the Middle Ages, the system of petty industry obtained generally, based upon the private property of the laborers in their means of production; in the country, the agriculture of the small peasant, freeman, or serf; in the towns, the handicrafts organized in guilds. The instruments of labor—land, agricultural implements, the workshop, the tool—were the instruments of labor of single individuals, adapted for the use of one worker, and, therefore, of necessity, small, dwarfish, circumscribed. But, for this very reason, they belonged as a rule to the producer himself. To concentrate these scattered, limited means of production, to enlarge them, to turn them into the powerful levers of production of the present day—this was precisely the historic role of capitalist production and of its upholder, the bourgeoisie. In the fourth section of *Capital*, Marx has explained in detail how since the fifteenth century this has been historically worked out through the three phases of simple cooperation, manufacture, and modern industry. But the bourgeoisie, as is shown there, could not transform these puny means of production into mighty productive forces without transforming them, at the same time, from means of production of the individual into *social* means of production only workable by a collectivity of men. The spinning wheel, the handloom, the blacksmith's hammer, were replaced by the spinning machine, the power loom, the steam hammer; the individual workshop, by the factory implying the cooperation of hundreds and thousands of workmen. In like manner, production itself changed from a series of individual into a series of social acts, and the production from individual to social products. The yarn, the cloth, the metal articles that now come out of the factory were the joint product of many workers, through whose hands they had successively to pass before they were ready. No one person could say of them: "*I* made that; this is *my* product."

But where, in a given society, the fundamental form of production is that spontaneous division of labor which creeps in gradually and not upon any preconceived plan, there the products take on the form of *commodities*, whose mutual exchange, buying and selling, enable the individual producers to satisfy their manifold wants. And this was the case in the Middle Ages. The peasant, e.g., sold to the artisan agricultural products and bought from him the products of handicraft. Into this society of individual producers, of commodity producers, the new mode of production thrust itself. In the midst of the old division of labor, grown up spontaneously and upon *no definite plan*, which had governed the whole of society, now arose division of labor upon *a definite plan*, as organized in the factory; side by side with *individual* production appeared *social* production. The products of both were sold in the same market, and, therefore, at prices at least approximately equal. But organization upon a definite plan was stronger than spontaneous division of labor. The factories working with the combined social forces of a collectivity of individuals produced their commodities far more cheaply than the individual small producers. Individual producers succumbed in one department after another. Socialized production revolutionized all the old methods of production. But its revolutionary character was, at the same time, so little recognized that it was, on the contrary, introduced as a means of increasing and developing the production of commodities. When it arose, it found ready-made, and made liberal use of, certain machinery for the production and exchange of commodities: merchants' capital, handicraft, wage labor. Socialized production thus introducing itself as a new form of the production of commodities, it was a matter of course that under it the old forms of appropriation remained in full swing, and were applied to its products as well.

In the medieval stage of evolution of the production of commodities, the question as to the owner of the product of labor could not arise. The individual producer, as a rule, had, from raw material belonging to himself, and generally his own handiwork, produced it with his own tools, by the labor of his own hands or of his family. There was no need for him to appropriate the new product. It belonged wholly to him, as a matter of course. His property in the product was, therefore, based *upon his own labor*. Even where external help was used, this was, as a rule, of little importance, and very generally was compensated by something other than wages. The apprentices and journeymen of the guilds worked less for board and wages than for education, in order that they might become master craftsmen themselves.

Then came the concentration of the means of production and of the producers in large workshops and manufactories, their trans-formation into actual socialized means of production and socialized producers. But the socialized producers and means of production and their products were still treated, after this change, just as they had been before, i.e., as the means of production and the products of indi-viduals. Hitherto, the owner of the instruments of labor had himself appropriated the product, because, as a rule, it was his own product and the assistance of others was the exception. Now, the owner of the instruments of labor always appropriated to himself the product, although it was no longer *his* product but exclusively the product of the *labor of others*. Thus, the products now produced socially were not appropriated by those who had actually set in motion the means of production and actually produced the commodities, but by the *capital-ists*. The means of production, and production itself, had become in essence socialized. But they were subjected to a form of appropriation which presupposes the private production of individuals, under which, therefore, every one owns his own product and brings it to market. The mode of production is subjected to this form of appropriation, although it abolishes the conditions upon which the latter rests.[7]

---

7  It is hardly necessary in this connection to point out that, even if the *form* of appropriation remains the same, the *character* of the appropriation is just as much revolutionized as production is by the changes described above. It is, of course, a very different matter whether I appropriate to myself my own product or that of another. Note in passing that wage labor, which contains the whole capitalist mode of production in embryo, is very ancient; in a sporadic, scattered form, it existed for centuries alongside slave labor. But

This contradiction, which gives to the new mode of production its capitalistic character, *contains the germ of the whole of the social antagonisms of today.* The greater the mastery obtained by the new mode of production over all important fields of production and in all manufacturing countries, the more it reduced individual production to an insignificant residuum, *the more clearly was brought out the incompatibility of socialized production with capitalistic appropriation.*

The first capitalists found, as we have said, alongside of other forms of labor, wage labor ready-made for them on the market. But it was exceptional, complementary, accessory, transitory wage labor. The agricultural laborer, though, upon occasion, he hired himself out by the day, had a few acres of his own land on which he could at all events live at a pinch. The guilds were so organized that the journeyman to today became the master of tomorrow. But all this changed, as soon as the means of production became socialized and concentrated in the hands of capitalists. The means of production, as well as the product, of the individual producer became more and more worthless; there was nothing left for him but to turn wageworker under the capitalist. Wage labor, aforetime the exception and accessory, now became the rule and basis of all production; aforetime complementary, it now became the sole remaining function of the worker. The wageworker for a time became a wageworker for life. The number of these permanent wageworkers was further enormously increased by the breaking up of the feudal system that occurred at the same time, by the disbanding of the retainers of the feudal lords, the eviction of the peasants from their homesteads, etc. The separation was made complete between the means of production concentrated in the hands of the capitalists, on the one side, and the producers, possessing nothing but their labor power, on the other. *The contradiction between socialized production and capitalistic appropriation manifested itself as the antagonism of proletariat and bourgeoisie.*

We have seen that the capitalistic mode of production thrust its way into a society of commodity producers, of individual producers, whose social bond was the exchange of their products. But every society based upon the production of commodities has this peculiarity: that the producers have lost control over their own social interrelations. Each man produces for himself with such means of production as he

---

the embryo could duly develop into the capitalistic mode of production only when the necessary historical preconditions had been furnished. [Engels.]

may happen to have, and for such exchange as he may require to satisfy his remaining wants. No one knows how much of his particular article is coming on the market, nor how much of it will be wanted. No one knows whether his individual product will meet an actual demand, whether he will be able to make good his costs of production or even to sell his commodity at all. Anarchy reigns in socialized production.

But the production of commodities, like every other form of production, has it peculiar, inherent laws inseparable from it; and these laws work, despite anarchy, in and through anarchy. They reveal themselves in the only persistent form of social interrelations, i.e., in exchange, and here they affect the individual producers as compulsory laws of competition. They are, at first, unknown to these producers themselves, and have to be discovered by them gradually and as the result of experience. They work themselves out, therefore, independently of the producers, and in antagonism to them, as inexorable natural laws of their particular form of production. The product governs the producers.

In medieval society, especially in the earlier centuries, production was essentially directed toward satisfying the wants of the individual. It satisfied, in the main, only the wants of the producer and his family. Where relations of personal dependence existed, as in the country, it also helped to satisfy the wants of the feudal lord. In all this there was, therefore, no exchange; the products, consequently, did not assume the character of commodities. The family of the peasant produced almost everything they wanted: clothes and furniture, as well as the means of subsistence. Only when it began to produce more than was sufficient to supply its own wants and the payments in kind to the feudal lords, only then did it also produce commodities. This surplus, thrown into socialized exchange and offered for sale, became commodities.

The artisan in the towns, it is true, had from the first to produce for exchange. But they, also, themselves supplied the greatest part of their individual wants. They had gardens and plots of land. They turned their cattle out into the communal forest, which, also, yielded them timber and firing. The women spun flax, wool, and so forth. Production for the purpose of exchange, production of commodities, was only in its infancy. Hence, exchange was restricted, the market narrow, the methods of production stable; there was local exclusiveness without, local unity within; the mark in the country; in the town, the guild.

But with the extension of the production of commodities, and especially with the introduction of the capitalist mode of production, the laws of commodity production, hitherto latent, came into action more openly and with greater force. The old bonds were loosened, the old exclusive limits broken through, the producers were more and more turned into independent, isolated producers of commodities. It became apparent that the production of society at large was ruled by absence of plan, by accident, by anarchy; and this anarchy grew to greater and greater height. But the chief means by aid of which the capitalist mode of production intensified this anarchy of socialized production was the exact opposite of anarchy. It was the increasing organization of production, upon a social basis, in every individual productive establishment. By this, the old, peaceful, stable condition of things was ended. Wherever this organization of production was introduced into a branch of industry, it brooked no other method of production by its side. The field of labor became a battleground. The great geographical discoveries, and the colonization following them, multiplied markets and quickened the transformation of handicraft into manufacture. The war did not simply break out between the individual producers of particular localities. The local struggles begat, in their turn, national conflicts, the commercial wars of the seventeenth and eighteenth centuries.

Finally, modern industry and the opening of the world market made the struggle universal, and at the same time gave it an unheard-of virulence. Advantages in natural or artificial conditions of production now decide the existence or nonexistence of individual capitalists, as well as of whole industries and countries. He that falls is remorselessly cast aside. It is the Darwinian struggle of the individual for existence transferred from nature to society with intensified violence. The conditions of existence natural to the animal appear as the final term of human development. The contradiction between socialized production and capitalistic appropriation now presents itself as *an antagonism between the organization of production in the individual workshop and the anarchy of production in society generally.*

The capitalistic mode of production moves in these two forms of the antagonism immanent to it from its very origin. It is never able to get out of that "vicious circle" which Fourier had already discovered. What Fourier could not, indeed, see in his time is that this circle is gradually narrowing; that the movement becomes more and more a spiral, and must come to an end, like the movement of planets, by collision with the center. It is the compelling force of anarchy in the production of society at large that more and more completely turns the great majority of men into proletarians; and it is the masses of the proletariat again who will finally put an end to anarchy in production. It is the compelling force of anarchy in social production that turns the limitless perfectibility of machinery under modern industry into a compulsory law by which every individual industrial capitalist must perfect his machinery more and more, under penalty of ruin.

But the perfecting of machinery is making human labor superfluous. If the introduction and increase of machinery means the displacement of millions of manual by a few machine workers, improvement in machinery means the displacement of more and more of the machine workers themselves. It means, in the last instance, the production of a number of available wageworkers in excess of the average needs of capital, the formation of a complete industrial reserve army, as I called it in 1845,[8] available at the times when industry is working at high pressure, to be cast out upon the street when the inevitable crash comes, a constant dead weight upon the limbs of the working class in its struggle for existence with capital, a regulator for keeping of wages down to the low level that suits the interests of capital.

Thus it comes about, to quote Marx, that machinery becomes the most powerful weapon in the war of capital against the working class; that the instruments of labor constantly tear the means of subsistence out of the hands of the laborer; that the very product of the worker is turned into an instrument for his subjugation.

Thus it comes about that the economizing of the instruments of labor becomes at the same time, from the outset, the most reckless waste of labor power, and robbery based upon the normal conditions under which labor functions; that machinery,

> the most powerful instrument for reducing labor time...becomes the most unfailing means for turning the whole lifetime of the worker and his family into labor time at capital's disposal for its own valorization. (*Capital* Vol. 1, Penguin, 532)

Thus it comes about that the overwork of some becomes the preliminary condition for the idleness of others, and that modern industry, which hunts after new consumers over the whole world, forces the

8    Engels, *The Condition of the Working-Class in England*, Moscow: Progress, 1973, 123–24.

consumption of the masses at home down to a starvation minimum, and in doing thus destroys its own home market.

> The law which always holds the relative surplus population or industrial reserve army in equilibrium with the extent and energy of accumulation rivets the worker to capital more firmly than the wedges of Hephaestus held Prometheus to the rock. It makes an accumulation of misery a necessary condition, corresponding to the accumulation of wealth. Accumulation of wealth at one pole is, therefore, at the same time accumulation of misery, the torment of labor, slavery, ignorance, brutalization, and moral degradation at the opposite pole, i.e., on the side of the class that produces its own product as capital. (*Capital* Vol. 1, Penguin, 799)

And to expect any other division of the products from the capitalist mode of production is the same as expecting the electrodes of a battery not to decompose acidulated water, not to liberate oxygen at the positive, hydrogen at the negative pole, so long as they are connected with the battery.

We have seen that the ever-increasing perfectibility of modern machinery is, by the anarchy of social production, turned into a compulsory law that forces the individual industrial capitalist always to improve his machinery, always to increase its productive force. The bare possibility of extending the field of production is transformed for him into a similarly compulsory law. The enormous expansive force of modern industry, compared with which that of gases is mere child's play, appears to us now as a *necessity* for expansion, both qualitative and quantitative, that laughs at all resistance. Such resistance is offered by consumption, by sales, by the markets for the products of modern industry. But the capacity for extension, extensive and intensive, of the markets is primarily governed by quite different laws that work much less energetically. The extension of the markets cannot keep pace with the extension of production. The collision becomes inevitable, and as this cannot produce any real solution so long as it does not break in pieces the capitalist mode of production, the collisions become periodic. Capitalist production has begotten another "vicious circle."

As a matter of fact, since 1825, when the first general crisis broke out, the whole industrial and commercial world, production and exchange among all civilized peoples and their more or less barbaric hangers-on, are thrown out of joint about once every 10 years. Commerce is at a standstill, the markets are glutted, products accumulate, as multitudinous as they are unsaleable, hard cash disappears, credit vanishes, factories are closed, the mass of the workers are in want of the means of subsistence, because they have produced too much of the means of subsistence; bankruptcy follows upon bankruptcy, execution upon execution. The stagnation lasts for years; productive forces and products are wasted and destroyed wholesale, until the accumulated mass of commodities finally filter off, more or less depreciated in value, until production and exchange gradually begin to move again. Little by little, the pace quickens. It becomes a trot. The industrial trot breaks into a canter, the canter in turn grows into the headlong gallop of a perfect steeplechase of industry, commercial credit, and speculation, which finally, after breakneck leaps, ends where it began—in the ditch of a crisis. And so over and over again. We have now, since the year 1825, gone through this five times, and at the present moment (1877) we are going through it for the sixth time. And the character of these crises is so clearly defined that Fourier hit all of them off when he described the first "*crise plethorique,*" a crisis from plethora.

In these crises, the contradiction between socialized production and capitalist appropriation ends in a violent explosion. The circulation of commodities is, for the time being, stopped. Money, the means of circulation, becomes a hindrance to circulation. All the laws of production and circulation of commodities are turned upside down. The economic collision has reached its apogee. *The mode of production is in rebellion against the mode of exchange.*

The fact that the socialized organization of production within the factory has developed so far that it has become incompatible with the anarchy of production in society, which exists side by side with and dominates it, is brought home to the capitalist themselves by the violent concentration of capital that occurs during crises, through the ruin of many large, and a still greater number of small, capitalists. The whole mechanism of the capitalist mode of production breaks down under the pressure of the productive forces, its own creations. It is no longer able to turn all this mass of means of production into capital. They lie fallow, and for that very reason the industrial reserve army must also lie fallow. Means of production, means of subsistence, available laborers, all the elements of production and of general wealth, are present in abundance. But "abundance becomes the source of distress and want" (Fourier), because it is the very thing that prevents the transformation of the means of production and subsistence into capital. For in capitalistic society, the means of production can only function when they have undergone a preliminary transformation into capital, into the means of exploiting human labor power. The necessity of this transformation into capital of the means of production and subsistence stands like a ghost between these and the workers. It alone prevents the coming together of the material and personal levers of production; it alone forbids the means of production to function, the workers to work and live. On the one hand, therefore, the capitalistic mode of production stands convicted of its own incapacity to further direct these productive forces. On the other, these productive forces themselves, with increasing energy, press forward to the removal of the existing contradiction, to the abolition of their quality as capital, to the *practical recognition of their character as social production forces.*

This rebellion of the productive forces, as they grow more and more powerful, against their quality as capital, this stronger and stronger command that their social character shall be recognized, forces the capitalist class itself to treat them more and more as social productive forces, so far as this is possible under capitalist conditions. The period of industrial high pressure, with its unbounded inflation of credit, not less than the crash itself, by the collapse of great capitalist establishments, tends to bring about that form of the socialization of great masses of the means of production which we meet with in the different kinds of joint-stock companies. Many of these means of production and of distribution are, from the outset, so colossal that, like the railways, they exclude all other forms of capitalistic expansion. At a further stage of evolution, this form also becomes insufficient. The producers on a large scale in a particular branch of an industry in a particular country unite in a "trust," a union for the purpose of regulating production. They determine the total amount to be produced, parcel it out among themselves, and thus enforce the selling price fixed beforehand. But trusts of this kind, as soon as business becomes bad, are generally liable to break up, and on this very account compel a yet greater concentration of association. The whole of a particular industry is turned into one gigantic joint-stock company; internal competition gives place to the internal monopoly of this one company. This has happened in 1890 with the English alkali production, which is now, after the fusion of 48 large works, in the hands of one company, conducted upon a single plan, and with a capital of £6,000,000.

In the trusts, freedom of competition changes into its very opposite—into monopoly; and the production without any definite plan of capitalistic society capitulates to the production upon a definite plan of the invading socialistic society. Certainly, this is so far still to the benefit and advantage of the capitalists. But, in this case, the exploitation is so palpable, that it must break down. No nation will put up with production conducted by trusts, with so barefaced an exploitation of the community by a small band of dividend-mongers.

In any case, with trusts or without, the official representative of capitalist society—the state—will ultimately have to undertake the direction of production.[9] This necessity for conversion into state property is felt first in the great institutions for intercourse and communication—the post office, the telegraphs, the railways.

If the crises demonstrate the incapacity of the bourgeoisie for managing any longer modern productive forces, the transformation of the great establishments for production and distribution into joint-stock companies, trusts, and state property, show how unnecessary the bourgeoisie are for that purpose. All the social functions of the capitalist are now performed by salaried employees. The capitalist has no further social function than that of pocketing dividends, tearing off

---

9  I say "have to." For only when the means of production and distribution have *actually* outgrown the form of management by joint-stock companies, and when, therefore, the taking them over by the state has become *economically* inevitable, only then—even if it is the state of today that effects this—is there an economic advance, the attainment of another step preliminary to the taking over of all productive forces by society itself. But of late, since Bismarck went in for state ownership of industrial establishments, a kind of spurious socialism has arisen, degenerating, now and again, into something of flunkyism, that without more ado declares *all* state-ownership, even of the Bismarkian sort, to be socialistic. Certainly, if the taking over by the state of the tobacco industry is socialistic, then Napoleon and Metternich must be numbered among the founders of socialism.

If the Belgian state, for quite ordinary political and financial reasons, itself constructed its chief railway lines; if Bismarck, not under any economic compulsion, took over for the state the chief Prussian lines, simply to be the better able to have them in hand in case of war, to bring up the railway employees as voting cattle for the government, and especially to create for himself a new source of income independent of parliamentary votes—this was, in no sense, a socialistic measure, directly or indirectly, consciously or unconsciously. Otherwise, the Royal Maritime Company, the Royal porcelain manufacture, and even the regimental tailor of the army would also be socialistic institutions, or even, as was seriously proposed by a sly dog in Frederick William III's reign, the taking over by the state of the brothels. [Engels.]

coupons, and gambling on the stock exchange, where the different capitalists despoil one another of their capital. At first, the capitalistic mode of production forces out the workers. Now, it forces out the capitalists, and reduces them, just as it reduced the workers, to the ranks of the surplus population, although not immediately into those of the industrial reserve army.

But, the transformation—either into joint-stock companies and trusts, or into state ownership—does not do away with the capitalistic nature of the productive forces. In the joint-stock companies and trusts, this is obvious. And the modern state, again, is only the organization that bourgeois society takes on in order to support the external conditions of the capitalist mode of production against the encroachments as well of the workers as of individual capitalists. The modern state, no matter what its form, is essentially a capitalist machine—the state of the capitalists, the ideal personification of the total national capital. The more it proceeds to the taking over of productive forces, the more does it actually become the national capitalist, the more citizens does it exploit. The workers remain wageworkers—proletarians. The capitalist relation is not done away with. It is, rather, brought to a head. But, brought to a head, it topples over. State ownership of the productive forces is not the solution of the conflict, but concealed within it are the technical conditions that form the elements of that solution.

This solution can only consist in the practical recognition of the social nature of the modern forces of production, and therefore in the harmonizing with the socialized character of the means of production. And this can only come about by society openly and directly taking possession of the productive forces which have outgrown all control, except that of society as a whole. The social character of the means of production and of the products today reacts against the producers, periodically disrupts all production and exchange, acts only like a law of nature working blindly, forcibly, destructively. But with the taking over by society of the productive forces, the social character of the means of production and of the products will be utilized by the producers with a perfect understanding of its nature, and instead of being a source of disturbance and periodical collapse, will become the most powerful lever of production itself.

Active social forces work exactly like natural forces: blindly, forcibly, destructively, so long as we do not understand, and reckon with, them.

But, when once we understand them, when once we grasp their action, their direction, their effects, it depends only upon ourselves to subject them more and more to our own will, and, by means of them, to reach our own ends. And this holds quite especially of the mighty productive forces of today. As long as we obstinately refuse to understand the nature and the character of these social means of action—and this understanding goes against the grain of the capitalist mode of production, and its defenders—so long these forces are at work in spite of us, in opposition to us, so long they master us, as we have shown above in detail.

But when once their nature is understood, they can, in the hands of the producers working together, be transformed from master demons into willing servants. The difference is as that between the destructive force of electricity in the lightning in the storm, and electricity under command in the telegraph and the voltaic arc; the difference between a conflagration, and fire working in the service of man. With this recognition, at last, of the real nature of the productive forces of today, the social anarchy of production gives place to a social regulation of production upon a definite plan, according to the needs of the community and of each individual. Then the capitalist mode of appropriation, in which the product enslaves first the producer, and then the appropriator, is replaced by the mode of appropriation of the products that is based upon the nature of the modern means of production; upon the one hand, direct social appropriation, as means to the maintenance and extension of production—on the other, direct individual appropriation, as means of subsistence and of enjoyment.

While the capitalist mode of production more and more completely transforms the great majority of the population into proletarians, it creates the power which, under penalty of its own destruction, is forced to accomplish this revolution. While it forces on more and more of the transformation of the vast means of production, already socialized, into state property, it shows itself the way to accomplishing this revolution. *The proletariat seizes political power and turns the means of production into state property.*

But, in doing this, it abolishes itself as proletariat, abolishes all class distinction and class antagonisms, abolishes also the state as state. Society, thus far, based upon class antagonisms, had need of the state. That is, of an organization of the particular class which was, *pro tempore*, the exploiting class, an organization for the purpose of preventing any interference from without with the existing conditions of production, and, therefore, especially, for the purpose of forcibly keeping the exploited classes in the condition of oppression corresponding with the given mode of production (slavery, serfdom, wage labor). The state was the official representative of society as a whole; the gathering of it together into a visible embodiment. But, it was this only in so far as it was the state of that class which itself represented, for the time being, society as a whole:

- in ancient times, the state of slaveowning citizens;
- in the Middle Ages, the feudal lords;
- in our own times, the bourgeoisie.

When, at last, it becomes the real representative of the whole of society, it renders itself unnecessary. As soon as there is no longer any social class to be held in subjection; as soon as class rule, and the individual struggle for existence based upon our present anarchy in production, with the collisions and excesses arising from these, are removed, nothing more remains to be repressed, and a special repressive force, a state, is no longer necessary. The first act by virtue of which the state really constitutes itself the representative of the whole of society—the taking possession of the means of production in the name of society—this is, at the same time, its last independent act as a state. State interference in social relations becomes, in one domain after another, superfluous, and then dies out of itself; the government of persons is replaced by the administration of things, and by the conduct of processes of production. The state is not "abolished." *It dies out.* This gives the measure of the value of the phrase: "*a free state*," both as to its justifiable use at times by agitators, and as to its ultimate scientific inefficiency; and also of the demands of the so-called anarchists for the abolition of the state out of hand.

Since the historical appearance of the capitalist mode of production, the appropriation by society of all the means of production has often been dreamed of, more or less vaguely, by individuals, as well as by sects, as the ideal of the future. But it could become possible, could become a historical necessity, only when the actual conditions for its realization were there. Like every other social advance, it becomes practicable, not by men understanding that the existence of classes is in contradiction to justice, equality, etc., not by the mere willingness to abolish these classes, but by virtue of certain new economic conditions. The separation of society into an exploiting and an exploited class, a ruling and an oppressed class, was the necessary consequences of the deficient and restricted development of production in former times. So long as the total social labor only yields a produce which but slightly exceeds that barely necessary for the existence of all; so long, therefore, as labor engages all or almost all the time of the great majority of the members of society—so long, of necessity, this society is divided into classes. Side by side with the great majority, exclusively bond slaves to labor, arises a class freed from directly productive labor, which looks after the general affairs of society: the direction of labor, state business, law, science, art, etc. It is, therefore, the law of division of labor that lies at the basis of the division into classes. But this does not prevent this division into classes from being carried out by means of violence and robbery, trickery and fraud. It does not prevent the ruling class, once having the upper hand, from consolidating its power at the expense of the working class, from turning its social leadership into an intensified exploitation of the masses.

But if, upon this showing, division into classes has a certain historical justification, it has this only for a given period, only under given social conditions. It was based upon the insufficiency of production. It will be swept away by the complete development of modern productive forces. And, in fact, the abolition of classes in society presupposes a degree of historical evolution at which the existence, not simply of this or that particular ruling class, but of any ruling class at all, and, therefore, the existence of class distinction itself, has become a obsolete anachronism. It presupposes, therefore, the development of production carried out to a degree at which appropriation of the means of production and of the products, and, with this, of political domination, of the monopoly of culture, and of intellectual leadership by a particular class of society, has become not only superfluous but economically, politically, intellectually, a hindrance to development.

This point is now reached. Their political and intellectual bankruptcy is scarcely any longer a secret to the bourgeoisie themselves. Their economic bankruptcy recurs regularly every ten years. In every crisis, society is suffocated beneath the weight of its own productive forces and products, which it cannot use, and stands helpless, face to face with the absurd contradiction that the producers have nothing to consume, because consumers are wanting. The expansive force of the means of production burst the bonds that the capitalist mode of production had imposed upon them. Their deliverance from these bonds is the one precondition for an unbroken, constantly accelerated development of the productive forces, and therewith for a practically unlimited increase of production itself. Nor is this all. The socialized appropriation of the means of production does away, not only with the present artificial restrictions upon production, but also with the positive waste and devastation of productive forces and products that are at the present time the inevitable concomitants of production, and that reach their height in the crises. Further, it sets free for the community at large a mass of means of production and of products, by doing away with the senseless extravagance of the ruling classes of today, and their political representatives. The possibility of securing for every member of society, by means of socialized production, an existence not only fully sufficient materially, and becoming day by day more full, but an existence guaranteeing to all the free development and exercise of their physical and mental faculties—this possibility is now for the first time here, but *it is here.*[10]

With the seizing of the means of production by society, production of commodities is done away with, and, simultaneously, the mastery of the product over the producer. Anarchy in social production is replaced by systematic, definite organization. The struggle for individual existence disappears. Then, for the first time, man, in a certain sense, is finally marked off from the rest of the animal kingdom, and emerges from mere animal conditions of existence into really human ones. The whole sphere of the conditions of life which environ man, and which have hitherto ruled man, now comes under the dominion and control of man, who for the first time becomes the real, conscious lord of nature, because he has now become master of his own social organization. The laws of his own social action, hitherto standing face

---

10   A few figures may serve to give an approximate idea of the enormous expansive force of the modern means of production, even under capitalist pressure. According to Mr. Giffen, the total wealth of Great Britain and Ireland amounted, in round numbers in

1814 to £2,200,000,000,
1865 to £6,100,000,000,
1875 to £8,500,000,000.

As an instance of the squandering of means of production and of products during a crisis, the total loss in the German iron industry alone, in the crisis of 1873-78, was given at the second German Industrial Congress (Berlin, February 21, 1878), as 22,750,000 pounds. [Engels.]

to face with man as laws of nature foreign to, and dominating him, will then be used with full understanding, and so mastered by him. Man's own social organization, hitherto confronting him as a necessity imposed by nature and history, now becomes the result of his own free action. The extraneous objective forces that have, hitherto, governed history, pass under the control of man himself. Only from that time will man himself, more and more consciously, make his own history—only from that time will the social causes set in movement by him have, in the main and in a constantly growing measure, the results intended by him. It is the ascent of man from the kingdom of necessity to the kingdom of freedom.

Let us briefly sum up our sketch of historical evolution.

I. *Medieval Society*—Individual production on a small scale. Means of production adapted for individual use; hence primitive, ungainly, petty, dwarfed in action. Production for immediate consumption, either of the producer himself or his feudal lord. Only where an excess of production over this consumption occurs is such excess offered for sale, enters into exchange. Production of commodities, therefore, only in its infancy. But already it contains within itself, in embryo, *anarchy in the production of society at large.*

II. *Capitalist Revolution*—transformation of industry, at first by means of simple cooperation and manufacture. Concentration of the means of production, hitherto scattered, into great workshops. As a consequence, their transformation from individual to social means of production—a transformation which does not, on the whole, affect the form of exchange. The old forms of appropriation remain in force. The capitalist appears. In his capacity as owner of the means of production, he also appropriates the products and turns them into commodities. Production has become a *social* act. Exchange and appropriation continue to be *individual* acts, the acts of individuals. *The social product is appropriated by the individual capitalist.* Fundamental contradiction, whence arise all the contradictions in which our present-day society moves, and which modern industry brings to light.

A.  Severance of the producer from the means of production. Condemnation of the worker to wage labor for life. *Antagonism between the proletariat and the bourgeoisie.*
B.  Growing predominance and increasing effectiveness of the laws governing the production of commodities. Unbridled competition. *Contradiction between socialized*

> *organization in the individual factory and social anarchy*
> *in the production as a whole.*

C.    On the one hand, perfecting of machinery, made by competition compulsory for each individual manufacturer, and complemented by a constantly growing displacement of laborers. *Industrial reserve army.* On the other hand, unlimited extension of production, also compulsory under competition, for every manufacturer. On both sides, unheard-of development of productive forces, excess of supply over demand, overproduction, glutting of the markets, crises every ten years, the vicious circle: excess here, of means of production and products—excess there, of laborers, without employment and without means of existence. But these two levers of production and of social well-being are unable to work together, because the capitalist form of production prevents the productive forces from working and the products from circulating, unless they are first turned into capital—which their very superabundance prevents. The contradiction has grown into an absurdity. *The mode of production rises in rebellion against the form of exchange.* The bourgeoisie are convicted of incapacity further to manage their own social productive forces.

D.    Partial recognition of the social character of the productive forces forced upon the capitalists themselves. Taking over of the great institutions for production and communication, first by joint-stock companies, later on by trusts, then by the state. The bourgeoisie demonstrated to be a superfluous class. All its social functions are now performed by salaried employees.

III. *Proletarian Revolution*—Solution of the contradictions. The proletariat seizes the public power, and by means of this transforms the socialized means of production, slipping from the hands of the bourgeoisie, into public property. By this act, the proletariat frees the means of production from the character of capital they have thus far borne, and gives their socialized character complete freedom to work itself out. Socialized production upon a predetermined plan becomes henceforth possible. The development of production makes the existence of different classes of society thenceforth an anachronism. In proportion as anarchy in social production vanishes, the political authority of the state dies out. Man, at last the master of his own form of social organization, becomes at the same time the lord over nature, his own master—free.

To accomplish this act of universal emancipation is the historical mission of the modern proletariat. To thoroughly comprehend the historical conditions and thus the very nature of this act, to impart to the now oppressed proletarian class a full knowledge of the conditions and of the meaning of the momentous act it is called upon to accomplish, this is the task of the theoretical expression of the proletarian movement, scientific socialism.

V.I. Lenin in 1918

# The State and Revolution

## V.I. Lenin

*This important work of Marxist theory was written by Lenin while working in clandestinity between August and September of 1917. In it he examines the analysis of the state put forward by opportunists and anarchists, quoting extensively from Engels's* Origin of the Family, Private Property, and the State *and* Anti-Dühring, *as well as Marx's* Civil War in France *and* The 18th Brumaire of Louis Bonaparte. *Basing himself on these earlier works he presents a comprehensive and authoritative Marxist analysis of the state. He emphasizes the need to smash the bourgeois state apparatus and argues that the proletarian "semi-state" will, from its inception, begin to wither away.*

# Preface to the First Edition

T
he question of the state is now acquiring particular importance both in theory and in practical politics. The imperialist
war has immensely accelerated and intensified the process of
transformation of monopoly capitalism into state monopoly capitalism. The monstrous oppression of the working people by the state,
which is merging more and more with the all-powerful capitalist
associations, is becoming increasingly monstrous. The advanced
countries—we mean their hinterland—are becoming military convict
prisons for the workers.

The unprecedented horrors and miseries of the protracted war are
making the people's position unbearable and increasing their anger.
The world proletarian revolution is clearly maturing. The question of
its relation to the state is acquiring practical importance.

The elements of opportunism that accumulated over the decades
of comparatively peaceful development have given rise to the trend
of social-chauvinism which dominated the official socialist parties
throughout the world. This trend—socialism in words and chauvinism in deeds (Plekhanov, Potresov, Breshkovskaya, Rubanovich,
and, in a slightly veiled form, Tsereteli, Chernov and Co. in Russia;
Scheidemann, Legien, David and others in Germany; Renaudel,
Guesde and Vandervelde in France and Belgium; Hyndman and the
Fabians[1] in England, etc., etc.)—is conspicuous for the base, servile
adaptation of the "leaders of socialism" to the interests not only of
"their" national bourgeoisie, but of "their" state, for the majority of

1 *Fabians*—members of the Fabian Society, a British reformist organization
founded in 1884. It grouped mostly bourgeois intellectuals—scholars, writers,
politicians—including Sydney and Beatrice Webb, Ramsay MacDonald and
Bernard Shaw. The Fabians denied the necessity for the proletarian class
struggle and for the socialist revolution. They contended that the transition
from capitalism to socialism could only be effected through minor social
reforms, that is, gradual changes. Lenin described Fabian ideas as "*an
extremely opportunist* trend" (V.I. Lenin, *Collected Works*, Vol. 13, p. 358).

In 1900 the Fabian Society became part of the British Labour Party.
"Fabian socialism" is a source of the Labour Party's ideology.

During the First World War the Fabians took a social-chauvinist stand.
For Lenin's characterisation of Fabian principles, see Lenin's article "British
Pacifism and the British Dislike of Theory" (V.I. Lenin, *Collected Works*,
Vol. 21, pp. 260–65).

the so-called Great Powers have long been exploiting and enslaving a whole number of small and weak nations. And the imperialist war is a war for the division and redivision of this kind of booty. The struggle to free the working people from the influence of the bourgeoisie in general, and of the imperialist bourgeoisie in particular, is impossible without a struggle against opportunist prejudices concerning the "state."

First of all we examine the theory of Marx and Engels of the state, and dwell in particular detail on those aspects of this theory which are ignored or have been distorted by the opportunists. Then we deal specially with the one who is chiefly responsible for these distortions, Karl Kautsky, the best-known leader of the Second International (1889–1914), which has met with such miserable bankruptcy in the present war. Lastly, we sum up the main results of the experience of the Russian revolutions of 1905 and particularly of 1917. Apparently, the latter is now (early August 1917) completing the first stage of its development; but this revolution as a whole can only be understood as a link in a chain of socialist proletarian revolutions being caused by the imperialist war. The question of the relation of the socialist proletarian revolution to the state, therefore, is acquiring not only practical political importance, but also the significance of a most urgent problem of the day, the problem of explaining to the masses what they will have to do before long to free themselves from capitalist tyranny.

*The Author*
August 1917

# Preface to the Second Edition

The present, second edition is published virtually unaltered, except that Section 3 had been added to Chapter II.

*The Author*
Moscow
December 17, 1918

# I
# Class Society and the State

## 1. The State: A Product of the Irreconcilability of Class Antagonisms

What is now happening to Marx's theory has, in the course of history, happened repeatedly to the theories of revolutionary thinkers and leaders of oppressed classes fighting for emancipation. During the lifetime of great revolutionaries, the oppressing classes constantly hounded them, received their theories with the most savage malice, the most furious hatred and the most unscrupulous campaigns of lies and slander. After their death, attempts are made to convert them into harmless icons, to canonize them, so to say, and to hallow their *names* to a certain extent for the "consolation" of the oppressed classes and with the object of duping the latter, while at the same time robbing the revolutionary theory of its *substance*, blunting its revolutionary edge and vulgarizing it. Today, the bourgeoisie and the opportunists within the labor movement concur in this doctoring of Marxism. They omit, obscure, or distort the revolutionary side of this theory, its revolutionary soul. They push to the foreground and extol what is or seems acceptable to the bourgeoisie. All the social-chauvinists are now "Marxists" (don't laugh!). And more and more frequently German bourgeois scholars, only yesterday specialists in the annihilation of Marxism, are speaking of the "national-German" Marx, who, they claim, educated the labor unions which are so splendidly organized for the purpose of waging a predatory war!

In these circumstances, in view of the unprecedently widespread distortion of Marxism, our prime task is to reestablish what Marx really taught on the subject of the state. This will necessitate a number of long quotations from the works of Marx and Engels themselves. Of course, long quotations will render the text cumbersome and not help at all to make it popular reading, but we cannot possibly dispense with them. All, or at any rate all most essential passages in the works of Marx and Engels on the subject of the state must by all means be quoted as fully as possible so that the reader may form an independent

opinion of the totality of the views of the founders of scientific socialism, and of the evolution of those views, and so that their distortion
by the "Kautskyism" now prevailing may be documentarily proved and
clearly demonstrated.

Let us begin with the most popular of Engels' works, *The Origin of
the Family, Private Property, and the State*, the sixth edition of which
was published in Stuttgart as far back as 1894. We have to translate
the quotations from the German originals, as the Russian translations,
while very numerous, are for the most part either incomplete or very
unsatisfactory.

Summing up his historical analysis, Engels says:

> The state is, therefore, by no means a power forced on society from
> without; just as little is it 'the reality of the ethical idea,' 'the image
> and reality of reason,' as Hegel maintains. Rather, it is a product of
> society at a certain stage of development; it is the admission that this
> society has become entangled in an insoluble contradiction with itself,
> that it has split into irreconcilable antagonisms which it is powerless
> to dispel. But in order that these antagonisms, these classes with con-
> flicting economic interests, might not consume themselves and society
> in fruitless struggle, it became necessary to have a power, seemingly
> standing above society, that would alleviate the conflict and keep it
> within the bounds of 'order'; and this power, arisen out of society but
> placing itself above it, and alienating itself more and more from it, is
> the state. (Pp.177–78, sixth German edition)[2]

This expresses with perfect clarity the basic idea of Marxism with
regard to the historical role and the meaning of the state. The state is
a product and a manifestation of the *irreconcilability* of class antagonisms. The state arises where, when and insofar as class antagonism
objectively *cannot* be reconciled. And, conversely, the existence of the
state proves that the class antagonisms are irreconcilable.

It is on this most important and fundamental point that the distortion of Marxism, proceeding along two main lines, begins.

On the one hand, the bourgeois, and particularly the petty bourgeois, ideologists, compelled under the weight of indisputable his-

---

2   See Frederick Engels, *The Origin of the Family, Private Property and
the State* (Karl Marx and Frederick Engels, *Selected Works*, Vol. 3, Moscow,
1973, 326–27).

On pp. 85–87, 89–91 of this volume, Lenin is quoting from the same
work by Engels (op. cit., pp. 327–30).

torical facts to admit that the state only exists where there are class antagonisms and a class struggle, "correct" Marx in such a way as to make it appear that the state is an organ for the *reconciliation* of classes. According to Marx, the state could neither have arisen nor maintained itself had it been possible to reconcile classes. From what the petty bourgeois and philistine professors and publicists say, with quite frequent and benevolent references to Marx, it appears that the state does reconcile classes. According to Marx, the state is an organ of class *rule*, an organ for the *oppression* of one class by another; it is the creation of "order," which legalizes and perpetuates this oppression by moderating the conflict between classes. In the opinion of the petty bourgeois politicians, however, order means the reconciliation of classes, and not the oppression of one class by another; to alleviate the conflict means reconciling classes and not depriving the oppressed classes of definite means and methods of struggle to overthrow the oppressors.

For instance, when, in the revolution of 1917, the question of the significance and role of the state arose in all its magnitude as a practical question demanding immediate action, and, moreover, action on a mass scale, all the Social Revolutionaries[3] and Mensheviks[4] descended at once to the petty-bourgeois theory that the "state" "reconciles" classes. Innumerable resolutions and articles by politicians of both these parties are thoroughly saturated with this petty-bourgeois and philistine "reconciliation" theory. That the state is an organ of the rule of a definite class which cannot be reconciled with its antipode (the class opposite to it) is something the petty-bourgeois democrats will never

---

3    *Social Revolutionaries* (S.R.s)—a petty-bourgeois party founded in Russia in late 1901 and early 1902 as a result of the amalgamation of various Narodnik groups and circles. Their views were an eclectic hodgepodge of Narodnik and revisionist ideas.
4    *Mensheviks*—The opposition faction in the RSDLP.  The word Menshevik means "minority" in Russian. This is in reference to the fact that the Mensheviks made up a minority at the 1903 Congress. They pursued a policy of class collaboration with the bourgeoisie. This meant that they subordinated the interests of the working class to the interests of the allegedly "progressive" wing of the bourgeoisie. They originated the "two-stage" theory of revolution: first a bourgeois-democratic revolution, *then*, sometime in the distant future, a socialist revolution. This mechanical conception of historical materialism led to their siding with the bourgeoisie and imperialist reaction during the Russian Revolution.

be able to understand. Their attitude to the state is one of the most striking manifestations of the fact that our Socialist Revolutionaries and Mensheviks are not socialists at all (a point that we Bolsheviks[5] have always maintained), but petty bourgeois democrats using near-socialist phraseology.

On the other hand, the "Kautskyite" distortion of Marxism is far more subtle. "Theoretically," it is not denied that the state is an organ of class rule, or that class antagonisms are irreconcilable. But what is overlooked or glossed over is this: if the state is the product of the irreconcilability of class antagonisms, if it is a power standing above society and "*alienating* itself from it," it is clear that the liberation of the oppressed class is impossible not only without a violent revolution, *but also without the destruction* of the apparatus of state power which was created by the ruling class and which is the embodiment of this "alienation." As we shall see later, Marx very explicitly drew this theoretically self-evident conclusion on the strength of a concrete historical analysis of the tasks of the revolution. And—as we shall show in detail further on—it is this conclusion which Kautsky has "forgotten" and distorted.

## 2. Special Bodies of Armed Men, Prisons, etc.

Engels continues:

As distinct from the old gentile [tribal or clan] order,[6] the state, first,

---

5    *Bolsheviks*—Lenin's faction in the Russian Social Democratic Labor Party (RSDLP). The word Bolshevik means "majority" in Russian. This is in reference to the fact that the Bolsheviks made up a majority at the 1903 Congress, however the Bolshevik Party only split from the RSDLP in 1912. They defended the class independence of the working class in relation to bourgeois parties, implacable firmness in questions of theory, as well as tactical and organizational flexibility.

6    *Gentile, or tribal, organization of society*—the primitive communal system, or the first socio-economic formation in history. The tribal commune was a community of blood relatives linked by economic and social ties. The tribal system went through the matriarchal and the patriarchal periods. The patriarchate culminated in primitive society becoming a class society and in the rise of the state. Relations of production under the primitive communal system were based on social ownership of the means of production and equalitarian distribution of all products. This corresponded in the main to the low level of the productive forces and to their character at the time.

    For the primitive communal system, see Karl Marx, *Conspectus of* divides its subjects *according to territory....*

This division seems "natural" to us, but it costs a prolonged struggle against the old organization according to generations or tribes.

> The second distinguishing feature is the establishment of a *public power* which no longer directly coincides with the population organizing itself as an armed force. This special, public power is necessary because a self-acting armed organization of the population has become impossible since the split into classes.... This public power exists in every state; it consists not merely of armed men but also of material adjuncts, prisons, and institutions of coercion of all kinds, of which gentile [clan] society knew nothing....

Engels elucidates the concept of the "power" which is called the state, a power which arose from society but places itself above it and alienates itself more and more from it. What does this power mainly consist of? It consists of special bodies of armed men having prisons, etc., at their command.

We are justified in speaking of special bodies of armed men, because the public power which is an attribute of every state "does not directly coincide" with the armed population, with its "self-acting armed organization".

Like all great revolutionary thinkers, Engels tries to draw the attention of the class-conscious workers to what prevailing philistinism regards as least worthy of attention, as the most habitual thing, hallowed by prejudices that are not only deep-rooted but, one might say, petrified. A standing army and police are the chief instruments of state power. But how can it be otherwise?

From the viewpoint of the vast majority of Europeans of the end of the nineteenth century, whom Engels was addressing, and who had not gone through or closely observed a single great revolution, it could not have been otherwise. They could not understand at all what a "self-acting armed organization of the population" was. When asked why it became necessary to have special bodies of armed men placed above society and alienating themselves from it (police and a standing army), the West-European and Russian philistines are inclined to utter a few phrases borrowed from Spencer of Mikhailovsky, to refer to the growing complexity of social life, the differentiation of func-

*Lewis Morgan's Ancient Society* and Frederick Engels' *The Origin of the Family, Private Property and the State* (Karl Marx and Frederick Engels, *Selected Works*, Vol. 3, Moscow, 1973, 204–334).

tions, and so on.

Such a reference seems "scientific," and effectively lulls the ordinary person to sleep by obscuring the important and basic fact, namely, the split of society into irreconcilable antagonistic classes.

Were it not for this split, the "self-acting armed organization of the population" would differ from the primitive organization of a stick-wielding herd of monkeys, or of primitive men, or of men united in clans, by its complexity, its high technical level, and so on. But such an organization would still be possible.

It is impossible because civilized society is split into antagonistic, and, moreover, irreconcilably antagonistic classes, whose "self-acting" arming would lead to an armed struggle between them. A state arises, a special power is created, special bodies of armed men, and every revolution, by destroying the state apparatus, shows us the naked class struggle, clearly shows us how the ruling class strives to restore the special bodies of armed men which serve *it*, and how the oppressed class strives to create a new organization of this kind, capable of serving the exploited instead of the exploiters.

In the above argument, Engels raises theoretically the very same question which every great revolution raises before us in practice, palpably and, what is more, on a scale of mass action, namely, the question of the relationship between "special" bodies of armed men and the "self-acting armed organization of the population." We shall see how this question is specifically illustrated by the experience of the European and Russian revolutions.

But to return to Engel's exposition.

He points out that sometimes—in certain parts of North America, for example—this public power is weak (he has in mind a rare exception in capitalist society, and those parts of North America in its pre-imperialist days where the free colonist predominated), but that, generally speaking, it grows stronger:

> It [the public power] grows stronger, however, in proportion as class antagonisms within the state become more acute, and as adjacent states become larger and more populous. We have only to look at our present-day Europe, where class struggle and rivalry in conquest have tuned up the public power to such a pitch that it threatens to swallow the whole of society and even the state.

This was written not later than the early nineties of the last century, Engel's last preface being dated June 16, 1891. The turn towards imperialism—meaning the complete domination of the trusts, the omnipotence of the big banks, a grand-scale colonial policy, and so forth—was only just beginning in France, and was even weaker in North America and in Germany. Since then "rivalry in conquest" has taken a gigantic stride, all the more because by the beginning of the second decade of the twentieth century the world had been completely divided up among these "rivals in conquest," i.e., among the predatory Great Powers. Since then, military and naval armaments have grown fantastically and the predatory war of 1914–17 for the domination of the world by Britain or Germany, for the division of the spoils, has brought the "swallowing" of all the forces of society by the rapacious state power close to complete catastrophe.

Engels could, as early as 1891, point to "rivalry in conquest" as one of the most important distinguishing features of the foreign policy of the Great Powers, while the social-chauvinist scoundrels have ever since 1914, when this rivalry, many times intensified, gave rise to an imperialist war, been covering up the defense of the predatory interests of "their own" bourgeoisie with phrases about "defense of the fatherland," "defense of the republic and the revolution," etc.!

## 3. The State—an Instrument for the Exploitation of the Oppressed Class

The maintenance of the special public power standing above society requires taxes and state loans.

"Having pubic power and the right to levy taxes," Engels writes, "the officials now stand, as organs of society, above society. The free, voluntary respect that was accorded to the organs of the gentile [clan] constitution does not satisfy them, even if they could gain it...."

Special laws are enacted proclaiming the sanctity and immunity of the officials. "The shabbiest police servant" has more "authority" than the representative of the clan, but even the head of the military power of a civilized state may well envy the elder of a clan the "unrestrained respect" of society.

The question of the privileged position of the officials as organs of state power is raised here. The main point indicated is: what is it that places them *above* society? We shall see how this theoretical question was answered in practice by the Paris Commune in 1871 and how it was obscured from a reactionary standpoint by Kautsky in 1912.

> Because the state arose from the need to hold class antagonisms in check, but because it arose, at the same time, in the midst of the conflict of these classes, it is, as a rule, the state of the most powerful, economically dominant class, which, through the medium of the state, becomes also the politically dominant class, and thus acquires new means of holding down and exploiting the oppressed class....

The ancient and feudal states were organs for the exploitation of the slaves and serfs; likewise,

> the modern representative state is an instrument of exploitation of wage labor by capital. By way of exception, however, periods occur in which the warring classes balance each other so nearly that the state power as ostensible mediator acquires, for the moment, a certain degree of independence of both....

Such were the absolute monarchies of the seventeenth and eighteenth centuries, the Bonapartism of the First and Second Empires in France, and the Bismarck regime in Germany.

Such, we may add, is the Kerensky government in republican Russia since it began to persecute the revolutionary proletariat, at a moment when, owing to the leadership of the petty-bourgeois democrats, the Soviets have *already* become impotent, while the bourgeoisie are not *yet* strong enough simply to disperse them.

In a democratic republic, Engels continues, "wealth exercises its power indirectly, but all the more surely," first, by means of the "direct corruption of officials" (America); secondly, by means of an "alliance of the government and the Stock Exchange" (France and America).

At present, imperialism and the domination of the banks have "developed" into an exceptional art both these methods of upholding and giving effect to the omnipotence of wealth in democratic republics of all descriptions. Since, for instance, in the very first months of the Russian democratic republic, one might say during the honeymoon of the "socialist" S.R.s and Mensheviks joined in wedlock to the bourgeoisie, in the coalition government, Mr. Palchinsky obstructed every measure intended for curbing the capitalists and their marauding practices, their plundering of the state by means of war contracts; and since later on Mr. Palchinsky, upon resigning from the Cabinet (and being, of course, replaced by another quite similar Palchinsky), was "rewarded" by the capitalists with a lucrative job with a salary of 120,000 rubles per annum—what would you call that? Direct or indirect bribery? An alliance of the government and the syndicates, or "merely" friendly relations? What role do the Chernovs, Tseretelis, Avksentyevs and Skobelevs play? Are they the "direct" or only the indirect allies of the millionaire treasury-looters?

Another reason why the omnipotence of "wealth" is more *certain* in a democratic republic is that it does not depend on defects in the political machinery or on the faulty political shell of capitalism. A democratic republic is the best possible political shell for capitalism, and, therefore, once capital has gained possession of this very best shell (through the Palchinskys, Chernovs, Tseretelis and Co.), it establishes its power so securely, so firmly, that no change of persons, institutions or parties in the bourgeois-democratic republic can shake it.

We must also note that Engels is most explicit in calling universal suffrage as well an instrument of bourgeois rule. Universal suffrage, he says, obviously taking account of the long experience of German Social Democracy, is "the gauge of the maturity of the working class. It cannot and never will be anything more in the present-day state."

The petty-bourgeois democrats, such as our Socialist Revolutionaries and Mensheviks, and also their twin brothers, all the social-chauvinists and opportunists of Western Europe, expect just this "more" from universal suffrage. They themselves share, and instill into the minds of the people, the false notion that universal suffrage "in the *present-day* state" is really capable of revealing the will of the majority of the working people and of securing its realization.

Here, we can only indicate this false notion, only point out that Engels's perfectly clear, precise and concrete statement is distorted at every step in the propaganda and agitation of the "official" (i.e., opportunist) socialist parties. A detailed exposure of the utter falsity of this notion which Engels brushes aside here is given in our further account of the views of Marx and Engels on the "*present-day*" state.

Engels gives a general summary of his views in the most popular of his works in the following words:

> The state, then, has not existed from all eternity. There have been societies that did without it, that had no idea of the state and state power. At a certain stage of economic development, which was necessarily bound up with the split of society into classes, the state became a necessity owing to this split. We are now rapidly approaching a stage in the development of production at which the existence of these classes not only will have ceased to be a necessity, but will become a positive hindrance to production. They will fall as inevitably as they arose at

an earlier stage. Along with them the state will inevitably fall. Society, which will reorganize production on the basis of a free and equal association of the producers, will put the whole machinery of state where it will then belong: into a museum of antiquities, by the side of the spinning-wheel and the bronze axe.

We do not often come across this passage in the propaganda and agitation literature of the present-day Social Democrats. Even when we do come across it, it is mostly quoted in the same manner as one bows before an icon, i.e., it is done to show official respect for Engels, and no attempt is made to gauge the breadth and depth of the revolution that this relegating of "the whole machinery of state to a museum of antiquities" implies. In most cases we do not even find an understanding of what Engels calls the state machine.

## 4. The "Withering Away" of the State, and Violent Revolution

Engels's words regarding the "withering away" of the state are so widely known, they are often quoted, and so clearly reveal the essence of the customary adaptation of Marxism to opportunism that we must deal with them in detail. We shall quote the whole argument from which they are taken.

*The proletariat seizes from state power and turns the means of production into state property to begin with.* But thereby it abolishes itself as the proletariat, abolishes all class distinctions and class antagonisms, and abolishes also the state as state. Society thus far, operating amid class antagonisms, needed the state, that is, an organization of the particular exploiting class, for the maintenance of its external conditions of production, and, therefore, especially, for the purpose of forcibly keeping the exploited class in the conditions of oppression determined by the given mode of production (slavery, serfdom or bondage, wage labor). The state was the official representative of society as a whole, its concentration in a visible corporation. But it was this only insofar as it was the state of that class which itself represented, for its own time, society as a whole: in ancient times, the state of slave-owning citizens; in the Middle Ages, of the feudal nobility; in our own time, of the bourgeoisie. When at last it becomes the real representative of the whole of society, it renders itself unnecessary. As soon as there is no longer any social class to be held in subjection, as soon as class rule, and the individual struggle for existence based upon the present anarchy in production, with the collisions and excesses arising from this struggle, are removed, nothing more remains to be held in subjection—nothing necessitating a special coercive force, a state. The first act by which the state really comes forward as the representative of the whole of society— the taking possession of the means of production in the name of society—is also its last independent act as a state. State interference in social relations becomes, in one domain after another, superfluous, and then dies down of itself. The government of persons is replaced by the administration of things, and by the conduct of processes of production. The state is not "abolished." *It withers away.* This gives the measure of the value of the phrase "a free people's state," both as to its justifiable use for a long time from an agitational point of view, and as to its ultimate scientific insufficiency; and also of the so-called anarchists' demand that the state be abolished overnight. (*Herr Eugen Dühring's Revolution in Science [Anti-Dühring]*, 301–03, third German edition.)[7]

It is safe to say that of this argument of Engels's, which is so remarkably rich in ideas, only one point has become an integral part of socialist thought among modern socialist parties, namely, that according to Marx that state "withers away"—as distinct from the anarchist doctrine of the "abolition" of the state. To prune Marxism to such an extent means reducing it to opportunism, for this "interpretation" only leaves a vague notion of a slow, even, gradual change, of absence of leaps and storms, of absence of revolution. The current, widespread, popular, if one may say so, conception of the "withering away" of the state undoubtedly means obscuring, if not repudiating, revolution.

Such an "interpretation," however, is the crudest distortion of Marxism, advantageous only to the bourgeoisie. In point of theory, it is based on disregard for the most important circumstances and considerations indicated in, say, Engels's "summary" argument we have just quoted in full.

In the first place, at the very outset of his argument, Engels says that, in seizing state power, the proletariat thereby "abolishes the state as state." It is not done to ponder over the meaning of this. Generally, it is either ignored altogether, or is considered to be something in

---

7  See Frederick Engels, *Anti-Dühring*, Moscow, 1969, pp. 332-33.

On pp. 93–95 of this volume, Lenin is quoting from the same work by Engels (op. cit., 220). This quote can also be found in the present volume on p. 72, on which "withers away" is translated "dies out." The meaning, however, remains unchanged.

the nature of "Hegelian weakness" on Engels's part. As a matter of fact, however, these words briefly express the experience of one of the greatest proletarian revolutions, the Paris Commune of 1871, of which we shall speak in greater detail in its proper place. As a matter of fact, Engels speaks here of the proletarian revolution "abolishing" the *bourgeois* state, while the words about the state withering away refer to the remnants of the *proletarian* state *after* the socialist revolution. According to Engels, the bourgeois state does not "wither away," but is "*abolished*" by the proletariat in the course of the revolution. What withers away after this revolution is the proletarian state or semi-state.

Secondly, the state is a "special coercive force." Engels gives this splendid and extremely profound definition here with the utmost lucidity. And from it follows that the "special coercive force" for the suppression of the proletariat by the bourgeoisie, of millions of working people by handfuls of the rich, must be replaced by a "special coercive force" for the suppression of the bourgeoisie by the proletariat (the dictatorship of the proletariat).[8] This is precisely what is meant by "abolition of the state as state." This is precisely the "act" of taking possession of the means of production in the name of society. And it is self-evident that *such* a replacement of one (bourgeois) "special force" by another (proletarian) "special force" cannot possibly take place in the form of "withering away."

Thirdly, in speaking of the state "withering away," and the even more graphic and colorful "dying down of itself", Engels refers quite clearly and definitely to the period after "the state has taken possession of the means of production in the name of the whole of society,"

---

8  In modern English, the word "dictatorship" has come to mean "the rule of a dictator or despot." However, this modern usage, that is, as the opposite of "democracy," did not exist until the 1880s and is not the way that Marxists, such as Lenin, use or understand the term.  For Marxists, "dictatorship" means the economic and political domination of one class over another.  For example, the United States is currently a "dictatorship of the bourgeoisie"—the rule of the capitalist class over the working class and petty bourgeoisie—based on private property of the means of production and the extraction of surplus value (profit) from the working class.  In turn, as Lenin will explain, the "dictatorship of the proletariat" means simply: the proletariat as a class in power.  In practice, it signifies the economic and political rule of the working class (the vast majority) over the rest of society (the tiny minority of capitalists and the petty bourgeoisie), based on nationalized property forms and socialized production, distribution, and exchange.

that is, *after* the socialist revolution. We all know that the political form of the "state" at that time is the most complete democracy. But it never enters the head of any of the opportunists, who shamelessly distort Marxism, that Engels is consequently speaking here of *democracy* "dying down of itself," or "withering away." This seems very strange at first sight. But it is "incomprehensible" only to those who have not thought about democracy *also* being a state and, consequently, also disappearing when the state disappears. Revolution alone can "abolish" the bourgeois state. The state in general, i.e., the most complete democracy, can only "wither away."

Fourthly, after formulating his famous proposition that "the state withers away," Engels at once explains specifically that this proposition is directed against both the opportunists and the anarchists. In doing this, Engels puts in the forefront that conclusion, drawn from the proposition that "the state withers away," which is directed against the opportunists.

One can wager that out of every 10,000 persons who have read or heard about the "withering away" of the state, 9,990 are completely unaware, or do not remember, that Engels directed his conclusions from that proposition not against anarchists *alone*. And of the remaining ten, probably nine do not know the meaning of a "free people's state" or why an attack on this slogan means an attack on the opportunists. This is how history is written! This is how a great revolutionary teaching is imperceptibly falsified and adapted to prevailing philistinism. The conclusion directed against the anarchists has been repeated thousands of times; it has been vulgarized, and rammed into people's heads in the shallowest form, and has acquired the strength of a prejudice, whereas the conclusion directed against the opportunists has been obscured and "forgotten"!

The "free people's state" was a programmatic demand and a catchword current among the German Social Democrats in the seventies. This catchword is devoid of all political content except that it describes the concept of democracy in a pompous philistine fashion. Insofar as it hinted in a legally permissible manner at a democratic republic, Engels was prepared to "justify" its use "for a time" from an agitational point of view. But it was an opportunist catchword, for it amounted to something more than prettifying bourgeois democracy, and was also failure to understand the socialist criticism of the state in general. We are in favor of a democratic republic as the best form of state for the proletariat under capitalism. But we have no right to forget that wage slavery is the lot of the people even in the most democratic bourgeois republic. Furthermore, every state is a "special force" for the suppression of the oppressed class. Consequently, *every* state is *not* "free" and *not* a "people's state." Marx and Engels explained this repeatedly to their party comrades in the seventies.

Fifthly, the same work of Engels's, whose arguments about the withering away of the state everyone remembers, also contains an argument of the significance of violent revolution. Engels's historical analysis of its role becomes a veritable panegyric on violent revolution. This, "no one remembers." It is not done in modern socialist parties to talk or even think about the significance of this idea, and it plays no part whatever in their daily propaganda and agitation among the people. And yet it is inseparably bound up with the 'withering away" of the state into one harmonious whole.

Here is Engels's argument:

> ...That force, however, plays yet another role [other than that of a diabolical power] in history, a revolutionary role; that, in the words of Marx, it is the midwife of every old society which is pregnant with a new one, that it is the instrument with which social movement forces its way through and shatters the dead, fossilized political forms—of this there is not a word in Herr Dühring. It is only with sighs and groans that he admits the possibility that force will perhaps be necessary for the overthrow of an economy based on exploitation—unfortunately, because all use of force demoralizes, he says, the person who uses it. And this in spite of the immense moral and spiritual impetus which has been given by every victorious revolution! And this in Germany, where a violent collision—which may, after all, be forced on the people— would at least have the advantage of wiping out the servility which has penetrated the nation's mentality following the humiliation of the Thirty Years' War.[9] And this person's mode of thought—dull, insipid,

9   Thirty Years' War (1618–48), the first European war, resulted from an aggravation of the antagonisms between various alignments of European states, and took the form of a struggle between Protestants and Catholics. It began with a revolt in Bohemia against the tyranny of the Hapsburg monarchy and the onslaught of Catholic reaction. The states which then entered the war formed two camps. The Pope, the Spanish and Austrian Hapsburgs and the Catholic princes of Germany, who rallied to the Catholic Church, opposed the Protestant countries—Bohemia, Denmark, Sweden, the Dutch Republic, and a number of German states that had accepted the Reformation. The Protestant countries were backed by the French kings,

and impotent—presumes to impose itself on the most revolutionary party that history has known! (p.193, third German edition, Part II, end of Chap.IV)

How can this panegyric on violent revolution, which Engels insistently brought to the attention of the German Social Democrats between 1878 and 1894, i.e., right up to the time of his death, be combined with the theory of the "withering away" of the state to form a single theory?

Usually the two are combined by means of eclecticism, by an unprincipled or sophistic selection made arbitrarily (or to please the powers that be) of first one, then another argument, and in ninety-nine cases out of a hundred, if not more, it is the idea of the "withering away" that is placed in the forefront. Dialectics are replaced by eclecticism — this is the most usual, the most widespread practice to be met with in present-day official Social Democratic literature in relation to Marxism. This sort of substitution is, of course, nothing new; it was observed even in the history of classical Greek philosophy. In falsifying Marxism in opportunist fashion, the substitution of eclecticism for dialectics is the easiest way of deceiving the people. It gives an illusory satisfaction; it seems to take into account all sides of the process, all trends of development, all the conflicting influences, and so forth, whereas in reality it provides no integral and revolutionary conception of the process of social development at all.

We have already said above, and shall show more fully later, that the theory of Marx and Engels of the inevitability of a violent revolution refers to the bourgeois state. The latter *cannot* be superseded by the proletarian state (the dictatorship of the proletariat) through the process of "withering away," but, as a general rule, only through a violent revolution. The panegyric Engels sang in its honor, and which fully corresponds to Marx's repeated statements (see the concluding passages of *The Poverty of Philosophy*[10] and the *Communist Manifesto*,[11] with their proud and open proclamation of the inevitability of a violent revolution; see what Marx wrote nearly 30 years later, in criti-

enemies of the Hapsburgs. Germany became the chief battlefield and object of military plunder and predatory claims. The war ended in 1648 with the signing of the Peace Treaty of Westphalia, which completed the political dismemberment of Germany.

10   See Karl Marx, *The Poverty of Philosophy*, Moscow, 1973, 151–52.

11   See Karl Marx and Frederick Engels, *The Manifesto of the Communist Party* in this volume, pp. 1–35.

cizing the Gotha Program of 1875,[12] when he mercilessly castigated the opportunist character of that program)—this panegyric is by no means a mere "impulse," a mere declamation or a polemical sally. The necessity of systematically imbuing the masses with *this* and precisely this view of violent revolution lies at the root of the *entire* theory of Marx and Engels. The betrayal of their theory by the now prevailing social-chauvinist and Kautskyite trends expresses itself strikingly in both these trends ignoring *such* propaganda and agitation.

The supersession of the bourgeois state by the proletarian state is impossible without a violent revolution. The abolition of the proletarian state, i.e., of the state in general, is impossible except through the process of "withering away."

A detailed and concrete elaboration of these views was given by Marx and Engels when they studied each particular revolutionary situation, when they analyzed the lessons of the experience of each particular revolution. We shall now pass to this, undoubtedly the most important, part of their theory.

---

12   *Gotha Program*—the program adopted by the Socialist Workers' Party of Germany in 1875, at the Gotha Congress, which united two German socialist parties, namely, the Eisenachers—led by August Bebel and Wilhelm Liebknecht and influenced by Marx and Engels—and the Lassalleans. The program betrayed eclecticism and was opportunist, because the Eisenachers had made concessions to the Lassalleans on major issues and accepted Lassallean formulations. Marx in his *Critique of the Gotha Programme*, and Engels in his letter to Bebel of March 18–28, 1875, devastated the Gotha Program, which they regarded as a serious step backwards compared with the Eisenach Program of 1869.

## II
# Experience of 1848–51

## 1. The Eve of the Revolution

The first works of mature Marxism—*The Poverty of Philosophy* and the *Communist Manifesto*—appeared just on the eve of the revolution of 1848. For this reason, in addition to presenting the general principles of Marxism, they reflect to a certain degree the concrete revolutionary situation of the time. It will, therefore, be more expedient, perhaps, to examine what the authors of these works said about the state immediately before they drew conclusions from the experience of the years 1848–51.

In *The Poverty of Philosophy*, Marx wrote:

> The working class, in the course of development, will substitute for the old bourgeois society an association which will preclude classes and their antagonism, and there will be no more political power proper, since political power is precisely the official expression of class antagonism in bourgeois society. (p.182, German edition, 1885)[13]

It is instructive to compare this general exposition of the idea of the state disappearing after the abolition of classes with the exposition contained in the *Communist Manifesto*, written by Marx and Engels a few months later—in November 1847, to be exact:

> ... In depicting the most general phases of the development of the proletariat, we traced the more or less veiled civil war, raging within existing society up to the point where that war breaks out into open revolution, and where the violent overthrow of the bourgeoisie lays the foundation for the sway of the proletariat....
>
> ... We have seen above that the first step in the revolution by the working class is to raise the proletariat to the position of the ruling class to win the battle of democracy.
>
> The proletariat will use its political supremacy to wrest, by degree, all capital from the bourgeoisie, to centralize all instruments of production in the hands of the state, i.e., of the proletariat organized as the ruling class; and to increase the total productive forces as rapidly as possible. (pp.31 and 37, seventh German edition, 1906)[14]

---

13  See Karl Marx, *The Poverty of Philosophy*, Moscow, 1973, P. 151.
14  See this volume, pp. 13, 22.

Here we have a formulation of one of the most remarkable and most important ideas of Marxism on the subject of the state, namely, the idea of the "dictatorship of the proletariat" (as Marx and Engels began to call it after the Paris Commune); and, also, a highly interesting definition of the state, which is also one of the "forgotten words" of Marxism: "*the state, i.e., the proletariat organized as the ruling class.*"

This definition of the state has never been explained in the prevailing propaganda and agitation literature of the official Social Democratic parties. More than that, it has been deliberately ignored, for it is absolutely irreconcilable with reformism, and is a slap in the face for the common opportunist prejudices and philistine illusions about the "peaceful development of democracy."

The proletariat needs the state — this is repeated by all the opportunists, social-chauvinists and Kautskyites, who assure us that this is what Marx taught. But they "*forget*" to add that, in the first place, according to Marx, the proletariat needs only a state which is withering away, i.e., a state so constituted that it begins to wither away immediately, and cannot but wither away. And, secondly, the working people need a "state, i.e., the proletariat organized as the ruling class."

The state is a special organization of force: it is an organization of violence for the suppression of some class. What class must the proletariat suppress? Naturally, only the exploiting class, i.e., the bourgeoisie. The working people need the state only to suppress the resistance of the exploiters, and only the proletariat can direct this suppression, can carry it out. For the proletariat is the only class that is consistently revolutionary, the only class that can unite all the working and exploited people in the struggle against the bourgeoisie, in completely removing it.

The exploiting classes need political rule to maintain exploitation, i.e., in the selfish interests of an insignificant minority against the vast majority of all people. The exploited classes need political rule in order to completely abolish all exploitation, i.e., in the interests of the vast majority of the people, and against the insignificant minority consisting of the modern slave-owners—the landowners and capitalists.

The petty-bourgeois democrats, those sham socialists who replaced the class struggle by dreams of class harmony, even pictured the socialist transformation in a dreamy fashion—not as the overthrow of the rule of the exploiting class, but as the peaceful submission of the minority to the majority which has become aware of its aims. This petty-bourgeois utopia, which is inseparable from the idea of the state being above classes, led in practice to the betrayal of the interests of the working classes, as was shown, for example, by the history of the French revolutions of 1848 and 1871, and by the experience of "socialist" participation in bourgeois Cabinets in Britain, France, Italy and other countries at the turn of the century.

All his life Marx fought against this petty-bourgeois socialism, now revived in Russia by the Socialist Revolutionary and Menshevik parties. He developed his theory of the class struggle consistently, down to the theory of political power, of the state.

The overthrow of bourgeois rule can be accomplished only by the proletariat, the particular class whose economic conditions of existence prepare it for this task and provide it with the possibility and the power to perform it. While the bourgeoisie break up and disintegrate the peasantry and all the petty-bourgeois groups, they weld together, unite and organize the proletariat. Only the proletariat—by virtue of the economic role it plays in large-scale production—is capable of being the leader of *all* the working and exploited people, whom the bourgeoisie exploit, oppress and crush, often not less but more than they do the proletarians, but who are incapable of waging an *independent* struggle for their emancipation.

The theory of class struggle, applied by Marx to the question of the state and the socialist revolution, leads as a matter of course to the recognition of the *political rule* of the proletariat, of its dictatorship, i.e., of undivided power directly backed by the armed force of the people. The overthrow of the bourgeoisie can be achieved only by the proletariat becoming the *ruling class*, capable of crushing the inevitable and desperate resistance of the bourgeoisie, and of organizing *all* the working and exploited people for the new economic system.

The proletariat needs state power, a centralized organization of force, an organization of violence, both to crush the resistance of the exploiters and to lead the enormous mass of the population—the peasants, the petty bourgeoisie, and semi-proletarians—in the work of organizing a socialist economy.

By educating the workers' party, Marxism educates the vanguard of the proletariat, capable of assuming power and *leading the whole people* to socialism, of directing and organizing the new system, of being the teacher, the guide, the leader of all the working and exploited people in organizing their social life without the bourgeoisie and against the bourgeoisie. By contrast, the opportunism now prevailing trains the members of the workers' party to be the representatives of the better-paid workers, who lose touch with the masses, "get along" fairly well under capitalism, and sell their birthright for a mass of pottage, i.e., renounce their role as revolutionary leaders of the people against the bourgeoisie.

Marx's theory of "the state, i.e., the proletariat organized as the ruling class" is inseparably bound up with the whole of his doctrine of the revolutionary role of the proletariat in history. The culmination of this rule is the proletarian dictatorship, the political rule of the proletariat.

But since the proletariat needs the state as a *special* form of organization of violence *against* the bourgeoisie, the following conclusion suggests itself: is it conceivable that such an organization can be created without first abolishing, destroying the state machine created by the bourgeoisie *for themselves*? The *Communist Manifesto* leads straight to this conclusion, and it is of this conclusion that Marx speaks when summing up the experience of the revolution of 1848–51.

## 2. The Revolution Summed Up

Marx sums up his conclusions from the revolution of 1848–51, on the subject of the state we are concerned with, in the following argument contained in *The Eighteenth Brumaire of Louis Bonaparte*:

> But the revolution is throughgoing. It is still journeying through purgatory. It does its work methodically. By December 2, 1851 [the day of Louis Bonaparte's coup d'état], it had completed one half of its preparatory work. It is now completing the other half. First it perfected the parliamentary power, in order to be able to overthrow it. Now that it has attained this, it is perfecting the *executive power*, reducing it to its purest expression, isolating it, setting it up against itself as the sole object, *in order to concentrate all its forces of destruction against it* [italics ours—Lenin]. And when it has done this second half of its preliminary work, Europe will leap from its seat and exultantly exclaim: well grubbed, old mole!
>
> This executive power with its enormous bureaucratic and military organization, with its vast and ingenious state machinery, with a host of officials numbering half a million, besides an army of another half million, this appalling parasitic body, which enmeshes the body of French society and chokes all its pores, sprang up in the days of the absolute monarchy, with the decay of the feudal system, which it helped to hasten." The first French Revolution developed centralization, "but at the

same time" it increased "the extent, the attributes and the number of agents of governmental power. Napoleon completed this state machinery." The legitimate monarchy and the July monarchy "added nothing but a greater division of labor....

...Finally, in its struggle against the revolution, the parliamentary republic found itself compelled to strengthen, along with repressive measures, the resources and centralization of governmental power. *All revolutions perfected this machine instead of smashing it* [italics ours]. The parties that contended in turn for domination regarded the possession of this huge state edifice as the principal spoils of the victor. (*The Eighteenth Brumaire of Louis Bonaparte,* pp. 98–99, fourth edition, Hamburg, 1907)[15]

In this remarkable argument, Marxism takes a tremendous step forward compared with the *Communist Manifesto*. In the latter, the question of the state is still treated in an extremely abstract manner, in the most general terms and expressions. In the above-quoted passage, the question is treated in a concrete manner, and the conclusion is extremely precise, definite, practical and palpable: all previous revolutions perfected the state machine, whereas it must be broken, smashed.

This conclusion is the chief and fundamental point in the Marxist theory of the state. And it is precisely this fundamental point which has been completely *ignored* by the dominant official Social Democratic parties and, indeed, *distorted* (as we shall see later) by the foremost theoretician of the Second International, Karl Kautsky.

The *Communist Manifesto* gives a general summary of history, which compels us to regard the state as the organ of class rule and leads us to the inevitable conclusion that the proletariat cannot overthrow the bourgeoisie without first winning political power, without attaining political supremacy, without transforming the state into the "proletariat organized as the ruling class"; and that this proletarian state will begin to wither away immediately after its victory because the state is unnecessary and cannot exist in a society in which there are no class antagonisms. The question as to how, from the point of view of historical development, the replacement of the bourgeois by the proletarian state is to take place is not raised here.

This is the question Marx raises and answers in 1852. True to his

---

15  See Karl Marx, *The Eighteenth Brumaire of Louis Bonaparte* (Karl Marx and Frederick Engels, *Selected Works*, Vol. 1, Moscow, 1973, 477).

On p. 105 of this volume, Lenin is quoting from Engels's preface to the third edition of the work (op. cit., 396).

philosophy of dialectical materialism, Marx takes as his basis the historical experience of the great years of revolution, 1848 to 1851. Here, as everywhere else, his theory is a *summing up of experience*, illuminated by a profound philosophical conception of the world and a rich knowledge of history.

The problem of the state is put specifically: How did the bourgeois state, the state machine necessary for the rule of the bourgeoisie, come into being historically? What changes did it undergo, what evolution did it perform in the course of bourgeois revolutions and in the face of the independent actions of the oppressed classes? What are the tasks of the proletariat in relation to this state machine?

The centralized state power that is peculiar to bourgeois society came into being in the period of the fall of absolutism. Two institutions most characteristic of this state machine are the bureaucracy and the standing army. In their works, Marx and Engels repeatedly show that the bourgeoisie are connected with these institutions by thousands of threads. Every worker's experience illustrates this connection in an extremely graphic and impressive manner. From its own bitter experience, the working class learns to recognize this connection. That is why it so easily grasps and so firmly learns the doctrine which shows the inevitability of this connection, a doctrine which the petty-bourgeois democrats either ignorantly and flippantly deny, or still more flippantly admit "in general," while forgetting to draw appropriate practical conclusions.

The bureaucracy and the standing army are a "parasite" on the body of bourgeois society—a parasite created by the internal antagonisms which rend that society, but a parasite which "chokes" all its vital pores. The Kautskyite opportunism now prevailing in official Social Democracy considers the view that the state is a *parasitic organism* to be the peculiar and exclusive attribute of anarchism. It goes without saying that this distortion of Marxism is of vast advantage to those philistines who have reduced socialism to the unheard-of disgrace of justifying and prettifying the imperialist war by applying to it the concept of "defense of the fatherland"; but it is unquestionably a distortion, nevertheless.

The development, perfection, and strengthening of the bureaucratic and military apparatus proceeded during all the numerous bourgeois revolutions which Europe has witnessed since the fall of feudalism. In particular, it is the petty bourgeoisie who are attracted to the side of the big bourgeoisie and are largely subordinated to them through this apparatus, which provides the upper sections of the peasants, small artisans, tradesmen, and the like with comparatively comfortable, quiet, and respectable jobs raising their holders *above* the people. Consider what happened in Russia during the six months following February 27, 1917. The official posts which formerly were given by preference to the Black Hundreds[16] have now become the spoils of the Cadets,[17] Mensheviks, and Social-Revolutionaries. Nobody has really thought of introducing any serious reforms. Every effort has been made to put them off "until the Constituent Assembly meets," and to steadily put off its convocation until after the war! But there has been no delay, no waiting for the Constituent Assembly, in the matter of dividing the spoils of getting the lucrative jobs of ministers, deputy ministers, governors-general, etc., etc.! The game of combinations that has been played in forming the government has been, in essence, only an expression of this division and redivision of the "spoils," which has been going on above and below, throughout the country, in every department of central and local government. The six months between February 27 and August 27, 1917, can be summed up, objectively summed up beyond all dispute, as follows: reforms shelved, distribution of official jobs accomplished and "mistakes" in the distribution corrected by a few redistributions.

But the more the bureaucratic apparatus is "redistributed" among the various bourgeois and petty-bourgeois parties (among the Cadets, Socialist Revolutionaries and Mensheviks in the case of Russia), the more keenly aware the oppressed classes, and the proletariat at their head, become of their irreconcilable hostility to the *whole* of bourgeois society. Hence the need for all bourgeois parties, even for the most democratic and "revolutionary-democratic" among them, to intensify repressive measures against the revolutionary proletariat, to strengthen the apparatus of coercion, i.e., the state machine. This course of events compels the revolution *"to concentrate all its forces of destruction"* against the state power, and to set itself the aim, not of improving the state machine, but of *smashing and destroying* it.

It was not logical reasoning, but actual developments, the actual

16  *Black Hundreds*—monarchist bands formed by the tsarist police to fight the revolutionary movement. They assassinated revolutionaries, attacked progressive intellectuals and carried out anti-Jewish pogroms.
17  *Cadets*—members of the Contitutional Democratic Party, the leading party of the liberal monarchist bourgeoisie in Russia.

experience of 1848–51, that led to the matter being presented in this way. The extent to which Marx held strictly to the solid ground of historical experience can be seen from the fact that, in 1852, he did not yet specifically raise the question of *what* was to take the place of the state machine to be destroyed. Experience had not yet provided material for dealing with this question, which history placed on the agenda later on, in 1871. In 1852, all that could be established with the accuracy of scientific observation was that the proletarian revolution had *approached* the task of "concentrating all its forces of destruction" against the state power, of "smashing" the state machine.

Here the question may arise: is it correct to generalize the experience, observations and conclusions of Marx, to apply them to a field that is wider than the history of France during the three years 1848–51? Before proceeding to deal with this question, let us recall a remark made by Engels and then examine the facts. In his introduction to the third edition of *The Eighteenth Brumaire*, Engels wrote:

> France is the country where, more than anywhere else, the historical class struggles were each time fought out to a finish, and where, consequently, the changing political forms within which they move and in which their results are summarized have been stamped in the sharpest outlines. The center of feudalism in the Middle Ages, the model country, since the Renaissance, of a unified monarchy based on social estates, France demolished feudalism in the Great Revolution and established the rule of the bourgeoisie in a classical purity unequalled by any other European land. And the struggle of the upward-striving proletariat against the ruling bourgeoisie appeared here in an acute form unknown elsewhere. (p.4, 1907 edition)

The last remark is out of date inasmuch as since 1871 there has been a lull in the revolutionary struggle of the French proletariat, although, long as this lull may be, it does not at all preclude the possibility that in the coming proletarian revolution France may show herself to be the classic country of the class struggle to a finish.

Let us, however, cast a general glance over the history of the advanced countries at the turn of the century. We shall see that the same process went on more slowly, in more varied forms, in a much wider field: on the one hand, the development of "parliamentary power" both in the republican countries (France, America, Switzerland), and in the monarchies (Britain, Germany to a certain extent, Italy, the Scandinavian countries, etc.); on the other hand, a struggle for power among the various bourgeois and petty-bourgeois parties which distributed and redistributed the "spoils" of office, with the foundations of bourgeois society unchanged; and, lastly, the perfection and consolidation of the "executive power," of its bureaucratic and military apparatus.

There is not the slightest doubt that these features are common to the whole of the modern evolution of all capitalist states in general. In the three years 1848–51 France displayed, in a swift, sharp, concentrated form, the very same processes of development which are peculiar to the whole capitalist world.

Imperialism—the era of bank capital, the era of gigantic capitalist monopolies, of the development of monopoly capitalism into state-monopoly capitalism—has clearly shown an unprecedented growth in its bureaucratic and military apparatus in connection with the intensification of repressive measures against the proletariat both in the monarchical and in the freest, republican countries.

World history is now undoubtedly leading, on an incomparably larger scale than in 1852, to the "concentration of all the forces" of the proletarian revolution on the "destruction" of the state machine.

What the proletariat will put in its place is suggested by the highly instructive material furnished by the Paris Commune.

## 3. The Presentation of the Question by Marx in 1852

In 1907, Mehring, in the magazine *Neue Zeit*[18] (Vol.XXV, 2, p.164), published extracts from Marx's letter to Weydemeyer dated March 5, 1852. This letter, among other things, contains the following remarkable observation:

> And now as to myself, no credit is due to me for discovering the existence of classes in modern society or the struggle between them. Long before me bourgeois historians had described the historical development of this class struggle and bourgeois economists, the economic

---

18  *Die Neue Zeit* (New Times) – theoretical journal of the German Social-Democratic Party, published in Stuttgart from 1883 to 1923. It was edited by Karl Kautsky till October 1917 and by Heinrich Cunow in the subsequent period. It published some of Marx's and Engels's writings for the first time. Engels offered advice to its editors and often criticized them for departures from Marxism.

In the second half of the nineties, upon Engels's death, the journal began systematically to publish revisionist articles, including a serial by Bernstein entitled "Problems of Socialism." which initiated a revisionist campaign against Marxism. During the First World War the journal adhered to a Centrist position, and virtually backed the social-chauvinists.

anatomy of classes. What I did that was new was to prove: (1) that the *existence of classes* is only bound up with *particular, historical phases in the development of production* (historische Entwicklungsphasen der Produktion), (2) that the class struggle necessarily leads to the *dictatorship of the proletariat,* (3) that this dictatorship itself only constitutes the transition to the *abolition of all classes* and to a *classless society.*[19]

In these words, Marx succeeded in expressing with striking clarity, first, the chief and radical difference between his theory and that of the foremost and most profound thinkers of the bourgeoisie; and, secondly, the essence of his theory of the state.

It is often said and written that the main point in Marx's theory is the class struggle. But this is wrong. And this wrong notion very often results in an opportunist distortion of Marxism and its falsification in a spirit acceptable to the bourgeoisie. For the theory of the class struggle was created *not* by Marx, *but* by the bourgeoisie *before* Marx, and, generally speaking, it is *acceptable* to the bourgeoisie. Those who recognize *only* the class struggle are not yet Marxists; they may be found to be still within the bounds of bourgeois thinking and bourgeois politics. To confine Marxism to the theory of the class struggle means curtailing Marxism, distorting it, reducing it to something acceptable to the bourgeoisie. Only he is a Marxist who *extends* the recognition of the class struggle to the recognition of the *dictatorship of the proletariat.* That is what constitutes the most profound distinction between the Marxist and the ordinary petty (as well as big) bourgeois. This is the touchstone on which the *real* understanding and recognition of Marxism should be tested. And it is not surprising that when the history of Europe brought the working class face to face with this question as a *practical* issue, not only all the opportunists and reformists, but all the Kautskyites (people who vacillate between reformism and Marxism) proved to be miserable philistines and petty-bourgeois democrats *repudiating* the dictatorship of the proletariat. Kautsky's pamphlet, *The Dictatorship of the Proletariat,* published in August 1918, i.e., long after the first edition of the present book, is a perfect example of petty-bourgeois distortion of Marxism and base renunciation of it *in deeds,* while hypocritically recognizing it *in words* (see my pamphlet, *The Proletarian Revolution and the Renegade Kautsky,* Petrograd and Moscow, 1918).

19    See Karl Marx and Frederick Engels, *Selected Correspondence,* Moscow, 1965).

Opportunism today, as represented by its principal spokesman, the ex-Marxist Karl Kautsky, fits in completely with Marx's character-ization of the *bourgeois* position quoted above, for this opportunism limits recognition of the class struggle to the sphere of bourgeois relations. (Within this sphere, within its framework, not a single edu-cated liberal will refuse to recognize the class struggle "in principle"!) Opportunism *does not extend* recognition of the class struggle to the cardinal point, to the period of *transition* from capitalism to commu-nism, of the *overthrow* and the complete *abolition* of the bourgeoisie. In reality, this period inevitably is a period of an unprecedentedly vio-lent class struggle in unprecedentedly acute forms, and, consequently, during this period the state must inevitably be a state that is demo-cratic *in a new way* (for the proletariat and the propertyless in general) and dictatorial *in a new way* (against the bourgeoisie).

Further. The essence of Marx's theory of the state has been mas-tered only by those who realize that the dictatorship of a *single* class is necessary not only for every class society in general, not only for the *proletariat* which has overthrown the bourgeoisie, but also for the entire *historical period* which separates capitalism from "classless society," from communism. Bourgeois states are most varied in form, but their essence is the same: all these states, whatever their form, in the final analysis are inevitably the *dictatorship of the bourgeoisie*. The transition from capitalism to communism is certainly bound to yield a tremendous abundance and variety of political forms, but the essence will inevitably be the same: *the dictatorship of the proletariat.*

# III
# Experience of the Paris Commune of 1871 Marx's Analysis

## 1. What Made the Communards' Attempt Heroic?

It is well known that in the autumn of 1870, a few months before the Commune, Marx warned the Paris workers that any attempt to overthrow the government would be the folly of despair. But when, in March 1871, a decisive battle was *forced* upon the workers and they accepted it, when the uprising had become a fact, Marx greeted the proletarian revolution with the greatest enthusiasm, in spite of unfavorable auguries. Marx did not persist in the pedantic attitude of condemning an "untimely" movement as did the ill-famed Russian renegade from Marxism, Plekhanov, who in November 1905 wrote encouragingly about the workers' and peasants' struggle, but after December 1905 cried, liberal fashion: "They should not have taken up arms."

Marx, however, was not only enthusiastic about the heroism of the Communards, who, as he expressed it, "stormed heaven." Although the mass revolutionary movement did not achieve its aim, he regarded it as a historic experience of enormous importance, as a certain advance of the world proletarian revolution, as a practical step that was more important than hundreds of programs and arguments. Marx endeavored to analyze this experiment, to draw tactical lessons from it and re-examine his theory in the light of it.

The only "correction" Marx thought it necessary to make to the *Communist Manifesto* he made on the basis of the revolutionary experience of the Paris Communards.

The last preface to the new German edition of the *Communist Manifesto*, signed by both its authors, is dated June 24, 1872. In this preface the authors, Karl Marx and Frederick Engels, say that the program of the *Communist Manifesto* "has in some details become out-of-date," and they go on to say: "...*One thing especially was proved by the Commune, viz., that 'the working class cannot simply lay hold of the ready-made state machinery and wield it for its own purposes'*...."[20]

---

20   See Karl Marx and Frederick Engels, *Selected Works*, Vol. 1, Moscow,

The authors took the words that are in single quotation marks in this passage from Marx's book, *The Civil War in France.*

Thus, Marx and Engels regarded one principal and fundamental lesson of the Paris Commune as being of such enormous importance that they introduced it as an important correction into the *Communist Manifesto.*

Most characteristically, it is this important correction that has been distorted by the opportunists, and its meaning probably is not known to nine-tenths, if not ninety-nine-hundredths, of the readers of the *Communist Manifesto.* We shall deal with this distortion more fully farther on, in a chapter devoted specially to distortions. Here it will be sufficient to note that the current, vulgar "interpretation" of Marx's famous statement just quoted is that Marx here allegedly emphasizes the idea of slow development in contradistinction to the seizure of power, and so on.

As a matter of fact, *the exact opposite is the case.* Marx's idea is that the working class must *break up, smash* the "ready-made state machinery," and not confine itself merely to laying hold of it.

On April 12, 1871, i.e., just at the time of the Commune, Marx wrote to Kugelmann:

> If you look up the last chapter of my *Eighteenth Brumaire,* you will find that I declare that the next attempt of the French Revolution will be no longer, as before, to transfer the bureaucratic-military machine from one hand to another, but to *smash* it [Marx's italics—the original is *zerbrechen*], and this is the precondition for every real people's revolution on the Continent. And this is what our heroic Party comrades in Paris are attempting. (*Neue Zeit,* Vol. XX, 1, 1901–02, 709.)[21] [22]

The words, "to smash the bureaucratic-military machine," briefly express the principal lesson of Marxism regarding the tasks of the proletariat during a revolution in relation to the state. And it is this lesson that has been not only completely ignored, but positively distorted by the prevailing, Kautskyite, "interpretation" of Marxism!

As for Marx's reference to *The Eighteenth Brumaire,* we have quoted the relevant passage in full above.

It is interesting to note, in particular, two points in the above-

1962, 22.
21   See Karl Marx and Frederick Engels, *Selected Correspondence.* Moscow, 1965, 262–63.
22   The letters of Marx to Kugelmann have appeared in Russian in no less than two editions, one of which I edited and supplied with a preface.

quoted argument of Marx. First, he restricts his conclusion to the Continent. This was understandable in 1871, when Britain was still the model of a purely capitalist country, but without a militarist clique and, to a considerable degree, without a bureaucracy. Marx therefore excluded Britain, where a revolution, even a people's revolution, then seemed possible, and indeed was possible, *without* the precondition of destroying "ready-made state machinery."

Today, in 1917, at the time of the first great imperialist war, this restriction made by Marx is no longer valid. Both Britain and America, the biggest and the last representatives—in the whole world—of Anglo-Saxon "liberty," in the sense that they had no militarist cliques and bureaucracy, have completely sunk into the all-European filthy, bloody morass of bureaucratic-military institutions which subordinate everything to themselves, and suppress everything. Today, in Britain and America, too, "the precondition for every real people's revolution" is the *smashing*, the *destruction* of the "ready-made state machinery" (made and brought up to the "European," general imperialist, perfection in those countries in the years 1914–17).

Secondly, particular attention should be paid to Marx's extremely profound remark that the destruction of the bureaucratic-military state machine is "the precondition for every real *people's* revolution." This idea of a "people's" revolution seems strange coming from Marx, so that the Russian Plekhanovites and Mensheviks, those followers of Struve who wish to be regarded as Marxists, might possibly declare such an expression to be a "slip of the pen" on Marx's part. They have reduced Marxism to such a state of wretchedly liberal distortion that nothing exists for them beyond the antithesis between bourgeois revolution and proletarian revolution, and even this antithesis they interpret in an utterly lifeless way.

If we take the revolutions of the twentieth century as examples we shall, of course, have to admit that the Portuguese and the Turkish revolutions are both bourgeois revolutions. Neither of them, however, is a "people's" revolution, since in neither does the mass of the people, their vast majority, come out actively, independently, with their own economic and political demands to any noticeable degree. By contrast, although the Russian bourgeois revolution of 1905–07 displayed no such "brilliant" successes as at time fell to the Portuguese and Turkish revolutions, it was undoubtedly a "real people's" revolution, since the mass of the people, their majority, the very lowest social groups, crushed by oppression and exploitation, rose independently and stamped on the entire course of the revolution the imprint of *their* own demands, *their* attempt to build in their own way a new society in place of the old society that was being destroyed.

In Europe, in 1871, the proletariat did not constitute the majority of the people in any country on the Continent. A "people's" revolution, one actually sweeping the majority into its stream, could be such only if it embraced both the proletariat and the peasants. These two classes then constituted the "people." These two classes are united by the fact that the "bureaucratic-military state machine" oppresses, crushes, exploits them. To *smash* this machine, *to break it up*, is truly in the interest of the "people," of their majority, of the workers and most of the peasants, is "the precondition" for a free alliance of the poor peasant and the proletarians, whereas without such an alliance democracy is unstable and socialist transformation is impossible.

As is well known, the Paris Commune was actually working its way toward such an alliance, although it did not reach its goal owing to a number of circumstances, internal and external.

Consequently, in speaking of a "real people's revolution," Marx, without in the least discounting the special features of the petty bourgeois (he spoke a great deal about them and often), took strict account of the actual balance of class forces in most of the continental countries of Europe in 1871. On the other hand, he stated that the "smashing" of the state machine was required by the interests of both the workers and the peasants, that it united them, that it placed before them the common task of removing the "parasite" and of replacing it by something new.

By what exactly?

## 2. What is to Replace the Smashed State Machine?

In 1847, in the *Communist Manifesto*, Marx's answer to this question was as yet a purely abstract one; to be exact, it was an answer that indicated the tasks, but not the ways of accomplishing them. The answer given in the *Communist Manifesto* was that this machine was to be replaced by "the proletariat organized as the ruling class," by the "winning of the battle of democracy."

Marx did not indulge in utopias; he expected the *experience* of the mass movement to provide the reply to the question as to the specific forms this organization of the proletariat as the ruling class would assume and as to the exact manner in which this organization would be combined with the most complete, most consistent "winning of the battle of democracy."

Marx subjected the experience of the Commune, meager as it was, to the most careful analysis in *The Civil War in France*. Let us quote the most important passages of this work. [All the following quotes in this chapter, with one exception, are so citied—Ed.]

Originating from the Middle Ages, there developed in the 19th century "the centralized state power, with its ubiquitous organs of standing army, police, bureaucracy, clergy, and judicature." With the development of class antagonisms between capital and labor, "state power assumed more and more the character of a public force organized for the suppression of the working class, of a machine of class rule. After every revolution, which marks an advance in the class struggle, the purely coercive character of the state power stands out in bolder and bolder relief." After the revolution of 1848–49, state power became "the national war instruments of capital against labor." The Second Empire consolidated this.

"The direct antithesis to the empire was the Commune." It was the "specific form" of "a republic that was not only to remove the monarchical form of class rule, but class rule itself."

What was this "specific" form of the proletarian, socialist republic? What was the state it began to create?

"...The first decree of the Commune...was the suppression of the standing army, and its replacement by the armed people."

This demand now figures in the program of every party calling itself socialist. The real worth of their programs, however, is best shown by the behavior of our Social Revolutionists and Mensheviks, who, right after the revolution of February 27, actually refused to carry out this demand!

> The Commune was formed of the municipal councillors, chosen by universal suffrage in the various wards of the town, responsible and revocable at any time. The majority of its members were naturally working men, or acknowledged representatives of the working class.... The police, which until then had been the instrument of the Government, was at once stripped of its political attributes, and turned into the responsible, and at all times revocable, agent of the Commune. So were the officials of all other branches of the administration. From the members of the Commune downwards, the public service had to be done at *workmen's wages*. The privileges and the representation allow-

ances of the high dignitaries of state disappeared along with the high dignitaries themselves....

Having once got rid of the standing army and the police, the instruments of physical force of the old government, the Commune proceeded at once to break the instrument of spiritual suppression, the power of the priests....

The judicial functionaries lost that sham independence... they were thenceforward to be elective, responsible, and revocable.[23]

The Commune, therefore, appears to have replaced the smashed state machine "only" by fuller democracy: abolition of the standing army; all officials to be elected and subject to recall. But as a matter of fact this "only" signifies a gigantic replacement of certain institutions by other institutions of a fundamentally different type. This is exactly a case of "quantity being transformed into quality": democracy, introduced as fully and consistently as is at all conceivable, is transformed from bourgeois into proletarian democracy; from the state (= a special force for the suppression of a particular class) into something which is no longer the state proper.

It is still necessary to suppress the bourgeoisie and crush their resistance. This was particularly necessary for the Commune; and one of the reasons for its defeat was that it did not do this with sufficient determination. The organ of suppression, however, is here the majority of the population, and not a minority, as was always the case under slavery, serfdom, and wage slavery. And since the majority of people *itself* suppresses its oppressors, a 'special force" for suppression *is no longer necessary!* In this sense, the state *begins to wither away*. Instead of the special institutions of a privileged minority (privileged officialdom, the chiefs of the standing army), the majority itself can directly fulfill all these functions, and the more the functions of state power are performed by the people as a whole, the less need there is for the existence of this power.

In this connection, the following measures of the Commune, emphasized by Marx, are particularly noteworthy: the abolition of all representation allowances, and of all monetary privileges to officials, the reduction of the remuneration of *all* servants of the state to the level of *"workmen's wages."* This shows more clearly than anything else

---

23     See Karl Marx, *The Civil War in France* (Karl Marx and Frederick Engels, *Selected Works*, Vol. 2, Moscow, 1973, 217–21).

On pp. 116, 121, 124–125 of this volume, Lenin is quoting from the same work by Marx (op. cit., 222, 220–23).

the turn from bourgeois to proletarian democracy, from the democracy of the oppressors to that of the oppressed classes, from the state as a *"special force"* for the suppression of a particular class to the suppression of the oppressors by the *general force* of the majority of the people— the workers and the peasants. And it is on this particularly striking point, perhaps the most important as far as the problem of the state is concerned, that the ideas of Marx have been most completely ignored! In popular commentaries, the number of which is legion, this is not mentioned. The thing done is to keep silent about it as if it were a piece of old-fashioned "naiveté," just as Christians, after their religion had been given the status of state religion, "forgot" the "naiveté" of primitive Christianity with its democratic revolutionary spirit.

The reduction of the remuneration of high state officials seems to be "simply" a demand of naïve, primitive democracy. One of the "founders" of modern opportunism, the ex-Social Democrat Eduard Bernstein, has more than once repeated the vulgar bourgeois jeers at "primitive" democracy. Like all opportunists, and like the present Kautskyites, he did not understand at all that, first of all, the transition from capitalism to socialism is *impossible* without a certain "reversion" to "primitive" democracy (for how else can the majority, and then the whole population without exception, proceed to discharge state functions?); and that, secondly, "primitive democracy" based on capitalism and capitalist culture is not the same as primitive democracy in prehistoric or precapitalist times. Capitalist culture has *created* large-scale production, factories, railways, the postal service, telephones, etc., and *on this basis* the great majority of the functions of the old "state power" have become so simplified and can be reduced to such exceedingly simple operations of registration, filing, and checking that they can be easily performed by every literate person, can quite easily be performed for ordinary "workmen's wages," and that these functions can (and must) be stripped of every shadow of privilege, of every semblance of "official grandeur."

All officials, without exception, elected and subject to recall *at any time*, their salaries reduced to the level of ordinary "workmen's wages"—these simple and "self-evident" democratic measures, while completely uniting the interests of the workers and the majority of the peasants, at the same time serve as a bridge leading from capitalism to socialism. These measures concern the reorganization of the state, the purely political reorganization of society; but, of course, they acquire their full meaning and significance only in connection with the "expropriation of the expropriators" either bring accomplished or in preparation, i.e., with the transformation of capitalist private ownership of the means of production into social ownership.

"The Commune," Marx wrote, "made that catchword of all bourgeois revolutions, cheap government, a reality, by abolishing the two greatest sources of expenditure—the army and the officialdom."

From the peasants, as from other sections of the petty bourgeoisie, only an insignificant few "rise to the top," "get on in the world" in the bourgeois sense, i.e., become either well-to-do, bourgeois, or officials in secure and privileged positions. In every capitalist country where there are peasants (as there are in most capitalist countries), the vast majority of them are oppressed by the government and long for its overthrow, long for "cheap" government. This can be achieved *only* by the proletariat; and by achieving it, the proletariat at the same time takes a step towards the socialist reorganization of the state.

## 3. Abolition of Parliamentarism

"The Commune," Marx wrote, "was to be a working, not a parliamentary, body, executive and legislative at the same time....

> Instead of deciding once in three or six years which member of the ruling class was to represent and repress [ver- and zertreten] the people in parliament, universal suffrage was to serve the people constituted in communes, as individual suffrage serves every other employer in the search for workers, foremen and accountants for his business.

Owing to the prevalence of social-chauvinism and opportunism, this remarkable criticism of parliamentarism, made in 1871, also belongs now to the "forgotten words" of Marxism. The professional Cabinet Ministers and parliamentarians, the traitors to the proletariat and the "practical" socialists of our day, have left all criticism of parliamentarism to the anarchists, and, on this wonderfully reasonable ground, they denounce *all* criticism of parliamentarism as "anarchism"!! It is not surprising that the proletariat of the "advanced" parliamentary countries, disgusted with such "socialists" as the Scheidemanns, Davids, Legiens, Sembats, Renaudels, Hendersons, Vanderveldes, Staunings, Brantings, Bissolatis, and Co., has been with increasing frequency giving its sympathies to anarcho-syndicalism, in spite of the fact that the latter is merely the twin brother of opportunism.

For Marx, however, revolutionary dialectics was never the empty fashionable phrase, the toy rattle, which Plekhanov, Kautsky and others have made of it. Marx knew how to break with anarchism ruthlessly for its inability to make use even of the "pigsty" of bourgeois parliamentarism, especially when the situation was obviously not revolutionary; but at the same time he knew how to subject parliamentarism to genuinely revolutionary proletarian criticism.

To decide once every few years which members of the ruling class is to repress and crush the people through parliament—this is the real essence of bourgeois parliamentarism, not only in parliamentary-constitutional monarchies, but also in the most democratic republics.

But if we deal with the question of the state, and if we consider parliamentarism as one of the institutions of the state, from the point of view of the tasks of the proletariat in *this* field, what is the way out of parliamentarism? How can it be dispensed with?

Once again, we must say: the lessons of Marx, based on the study of the Commune, have been so completely forgotten that the present-day "Social Democrat" (i.e., present-day traitor to socialism) really cannot understand any criticism of parliamentarism other than anarchist or reactionary criticism.

The way out of parliamentarism is not, of course, the abolition of representative institutions and the elective principle, but the conversion of the representative institutions from talking shops into "working" bodies. "The Commune was to be a working, not a parliamentary, body, executive and legislative at the same time."

"A working, not a parliamentary body"—this is a blow straight from the shoulder at the present-day parliamentarians and parliamentary "lap dogs" of Social Democracy! Take any parliamentary country, from America to Switzerland, from France to Britain, Norway and so forth—in these countries the real business of "state" is performed behind the scenes and is carried on by the departments, chancelleries, and General Staffs. Parliament is given up to talk for the special purpose of fooling the "common people." This is so true that even in the Russian republic, a bourgeois-democratic republic, all these sins of parliamentarism came out at once, even before it managed to set up a real parliament. The heroes of rotten philistinism, such as the Skobelevs and Tseretelis, the Chernovs and Avksentyevs, have even succeeded in polluting the Soviets after the fashion of the most disgusting bourgeois parliamentarism, in converting them into mere talking shops. In the Soviets, the "socialist" Ministers are fooling the credulous rustics with phrase-mongering and resolutions. In the government itself a sort of permanent shuffle is going on in order that, on the one hand, as many Socialist Revolutionaries and Mensheviks as possible may in turn get near the "pie," the lucrative and honorable posts, and that, on the other hand, the "attention" of the people may be "engaged." Meanwhile the chancelleries and army staffs "do" the business of "state."

*Dyelo Naroda*, the organ of the ruling Socialist Revolutionary Party, recently admitted in a leading article—with the matchless frankness of people of "good society," in which "all" are engaged in political prostitution—that even in the ministries headed by the "socialists" (save the mark!), the whole bureaucratic apparatus is in fact unchanged, is working in the old way and quite "freely" sabotaging revolutionary measures! Even without this admission, does not the actual history of the participation of the Socialist Revolutionaries and Mensheviks in the government prove this? It is noteworthy, however, that in the ministerial company of the Cadets, the Chernovs, Rusanovs, Zenzinovs, and other editors of *Dyelo Naroda* have so completely lost all sense of shame as to brazenly assert, as if it were a mere bagatelle, that in "their" ministries everything is unchanged!! Revolutionary-democratic phrases to gull the rural Simple Simons, and bureaucracy and red tape to "gladden the hearts" of the capitalists—that is the essence of the "honest" coalition.

The Commune substitutes for the venal and rotten parliamentarism of bourgeois society institutions in which freedom of opinion and discussion does not degenerate into deception, for the parliamentarians themselves have to work, have to execute their own laws, have themselves to test the results achieved in reality, and to account directly to their constituents. Representative institutions remain, but there is *no* parliamentarism here as a special system, as the division of labor between the legislative and the executive, as a privileged position for the deputies. We cannot imagine democracy, even proletarian democracy, without representative institutions, but we can and must imagine democracy without parliamentarism, if criticism of bourgeois society is not mere words for us, if the desire to overthrow the rule of the bourgeoisie is our earnest and sincere desire, and not a mere "election" cry for catching workers' votes, as it is with the Mensheviks and Socialist Revolutionaries, and also the Scheidemanns and Legiens, the Semblats and Vandeveldes.

It is extremely instructive to note that, in speaking of the function of *those* officials who are necessary for the Commune and for proletarian democracy, Marx compares them to the workers of "every other employer," that is, of the ordinary capitalist enterprise, with its "workers, foremen, and accountants."

There is no trace of utopianism in Marx, in the sense that he made up or invented a "new" society. No, he studied the *birth* of the new society *out of* the old, and the forms of transition from the latter to the former, as a natural-historical process. He examined the actual experience of a mass proletarian movement and tried to draw practical lessons from it. He "learned" from the Commune, just as all the great revolutionary thinkers learned unhesitatingly from the experience of great movements of the oppressed classes, and never addressed them with pedantic "homilies" (such as Plekhanov's: "They should not have taken up arms" or Tsereteli's: "A class must limit itself").

Abolishing the bureaucracy at once, everywhere and completely, is out of the question. It is a utopia. But to *smash* the old bureaucratic machine at once and to begin immediately to construct a new one that will make possible the gradual abolition of all bureaucracy—this is *not* a utopia, it is the experience of the Commune, the direct and immediate task of the revolutionary proletariat.

Capitalism simplifies the functions of "state" administration; it makes it possible to cast "bossing" aside and to confine the whole matter to the organization of the proletarians (as the ruling class), which will hire "workers, foremen and accountants" in the name of the whole of society.

We are not utopians, we do not "dream" of dispensing *at once* with all administration, with all subordination. These anarchist dreams, based upon incomprehension of the tasks of the proletarian dictatorship, are totally alien to Marxism, and, as a matter of fact, serve only to postpone the socialist revolution until people are different. No, we want the socialist revolution with people as they are now, with people who cannot dispense with subordination, control, and "foremen and accountants."

The subordination, however, must be to the armed vanguard of all the exploited and working people, i.e., to the proletariat. A beginning can and must be made at once, overnight, to replace the specific "bossing" of state officials by the simple functions of "foremen and accountants," functions which are already fully within the ability of the average town dweller and can well be performed for "workmen's wages."

*We*, the workers, shall organize large-scale production on the basis of what capitalism has already created, relying on our own experience as workers, establishing strict, iron discipline backed up by the state power of the armed workers. We shall reduce the role of state officials to that of simply carrying out our instructions as responsible, revocable, modestly paid "foremen and accountants" (of course, with the aid of technicians of all sorts, types and degrees). This is *our* proletarian task, this is what we can and must *start* with in accomplishing the proletarian revolution. Such a beginning, on the basis of large-scale production, will of itself lead to the gradual "withering away" of all bureaucracy, to the gradual creation of an order—an order without inverted commas, an order bearing no similarity to wage slavery—an order under which the functions of control and accounting, becoming more and more simple, will be performed by each in turn, will then become a habit and will finally die out as the *special* functions of a special section of the population.

A witty German Social Democrat of the seventies of the last century called the *postal service* an example of the socialist economic system. This is very true. At the present the postal service is a business organized on the lines of state-*capitalist* monopoly. Imperialism is gradually transforming all trusts into organizations of a similar type, in which, standing over the "common" people, who are overworked and starved, one has the same bourgeois bureaucracy. But the mechanism of social management is here already to hand. Once we have overthrown the capitalists, crushed the resistance of these exploiters with the iron hand of the armed workers, and smashed the bureaucratic machinery of the modern state, we shall have a splendidly-equipped mechanism, freed from the "parasite," a mechanism which can very well be set going by the united workers themselves, who will hire technicians, foremen and accountants, and pay them *all*, as indeed *all* "state" officials in general, workmen's wages. Here is a concrete, practical task which can immediately be fulfilled in relation to all trusts, a task whose fulfillment will rid the working people of exploitation, a task which takes account of what the Commune had already begun to practice (particularly in building up the state).

To organize the *whole* economy on the lines of the postal service so that the technicians, foremen and accountants, as well as *all* officials, shall receive salaries no higher than "a workman's wage," all under the control and leadership of the armed proletariat—this is our immediate aim. This is the state and this is the economic foundation we need. This is what will bring about the abolition of parliamentarism and the preservation of representative institutions. This is what will rid the laboring classes of the bourgeoisie's prostitution of these institutions.

## 4. Organization of National Unity

> In a brief sketch of national organization which the Commune had no time to develop, it states explicitly that the Commune was to be the political form of even the smallest village....

The communes were to elect the "National Delegation" in Paris.

> ... The few but important functions which would still remain for a central government were not to be suppressed, as had been deliberately misstated, but were to be transferred to communal, i.e., strictly responsible, officials.
>
> ... National unity was not to be broken, but, on the contrary, organized by the communal constitution; it was to become a reality by the destruction of state power which posed as the embodiment of that unity yet wanted to be independent of, and superior to, the nation, on whose body it was but a parasitic excrescence. While the merely repressive organs of the old governmental power were to be amputated, its legitimate functions were to be wrested from an authority claiming the right to stand above society, and restored to the responsible servants of society.

The extent to which the opportunists of present-day Social Democracy have failed—perhaps it would be more true to say, have refused—to understand these observations of Marx is best shown by that book of Herostratean fame of the renegade Bernstein, *The Premises of Socialism and the Tasks of the Social-Democrats*. It is in connection with the above passage from Marx that Bernstein wrote that "as far as its political content is concerned," this program "displays, in all its essential features, the greatest similarity to the federalism of Proudhon.... In spite of all the other points of difference between Marx and the 'petty-bourgeois' Proudhon [Bernstein places the word "petty-bourgeois" in inverted commas, to make it sound ironical] on these points, their lines of reasoning run as close as could be."

"Of course," Bernstein continues, "the importance of the municipalities is growing, but it seems doubtful to me whether the first job of democracy would be such a dissolution [Auflösung] of the modern states and such a complete transformation [Umwandlung] of their organization as is visualized by Marx and Proudhon (the formation of a National Assembly from delegates of the provincial of district assemblies, which, in their turn, would consist of delegates from the communes), so that consequently the previous mode of national representation would disappear. (Bernstein, *Premises*, German edition, 1899, pp.134 and 136)

To confuse Marx's view on the "destruction of state power, a parasitic excrescence," with Proudhon's federalism is positively monstrous! But it is no accident, for it never occurs to the opportunist that Marx does not speak here at all about federalism as opposed to centralism, but about smashing the old, bourgeois state machine which exists in all bourgeois countries.

The only thing that does occur to the opportunist is what he sees around him, in an environment of petty-bourgeois philistinism and "reformist" stagnation, namely, only "municipalities"! The opportunist has even grown out of the habit of thinking about proletarian revolution.

It is ridiculous. But the remarkable thing is that nobody argued with Bernstein on this point. Bernstein has been refuted by many, especially by Plekhanov in Russian literature and by Kautsky in European literature, but neither of them has said *anything* about *this* distortion of Marx by Bernstein.

The opportunist has so much forgotten how to think in a revolutionary way and to dwell on revolution that he attributes "federalism" to Marx, whom he confuses with the founder of anarchism, Proudhon. As for Kautsky and Plekhanov, who claim to be orthodox Marxists and defenders of the theory of revolutionary Marxism, they are silent on this point! Here is one of the roots of the extreme vulgarization of the views on the difference between Marxism and anarchism, which is characteristic of both the Kautskyites and the opportunists, and which we shall discuss again later.

There is not a trace of federalism in Marx's above-quoted observation on the experience of the Commune. Marx agreed with Proudhon on the very point that the opportunist Bernstein did not see. Marx disagreed with Proudhon on the very point on which Bernstein found a similarity between them.

Marx agreed with Proudhon in that they both stood for the "smashing" of the modern state machine. Neither the opportunists nor the

Kautskyites wish to see the similarity of views on this point between Marxism and anarchism (both Proudhon and Bakunin) because this is where they have departed from Marxism.

Marx disagreed both with Proudhon and Bakunin precisely on the question of federalism (not to mention the dictatorship of the proletariat). Federalism as a principle follows logically from the petty-bourgeois views of anarchism. Marx was a centralist. There is no departure whatever from centralism in his observations just quoted. Only those who are imbued with the philistine "superstitious belief" in the state can mistake the destruction of the bourgeois state machine for the destruction of centralism!

Now if the proletariat and the poor peasants take state power into their own hands, organize themselves quite freely in communes, and *unite* the action of all the communes in striking at capital, in crushing the resistance of the capitalists, and in transferring the privately-owned railways, factories, land and so on to the *entire* nation, to the whole of society, won't that be centralism? Won't that be the most consistent democratic centralism and, moreover, proletarian centralism?

Bernstein simply cannot conceive of the possibility of voluntary centralism, of the voluntary amalgamation of the communes into a nation, of the voluntary fusion of the proletarian communes, for the purpose of destroying bourgeois rule and the bourgeois state machine. Like all philistines, Bernstein pictures centralism as something which can be imposed and maintained solely from above, and solely by the bureaucracy and military clique.

As though foreseeing that his views might be distorted, Marx expressly emphasized that the charge that the Commune had wanted to destroy national unity, to abolish the central authority, was a deliberate fraud. Marx purposely used the words: "National unity was... to be organized", so as to oppose conscious, democratic, proletarian centralism to bourgeois, military, bureaucratic centralism.

But there are none so deaf as those who will not hear. And the very thing the opportunists of present-day Social Democracy do not want to hear about is the destruction of state power, the amputation of the parasitic excrescence.

## 5. Abolition of the Parasite State

We have already quoted Marx's words on the subject, and we must now supplement them.

It is generally the fate of new historical creations," he wrote, "to be mistaken for the counterpart of older and even defunct forms of social life, to which they may bear a certain likeness. Thus, this new Commune, which breaks [*bricht*, smashes] the modern state power, has been regarded as a revival of the medieval communes... as a federation of small states (as Montesquieu and the Girondins[24] visualized it)... as an exaggerated form of the old struggle against overcentralization....

... The Communal Constitution would have restored to the social body all the forces hitherto absorbed by that parasitic excrescence, the 'state,' feeding upon and hampering the free movement of society. By this one act it would have initiated the regeneration of France....

... The Communal Constitution would have brought the rural producers under the intellectual lead of the central towns of their districts, and there secured to them, in the town working men, the natural trustees of their interests. The very existence of the Commune involved, as a matter of course, local self-government, but no longer as a counterpoise to state power, now become superfluous.

"Breaking state power," which was a "parasitic excrescence"; its "amputation," its "smashing"; "state power, now become superfluous"—these are the expressions Marx used in regard to the state when appraising and analyzing the experience of the Commune.

All this was written a little less than half a century ago; and now one has to engage in excavations, as it were, in order to bring undistorted Marxism to the knowledge of the mass of the people. The conclusions drawn from the observation of the last great revolution which Marx lived through were forgotten just when the time for the next great proletarian revolutions had arrived.

... The multiplicity of interpretations to which the Commune has been subjected, and the multiplicity of interests which expressed themselves in it show that it was a thoroughly flexible political form, while all previous forms of government had been essentially repressive. Its true secret was this: it was essentially *a working-class government,* the result of the struggle of the producing against the appropriating class, the political form at last discovered under which the economic emancipation of labor could be accomplished....

Except on this last condition, the Communal Constitution would have been an impossibility and a delusion....

---

24     *The Girondists*—a political grouping during the French bourgeois revolution of the late eighteenth century, expressed the interests of the moderate bourgeoisie. They wavered between revolution and counter-revolution, and made deals with the monarchy.

The utopians busied themselves with "discovering" political forms under which the socialist transformation of society was to take place. The anarchists dismissed the question of political forms altogether. The opportunists of present-day Social Democracy accepted the bourgeois political forms of the parliamentary democratic state as the limit which should not be overstepped; they battered their foreheads praying before this "model," and denounced as anarchism every desire to *break* these forms.

Marx deduced from the whole history of socialism and the political struggle that the state was bound to disappear, and that the transitional form of its disappearance (the transition from state to non-state) would be the "proletariat organized as the ruling class." Marx, however, did not set out to *discover* the political *forms* of this future stage. He limited himself to carefully observing French history, to analyzing it, and to drawing the conclusion to which the year 1851 had led, namely, that matters were moving towards destruction of the bourgeois state machine.

And when the mass revolutionary movement of the proletariat burst forth, Marx, in spite of its failure, in spite of its short life and patent weakness, began to study the forms it had *discovered.*

The Commune is the form "at last discovered" by the proletarian revolution, under which the economic emancipation of labor can take place.

The Commune is the first attempt by a proletarian revolution to *smash* the bourgeois state machine; and it is the political form "at last discovered," by which the smashed state machine can and must be *replaced.*

We shall see further on that the Russian revolutions of 1905 and 1917, in different circumstances and under different conditions, continue the work of the Commune and confirm Marx's brilliant historical analysis.

# IV
# Supplementary Explanations by Engels

Marx gave the fundamentals concerning the significance of the experience of the Commune. Engels returned to the same subject time and again, and explained Marx's analysis and conclusions, sometimes elucidating other aspects of the question with such power and vividness that it is necessary to deal with his explanations specially.

## 1. The Housing Question

In his work, *The Housing Question* (1872), Engels already took into account the experience of the Commune, and dealt several times with the tasks of the revolution in relation to the state. It is interesting to note that the treatment of this specific subject clearly revealed, on the one hand, points of similarity between the proletarian state and the present state—points that warrant speaking of the state in both cases—and, on the other hand, points of difference between them, or the transition to the destruction of the state.

> How is the housing question to be settled then? In present-day society, it is settled just as any other social question: by the gradual economic leveling of demand and supply, a settlement which reproduces the question itself again and again and therefore is no settlement. How a social revolution would settle this question not only depends on the circumstances in each particular case, but is also connected with much more far-reaching questions, one of the most fundamental of which is the abolition of the antithesis between town and country. As it is not our task to create utopian systems for the organization of the future society, it would be more than idle to go into the question here. But one thing is certain: there is already a sufficient quantity of houses in the big cities to remedy immediately all real 'housing *shortage*,' provided they are used judiciously. This can naturally only occur through the expropriation of the present owners and by quartering in their houses homeless workers or workers overcrowded in their present homes. As soon as the proletariat has won political power, such a measure

prompted by concern for the common good will be just as easy to carry out as are other expropriations and billetings by the present-day state. (German edition, 1887, p. 22) [25]

The change in the form of state power is not examined here, but only the content of its activity. Expropriations and billetings take place by order even of the present state. From the formal point of view, the proletarian state will also "order" the occupation of dwellings and expropriation of houses. But it is clear that the old executive apparatus, the bureaucracy, which is connected with the bourgeoisie, would simply be unfit to carry out the orders of the proletarian state.

> ... It must be pointed out that the 'actual seizure' of all the instruments of labor, the taking possession of industry as a whole by the working people, is the exact opposite of the Proudhonist 'redemption.' In the latter case the individual worker becomes the owner of the dwelling, the peasant farm, the instruments of labor; in the former case, the 'working people' remain the collective owners of the houses, factories and instruments of labor, and will hardly permit their use, at least during a transitional period, by individuals or associations without compensation for the cost. In the same way, the abolition of property in land is not the abolition of ground rent but its transfer, if in a modified form, to society. The actual seizure of all the instruments of labor by the working people, therefore, does not at all preclude the retention of rent relations. (p.68)

We shall examine the question touched upon in this passage, namely, the economic basis for the withering away of the state, in the next chapter. Engels expresses himself most cautiously, saying that the proletarian state would "hardly" permit the use of houses without payment, "at least during a transitional period." The letting of houses owed by the whole people to individual families presupposes the collection of rent, a certain amount of control, and the employment of some standard in allotting the housing. All this calls for a certain form of state, but it does not at all call for a special military bureaucratic apparatus, with officials occupying especially privileged positions. The transition to a situation in which it will be possible to supply dwellings rent-free depends on the complete "withering away" of the state.

---

25 See Frederick Engels, *The Housing Question* (Karl Marx and Frederick Engels, *Selected Works*, Vol. 2, Moscow, 1973, 317–18).

On pp. 128 of this volume, Lenin is quoting from the same work by Engels (op. cit., 370, 355).

Speaking of the Blanquists' adoption of the fundamental position of Marxism after the Commune and under the influence of its experience, Engels, in passing, formulates this position as follows: "... Necessity of political action by the proletariat and of its dictatorship as the transition to the abolition of classes and, with them, of the state...." (p.55)

Addicts of hair-splitting criticism, or bourgeois "exterminators of Marxism," will perhaps see a contradiction between this *recognition* of the "abolition of the state" and repudiation of this formula as an anarchist one in the above passage from *Anti-Dühring*. It would not be surprising if the opportunists classed Engels, too, as an "anarchist," for it is becoming increasingly common with the social-chauvinists to accuse the internationalists of anarchism.

Marxism has always taught that with the abolition of classes the state will also be abolished. The well-known passage on the "withering away of the state" in *Anti-Dühring* accuses the anarchists not simply of favoring the abolition of the state, but of preaching that the state can be abolished "overnight."

As the now prevailing "Social Democratic" doctrine completely distorts the relation of Marxism to anarchism on the question of the abolition of the state, it will be particularly useful to recall a certain controversy in which Marx and Engels came out against the anarchists.

## 2. Controversy with the Anarchists

This controversy took place in 1873. Marx and Engels contributed articles against the Proudhonists, "autonomists" or "anti-authoritarians," to an Italian socialist annual, and it was not until 1913 that these articles appeared in German in *Neue Zeit*.[26] "If the political struggle of the working class assumes revolutionary form," wrote Marx, ridiculing the anarchists for their repudiation of politics, "and if the workers set up their revolutionary dictatorship in place of the dictatorship of the bourgeoisie, they commit the terrible crime of violating principles, for in order to satisfy their wretched, vulgar everyday needs and to crush the resistance of the bourgeoisie, they give the state a revolutionary

26  Lenin is referring to the articles "L'indifferenza in materia politica" by Karl Marx and "Dell' Autorita" by Frederick Engels (*Almanacco Republicano per l'anno* 1874).

On pp. 129–30 of this volume, Lenin is quoting from the same articles.

and transient form, instead of laying down their arms and abolishing the state." (*Neue Zeit* Vol.XXXII, 1, 1913–14, p.40)

It was solely against this kind of "abolition" of the state that Marx fought in refuting the anarchists! He did not at all oppose the view that the state would disappear when classes disappeared, or that it would be abolished when classes were abolished. What he did oppose was the proposition that the workers should renounce the use of arms, organized violence, *that is, the state*, which is to serve to "crush the resistance of the bourgeoisie."

To prevent the true meaning of his struggle against anarchism from being distorted, Marx expressly emphasized the "revolutionary and *transient* form" of the state which the proletariat needs. The proletariat needs the state only temporarily. We do not after all differ with the anarchists on the question of the abolition of the state as the *aim*. We maintain that, to achieve this aim, we must temporarily make use of the instruments, resources, and methods of state power *against* the exploiters, just as the temporary dictatorship of the oppressed class is necessary for the abolition of classes. Marx chooses the sharpest and clearest way of stating his case against the anarchists: After overthrowing the yoke of the capitalists, should the workers "lay down their arms," or use them against the capitalists in order to crush their resistance? But what is the systematic use of arms by one class against another if not a "transient form" of state?

Let every Social Democrat ask himself: Is *that* how he has been posing the question of the state in controversy with the anarchists? Is that how it has been posed by the vast majority of the official socialist parties of the Second International?

Engels expounds the same ideas in much greater detail and still more popularly. First of all he ridicules the muddled ideas of the Proudhonists, who call themselves "anti-authoritarians," i.e., repudiated all authority, all subordination, all power. Take a factory, a railway, a ship on the high seas, said Engels: is it not clear that not one of these complex technical establishments, based on the use of machinery and the systematic cooperation of many people, could function without a certain amount of subordination and, consequently, without a certain amount of authority or power?

> ... When I counter the most rabid anti-authoritarians with these arguments, the only answer they can give me is the following: Oh, that's true, except that here it is not a question of authority with which we

vest our delegates, *but of a commission!* These people imagine they can change a thing by changing its name....

Having thus shown that authority and autonomy are relative terms, that the sphere of their application varies with the various phases of social development, that it is absurd to take them as absolutes, and adding that the sphere of application of machinery and large-scale production is steadily expanding, Engels passes from the general discussion of authority to the question of the state. "Had the autonomists," he wrote, "contented themselves with saying that the social organization of the future would allow authority only within the bounds which the conditions of production make inevitable, one could have come to terms with them. But they are blind to all facts that make authority necessary and they passionately fight the word."

> Why do the anti-authoritarians not confine themselves to crying out against political authority, the state? All socialists are agreed that the state, and with it political authority, will disappear as a result of the coming social revolution, that is, that public functions will lose their political character and become mere administrative functions of watching over social interests. But the anti-authoritarians demand that the political state be abolished at one stroke, even before the social relations that gave birth to it have been destroyed. They demand that the first act of the social revolution shall be the abolition of authority. Have these gentlemen ever seen a revolution? A revolution is certainly the most authoritarian thing there is; it is an act whereby one part of the population imposes its will upon the other part by means of rifles, bayonets and cannon, all of which are highly authoritarian means. And the victorious party must maintain its rule by means of the terror which its arms inspire in the reactionaries. Would the Paris Commune have lasted more than a day if it had not used the authority of the armed people against the bourgeoisie? Cannot we, on the contrary, blame it for having made too little use of that authority? Therefore, one of two things: either that anti-authoritarians don't know what they are talking about, in which case they are creating nothing but confusion. Or they do know, and in that case they are betraying the cause of the proletariat. In either case they serve only reaction. (p.39)

This argument touches upon questions which should be examined in connection with the relationship between politics and economics during the withering away of the state (the next chapter is devoted to this). These questions are: the transformation of public functions from political into simple functions of administration, and the "political state." This last term, one particularly liable to misunderstanding, indicates the process of the withering away of the state: at a certain stage of this process, the state which is withering away may be called a non-political state.

Again, the most remarkable thing in this argument of Engels is the way he states his case against the anarchists. Social Democrats, claiming to be disciples of Engels, have argued on this subject against the anarchists millions of times since 1873, but they have *not* argued as Marxists could and should. The anarchist idea of abolition of the state is muddled and *non-revolutionary*—that is how Engels put it. It is precisely the revolution in its rise and development, with its specific tasks in relation to violence, authority, power, the state, that the anarchists refuse to see.

The usual criticism of anarchism by present-day Social Democrats has boiled down to the purest philistine banality: "We recognize the state, whereas the anarchists do not!" Naturally, such banality cannot but repel workers who are at all capable of thinking and revolutionary-minded. What Engels says is different. He stresses that all socialists recognize that the state will disappear as a result of the socialist revolution. He then deals specifically with the question of the revolution—the very question which, as a rule, the Social Democrats evade out of opportunism, leaving it, so to speak, exclusively for the anarchists "to work out." And when dealing with this question, Engels takes the bull by the horns; he asks: should not the Commune have made *more* use of the *revolutionary* power of the *state*, that is, of the proletariat armed and organized as the ruling class?

Prevailing official Social Democracy usually dismissed the question of the concrete tasks of the proletariat in the revolution either with a philistine sneer, or, at best, with the sophistic evasion: "The future will show." And the anarchists were justified in saying about such Social Democrats that they were failing in their task of giving the workers a revolutionary education. Engels draws upon the experience of the last proletarian revolution precisely for the purpose of making a most concrete study of what should be done by the proletariat, and in what manner, in relation to both the banks and the state.

## 3. Letter to Bebel

One of the most, if not *the* most, remarkable observation on the state in the works of Marx and Engels is contained in the following passage in Engels's letter to Bebel dated March 18–28, 1875. This letter, we may observe in parenthesis, was, as far as we know, first published by Bebel in the second volume of his memoirs (*Aus meinem Leben*), which appeared in 1911, i.e., 36 years after the letter had been written and sent.

Engels wrote to Bebel criticizing the same draft of the Gotha Program which Marx criticized in his famous letter to Bracke. Referring specially to the question of the state, Engels said:

> The free people's state has been transformed into the free state. Taken in its grammatical sense, a free state is one where the state is free in relation to its citizens, hence a state with a despotic government. The whole talk about the state should be dropped, especially since the Commune, which was no longer a state in the proper sense of the word. The "people's state" has been thrown in our faces by the anarchists to the point of disgust, although already Marx's book against Proudhon and later the *Communist Manifesto* say plainly that with the introduction of the socialist order of society the state dissolves of itself [sich auflöst] and disappears. As the state is only a transitional institution which is used in the struggle, in the revolution, to hold down one's adversaries by force, it is sheer nonsense to talk of a "free people's state"; so long as the proletariat still *needs* the state, it does not need it in the interests of freedom but in order to hold down its adversaries, and as soon as it becomes possible to speak of freedom the state as such ceases to exist. We would therefore propose replacing the *state* everywhere by *Gemeinwesen*, a good old German word which can very well take the place of the French word *commune*. (pp. 321-22 of the German original.)[27]

It should be borne in mind that this letter refers to the party program which Marx criticized in a letter dated only a few weeks later than the above (Marx's letter is dated May 5, 1875), and that at the time Engels was living with Marx in London. Consequently, when he says "we" in the last sentence, Engels undoubtedly, in his own as well as in Marx's name, suggests to the leader of the German workers' party that the word "state" *be struck out of the program* and replaced by the word "*community.*"

What a howl about "anarchism" would be raised by the leading lights of present-day "Marxism," which has been falsified for the con-

27     See Karl Marx and Frederick Engels, *Selected Correspondence*, Moscow, 1965, 293–94.

venience of the opportunists, if such an amendment of the program were suggested to them!

Let them howl. This will earn them the praises of the bourgeoisie.

And we shall go on with our work. In revising the program of our Party, we must by all means take the advice of Engels and Marx into consideration in order to come nearer the truth, to restore Marxism by ridding it of distortions, to guide the struggle of the working class for its emancipation more correctly. Certainly no one opposed to the advice of Engels and Marx will be found among the Bolsheviks. The only difficulty that may perhaps arise will be in regard to the term. In German there are two words meaning "community," of which Engels used the one which does not denote a single community, but their totality, a system of communities. In Russian there is no such word, and we may have to choose the French word "commune," although this also has its drawbacks.

"The Commune was no longer a state in the proper sense of the word"—this is the most theoretically important statement Engels makes. After what has been said above, this statement is perfectly clear. The Commune *was ceasing* to be a state since it had to suppress, not the majority of the population, but a minority (the exploiters). It had smashed the bourgeois state machine. In place of a *special* coercive force the population itself came on the scene. All this was a departure from the state in the proper sense of the word. And had the Commune become firmly established, all traces of the state in it would have "withered away" of themselves; it would not have had to "abolish" the institutions of the state—they would have ceased to function as they ceased to have anything to do.

"The 'people's state' has been thrown in our faces by the anarchists." In saying this, Engels above all has in mind Bakunin and his attacks on the German Social Democrats. Engels admits that these attacks were justified *insofar* as the "people's state" was as much an absurdity and as much a departure from socialism as the "free people's state." Engels tried to put the struggle of the German Social Democrats against the anarchists on the right lines, to make this struggle correct in principle, to rid it of opportunist prejudices concerning the "state." Unfortunately, Engels's letter was pigeon-holed for 36 years. We shall see farther on that, even after this letter was published, Kautsky persisted in virtually the same mistakes against which Engels had warned.

Bebel replied to Engels in a letter dated September 21, 1875, in which he wrote, among other things, that he "fully agreed" with Engels's opinion of the draft program, and that he had reproached Liebknecht with readiness to make concessions (p.334 of the German edition of Bebel's memoirs, Vol.II). But if we take Bebel's pamphlet, *Our Aims*, we find there views on the state that are absolutely wrong. "The state must... be transformed from one based on *class rule* into a *people's state*." (*Unsere Ziele*, German Edition, 1886, p.14)

This was printed in the *ninth* (ninth!) edition of Bebel's pamphlet! It is not surprising that opportunist views on the state, so persistently repeated, were absorbed by the German Social Democrats, especially as Engels's revolutionary interpretations had been safely pigeonholed, and all the conditions of life were such as to "wean" them from revolution for a long time.

## 4. Criticism of the Draft of the Erfurt Programme

In analyzing Marxist teachings on the state, the criticism of the draft of the Erfurt Program,[28] sent by Engels to Kautsky on June 29, 1891, and published only 10 years later in *Neue Zeit*, cannot be ignored; for it is with the *opportunist* views of the Social Democrats on questions of state organization that this criticism is mainly concerned.

We shall note in passing that Engels also makes an exceedingly valuable observation on economic questions, which shows how attentively and thoughtfully he watched the various changes occurring in modern capitalism, and how for this reason he was able to foresee to a certain extent the tasks of our present, the imperialist, epoch. Here is

---

28    *Erfurt Programme*—the program adopted by the German Social Democratic Party at its Erfurt Congress in October 1891. A step forward compared with the Gotha Program (1875), it was based on Marx's doctrine of the inevitable downfall of the capitalist mode of production and its replacement by the socialist mode. It stressed the necessity for the working class to wage a political struggle, pointed out the party's role as the leader of that struggle, and so on. But it also made serious concessions to opportunism. Engels criticized the original draft of the program in detail in his work *A Critique of the Draft Social-Democratic Programme of 1891* It was virtually a critique of the opportunism of the Second International as a whole. But the German Social Democratic leaders concealed Engels's critique from the rank and file, and disregarded his highly important comments in drawing up the final text of the program. Lenin considered the fact that the Erfurt Program said nothing about the dictatorship of the proletariat to be its chief defect and a cowardly concession to opportunism.

that observation: referring to the word "planlessness" (Planlosigkeit), used in the draft program, as characteristic of capitalism, Engels wrote:

> When we pass from joint-stock companies to trusts which assume control over, and monopolize, whole industries, it is not only private production that ceases, but also planlessness. (*Neue Zeit*, Vol. XX, 1, 1901–02, p.8)

Here was have what is most essential in the theoretical appraisal of the latest phase of capitalism, i.e., imperialism, namely, that capitalism becomes monopoly *capitalism*. The latter must be emphasized because the erroneous bourgeois reformist assertion that monopoly capitalism or state-monopoly capitalism is *no longer* capitalism, but can now be called "state socialism" and so on, is very common. The trusts, of course, never provided, do not now provide, and cannot provide complete planning. But however much they do plan, however much the capitalist magnates calculate in advance the volume of production on a national and even on an international scale, and however much they systematically regulate it, we still remain under *capitalism*—at its new stage, it is true, but still capitalism, without a doubt. The "proximity" of *such* capitalism to socialism should serve genuine representatives of the proletariat as an argument proving the proximity, facility, feasibility, and urgency of the socialist revolution, and not at all as an argument for tolerating the repudiation of such a revolution and the efforts to make capitalism look more attractive, something which all reformists are trying to do.

But to return to the question of the state. In his letter Engels makes three particularly valuable suggestions: first, in regard to the republic; second, in regard to the connection between the national question and state organization; and, third, in regard to local self-government.

In regard to the republic, Engels made this the focal point of this criticism of the draft of the Erfurt Program. And when we recall the importance which the Erfurt Program acquired for all the Social Democrats of the world, and that it became the model for the whole Second International, we may say without exaggeration that Engels thereby criticizes the opportunism of the whole Second International.

"The political demands of the draft," Engels wrote, "have one great fault. *It lacks* [Engels' italics] precisely what should have been said."

And, later on, he makes it clear that the German Constitution is, strictly speaking, a copy of the extremely reactionary Constitution of

1850, that the Reichstag is only, as Wilhelm Liebknecht put it, "the fig leaf of absolutism" and that to wish "to transform all the instruments of labor into common property" on the basis of a constitution which legalizes the existence of petty states and the federation of petty German states is an "obvious absurdity."

"To touch on that is dangerous, however," Engels added, knowing only too well that it was impossible legally to include in the program the demand for a republic in Germany. But he refused to merely accept this obvious consideration which satisfied "everybody." He continued:

> Nevertheless, somehow or other, the thing has to be attacked. How necessary this is is shown precisely at the present time by opportunism, which is gaining ground [einreissende] in a large section of the Social Democrat press. Fearing a renewal of the Anti-Socialist Law,[29] or recalling all manner of overhasty pronouncements made during the reign of that law, they now want the Party to find the present legal order in Germany adequate for putting through all Party demands by peaceful means....

Engels particularly stressed the fundamental fact that the German Social Democrats were prompted by fear of a renewal of the Anti-Socialist Law, and explicitly described it as opportunism; he declared that precisely because there was no republic and no freedom in Germany, the dreams of a "peaceful" path were perfectly absurd. Engels was careful not to tie his hands. He admitted that in repub-

29  *The Anti-Socialist Law* (Exceptional Law Against the Socialists) was enacted in Germany by the Bismarck government in 1878 to combat the working-class and socialist movement. Under this law, all Social Democratic Party organizations, all mass organizations of the workers, and the working-class press were banned, socialist literature was confiscated and the Social Democrats were persecuted, to the point of banishment. These repressive measures did not, however, break the Social Democratic Party, which readjusted itself to illegal conditions. *Der Sozial-Demokrat*, the party's Central Organ, was published abroad and party congresses were held at regular intervals (1880, 1883 and 1887). In Germany herself, the Social Democratic organizations and groups were coming back to life underground, an illegal Central Committee leading their activities. Besides, the Party widely used legal opportunities to establish closer links with the working people, and its influence was growing steadily. At the Reichstag elections in 1890, it polled three times as many votes as in 1878. Marx and Engels did much to help the Social Democrats. In 1890 popular pressure and the growing working-class movement led to the annulment of the Anti-Socialist Law.

lican or very free countries "one can conceive" (only "conceive"!) of a peaceful development towards socialism, but in Germany, he repeated,

> ... in Germany, where the government is almost omnipotent and the Reichstag and all other representative bodies have no real power, to advocate such a thing in Germany, where, moreover, there is no need to do so, means removing the fig leaf from absolutism and becoming oneself a screen for its nakedness.

The great majority of the official leaders of the German Social Democratic Party, which pigeon-holed this advice, have really proved to be a screen for absolutism.

> ... In the long run such a policy can only lead one's own party astray. They push general, abstract political questions into the foreground, thereby concealing the immediate concrete questions, which at the moment of the first great events, the first political crisis, automatically pose themselves. What can result from this except that at the decisive moment the party suddenly proves helpless and that uncertainty and discord on the most decisive issues reign in it because these issues have never been discussed? ...
>
> The forgetting of the great, the principal considerations for the momentary interests of the day, this struggling and striving for the success of the moment regardless of later consequences, this sacrifice of the future of the movement for its present may be "honestly" meant, but it is and remains opportunism, and "honest" opportunism is perhaps the most dangerous of all....
>
> If one thing is certain it is that our party and the working class can only come to power in the form of the democratic republic. This is even the specific form for the dictatorship of the proletariat, as the Great French Revolution has already shown....

Engels repeated here in a particularly striking form the fundamental idea which runs through all of Marx's works, namely, that the democratic republic is the nearest approach to the dictatorship of the proletariat. For such a republic, without in the least abolishing the rule of capital, and, therefore, the oppression of the masses and the class struggle, inevitably leads to such an extension, development, unfolding, and intensification of this struggle that, as soon as it becomes possible to meet the fundamental interests of the oppressed masses, this possibility is realized inevitably and solely through the dictatorship of the proletariat, through the leadership of those masses by the proletariat. These, too, are "forgotten words" of Marxism for the whole of the Second International, and the fact that they have been forgotten was demonstrated with particular vividness by the history of the Menshevik Party during the first six months of the Russian revolution of 1917.

On the subject of a federal republic, in connection with the national composition of the population, Engels wrote:

> What should take the place of the present-day Germany [with its reactionary monarchical Constitution and its equally reactionary division into petty states, a division which perpetuates all the specific features of "Prussianism" instead of dissolving them in Germany as a whole]? In my view, the proletariat can only use the form of the one and indivisible republic. In the gigantic territory of the United States, a federal republic is still, on the whole, a necessity, although in the Eastern states it is already becoming a hindrance. It would be a step forward in Britain where the two islands are peopled by four nations and in spite of a single Parliament three different systems of legislation already exist side by side. In little Switzerland, it has long been a hindrance, tolerable only because Switzerland is content to be a purely passive member of the European state system. For Germany, federalization on the Swiss model would be an enormous step backward. Two points distinguish a union state from a completely unified state: first, that each member state, each canton, has its own civil and criminal legislative and judicial system, and, second, that alongside a popular chamber there is also a federal chamber in which each canton, whether large or small, votes as such.

In Germany, the union state is the transition to the completely unified state, and the "revolution from above" of 1866 and 1870 must not be reversed but supplemented by a "movement from below."

Far from being indifferent to the forms of state, Engels, on the contrary, tried to analyze the transitional forms with the utmost thoroughness in order to establish, in accordance with the concrete historical peculiarities of each particular case, *from what and to what* the given transitional form is passing.

Approaching the matter from the standpoint of the proletariat and the proletarian revolution, Engels, like Marx, upheld democratic centralism, the republic—one and indivisible. He regarded the federal republic either as an exception and a hindrance to development, or as a transition from a monarchy to a centralized republic, as a "step forward" under certain special conditions. And among these special conditions, he puts the national question to the fore.

Although mercilessly criticizing the reactionary nature of small states, and the screening of this by the national question in certain concrete cases, Engels, like Marx, never betrayed the slightest desire to brush aside the national question—a desire of which the Dutch and Polish Marxists, who proceed from their perfectly justified opposition to the narrow philistine nationalism of "their" little states, are often guilty.

Even in regard to Britain, where geographical conditions, a common language and the history of many centuries would seem to have "put an end" to the national question in the various small divisions of the country—even in regard to that country, Engels reckoned with the plain fact that the national question was not yet a thing of the past, and recognized in consequence that the establishment of a federal republic would be a "step forward." Of course, there is not the slightest hint here of Engels abandoning the criticism of the shortcomings of a federal republic or renouncing the most determined advocacy of, and struggle for, a unified and centralized democratic republic.

But Engels did not at all mean democratic centralism in the bureaucratic sense in which the term is used by bourgeois and petty-bourgeois ideologists, the anarchists among the latter. His idea of centralism did not in the least preclude such broad local self-government as would combine the voluntary defense of the unity of the state by the "communes" and districts, and the complete elimination of all bureaucratic practices and all "ordering" from above. Carrying forward the programmatic views of Marxism on the state, Engels wrote:

> So, then, a unified republic—but not in the sense of the present French Republic, which is nothing but the Empire established in 1798 without the Emperor. From 1792 to 1798 each French department, each commune [Gemeinde], enjoyed complete self-government on the American model, and this is what we too must have. How self-government is to be organized and how we can manage, without a bureaucracy has been shown to us by America and the first French Republic, and is being shown even today by Australia, Canada and the other English colonies. And a provincial [regional] and communal self-government of this type is far freer than, for instance, Swiss federalism, under which, it is true, the canton is very independent in relation to the Bund [i.e., the federated state as a whole], but is also independent in relation to the district [Bezirk] and the commune. The cantonal governments appoint the district governors [Bezirksstatthalter] and prefects—which is unknown in English-speaking countries and which we want to abolish here as resolutely in the future as the Prussian Landräte and Regierungsräte [commissioners, district police chiefs, governors, and

in general all officials appointed from above].

Accordingly, Engels proposes the following words for the self-government clause in the program:

> Complete self-government for the provinces [gubernias or regions], districts and communes through officials elected by universal suffrage. The abolition of all local and provincial authorities appointed by the state.

I have already had occasion to point out—in *Pravda* (No.68, May 28, 1917), which was suppressed by the government of Kerensky and other "socialist" Ministers—how on this point (of course, not on this point alone by any means) our pseudo-socialist representatives of pseudo-revolutionary pseudo-democracy have made glaring departures *from democracy*. Naturally, people who have bound themselves by a "coalition" to the imperialist bourgeoisie have remained deaf to this criticism.

It is extremely important to note that Engels, armed with facts, disproved by a most precise example the prejudice which is very widespread, particularly among petty-bourgeois democrats, that a federal republic necessarily means a greater amount of freedom than a centralized republic. This is wrong. It is disproved by the facts cited by Engels regarding the centralized French Republic of 1792–98 and the federal Swiss Republic. The really democratic centralized republic gave *more* freedom that the federal republic. In other words, the *greatest* amount of local, regional, and other freedom known in history was accorded by a *centralized* and not a federal republic.

Insufficient attention has been and is being paid in our Party propaganda and agitation to this fact, as, indeed, to the whole question of the federal and the centralized republic and local self-government.

### 5. The 1891 Preface to Marx's "The Civil War in France"

In his preface to the third edition of *The Civil War in France* (this preface is dated March 18, 1891, and was originally published in *Neue Zeit*), Engels, in addition to some interesting incidental remarks on questions concerning the attitude towards the state, gave a remarkably vivid summary of the lessons of the Commune.[30] This summary, made

30   See Karl Marx and Frederick Engels, *Selected Works*, Vol. 2, Moscow, 1973, 178–89.

   On pp. 142–45 of this volume, Lenin is quoting from the same work (op. cit., 179–80, 184, 187–89).

more profound by the entire experience of the twenty years that separated the author from the Commune, and directed expressly against the "superstitious belief in the state" so widespread in Germany, may justly be called the *last word* of Marxism on the question under consideration.

In France, Engels observed, the workers emerged with arms from every revolution;

> therefore the disarming of the workers was the first commandment for the bourgeois, who were at the helm of the state. Hence, after every revolution won by the workers, a new struggle, ending with the defeat of the workers.

This summary of the experience of bourgeois revolutions is as concise as it is expressive. The essence of the matter—among other things, on the question of the state (*has the oppressed class arms?*)—is here remarkably well-grasped. It is precisely this essence that is most often evaded by both professors influenced by bourgeois ideology, and by petty-bourgeois democrats. In the Russian revolution of 1917, the honor (Cavaignac honor) of blabbing this secret of bourgeois revolutions fell to the Menshevik, would-be Marxist, Tsereteli. In his "historic" speech of June 11, Tsereteli blurted out that the bourgeoisie were determined to disarm the Petrograd workers—presenting, of course, this decision as his own, and as a necessity for the "state" in general!

Tsereteli's historical speech of June 11 will, of course, serve every historian of the revolution of 1917 as a graphic illustration of how the Social Revolutionary and Menshevik bloc, led by Mr. Tsereteli, deserted to the bourgeoisie *against* the revolutionary proletariat.

Another incidental remark of Engels's, also connected with the question of the state, deals with religion. It is well known that the German Social Democrats, as they degenerated and became increasingly opportunist, slipped more and more frequently into the philistine misinterpretation of the celebrated formula: "Religion is to be declared a private matter." That is, the formula was twisted to mean that religion was a private matter *even for the party* of the revolutionary proletariat!! It was against this complete betrayal of the revolutionary program of the proletariat that Engels vigorously protested. In 1891 he saw only the *very feeble* beginnings of opportunism in his party, and, therefore, he expressed himself with extreme caution:

> As almost only workers, or recognized representatives of the workers,

sat in the Commune, its decisions bore a decidedly proletarian character. Either they decreed reforms which the republican bourgeoisie had failed to pass solely out of cowardice, but which provided a necessary basis for the free activity of the working class—such as the realization of the principle that *in relation to the state* religion is a purely private matter—or the Commune promulgated decrees which were in the direct interest of the working class and in part cut deeply into the old order of society.

Engels deliberately emphasized the words "in relation to the state" as a straight thrust at German opportunism, which had declared religion to be a private matter *in relation to the party*, thus degrading the party of the revolutionary proletariat to the level of the most vulgar "free-thinking" philistinism, which is prepared to allow a non-denominational status, but which renounces the *party* struggle against the opium of religion which stupefies the people.

The future historian of the German Social Democrats, in tracing the roots of their shameful bankruptcy in 1914, will find a fair amount of interesting material on this question, beginning with the evasive declarations in the articles of the party's ideological leader, Kautsky, which throw the door wide open to opportunism, and ending with the attitude of the party towards the "Los-von-Kirche-Bewegung"[31] (the "Leave-the-Church" movement) in 1913.

But let us see how, twenty years after the Commune, Engels summed up its lessons for the fighting proletariat.

Here are the lessons to which Engels attached prime importance:

... It was precisely the oppressing power of the former centralized

31  The *Los-von-Kirche-Bewegung* (the "Leave-the-Church" movement), or *Kirchenaustrittsbewegung* (Movement to Secede from the Church) assumed a vast scale in Germany before the First World War. In January 1914 *Neue Zeit* began, with the revisionist Paul Göhre's article "Kirchenaustrittsbewegung und Sozialdemokratie" ("The Movement to Secede from the Church and Social Democracy"), to discuss the attitude of the German Social Democratic Party to the movement. During that discussion prominent German Social Democratic leaders failed to rebuff Göhre, who affirmed that the party should remain neutral towards the Movement to Secede from the Church and forbid its members to engage in propaganda against religion and the Church on behalf of the party.

Lenin took notice of the discussion while working on material for *Imperialism, the Highest Stage of Capitalism* (see *Collected Works*, Vol. 39, 591).

government, army, political parties, bureaucracy, which Napoleon had
created in 1798 and which every new government had since then taken
over as a welcome instrument and used against its opponents—it was
this power which was to fall everywhere, just as it had fallen in Paris.

From the very outset the Commune had to recognize that the working class, once in power, could not go on managing with the old state
machine; that in order not to lose again its only just-gained supremacy,
this working class must, on the one hand, do away with all the old
machinery of oppression previously used against it itself, and, on the
other, safeguard itself against its own deputies and officials, by declaring them all, without exception, subject to recall at any time....

Engels emphasized once again that not only under a monarchy, but
*also in a democratic republic* the state remains a state, i.e., it retains its
fundamental distinguishing feature of transforming the officials, the
"servants of society," its organs, into the *masters* of society.

Against this transformation of the state and the organs of the state from
servants of society into masters of society—an inevitable transformation in all previous states—the Commune used two infallible means. In
the first place, it filled all posts—administrative, judicial, and educational—by election on the basis of universal suffrage of all concerned,
subject to recall at any time by the electors. And, in the second place, it
paid all officials, high or low, only the wages received by other workers. The highest salary paid by the Commune to anyone was 6,000
francs. In this way a dependable barrier to place-hunting and careerism
was set up, even apart from the binding mandates to delegates to representative bodies, which were added besides....

Engels here approached the interesting boundary line at which consistent democracy, on the one hand, is *transformed* into socialism and,
on the other, *demands* socialism. For, in order to abolish the state, it is
necessary to convert the functions of the civil service into the simple
operations of control and accounting that are within the scope and
ability of the vast majority of the population, and, subsequently, of
every single individual. And if careerism is to be abolished completely,
it must be made *impossible* for "honorable" though profitless posts in
the Civil Service to be used as a springboard to highly lucrative posts
in banks or joint-stock companies, as *constantly* happens in all the freest capitalist countries.

Engels, however, did not make the mistake some Marxists make in
dealing, for example, with the question of the right of nations to self-

determination, when they argue that it is impossible under capitalism and will be superfluous under socialism. This seemingly clever but actually incorrect statement might be made in regard to *any* democratic institution, including moderate salaries for officials, because fully consistent democracy is impossible under capitalism, and under socialism all democracy *will wither away*.

This is a sophism like the old joke about a man becoming bald by losing one more hair.

To develop democracy *to the utmost*, to find the *forms* for this development, to test them *by practice*, and so forth—all this is one of the component tasks of the struggle for the social revolution. Taken separately, no kind of democracy will bring socialism. But in actual life democracy will never be "taken separately"; it will be "taken together" with other things, it will exert its influence on economic life as well, will stimulate *its* transformation; and in its turn it will be influenced by economic development, and so on. This is the dialectics of living history.

Engels continued:

> ... This shattering [Sprengung] of the former state power and its replacement by a new and truly democratic one is described in detail in the third section of *The Civil War*. But it was necessary to touch briefly here once more on some of its features, because in Germany particularly the superstitious belief in the state has passed from philosophy into the general consciousness of the bourgeoisie and even of many workers. According to the philosophical conception, the state is the "realization of the idea," or the Kingdom of God on earth, translated into philosophical terms, the sphere in which eternal truth and justice are, or should be, realized. And from this follows a superstitious reverence for the state and everything connected with it, which takes root the more readily since people are accustomed from childhood to imagine that the affairs and interests common to the whole of society could not be looked after other than as they have been looked after in the past, that is, through the state and its lucratively positioned officials. And people think they have taken quite an extraordinary bold step forward when they have rid themselves of belief in hereditary monarchy and swear by the democratic republic. In reality, however, the state is nothing but a machine for the oppression of one class by another, and indeed in the democratic republic no less than in the monarchy. And at best it is an evil inherited by the proletariat after its victorious struggle for class supremacy, whose worst sides the victorious proletariat will have to lop off as speedily as possible, just as the Commune had to,

until a generation reared in new, free social conditions is able to discard the entire lumber of the state.

Engels warned the Germans not to forget the principles of socialism with regard to the state in general in connection with the substitution of a republic for the monarchy. His warnings now read like a veritable lesson to the Tseretelis and Chernovs, who in their "coalition" practice have revealed a superstitious belief in, and a superstitious reverence for, the state!

Two more remarks.

> 1. Engels's statement that in a democratic republic, "no less" than in a monarchy, the state remains a "machine for the oppression of one class by another" by no means signifies that the *form* of oppression makes no difference to the proletariat, as some anarchists *"teach."* A wider, freer and more open *form* of the class struggle and of class oppression vastly assists the proletariat in its struggle for the abolition of classes in general.
> 2. Why will only a new generation be able to discard the entire lumber of the state? This question is bound up with that of overcoming democracy, with which we shall deal now.

## 6. Engels on the Overcoming of Democracy

Engels came to express his views on this subject when establishing that the term "Social Democrat" was *scientifically* wrong.

In a preface to an edition of his articles of the seventies on various subjects, mostly on "international" questions (*Internationales aus dem Volkstaat*), dated January 3, 1894, i.e., written a year and a half before his death, Engels wrote that in all his articles he used the word "Communist," and not "SocialDemocrat," because at that time the Proudhonists in France and the Lassalleans[32] in Germany called

---

32    *Lassalleans*—supporters of the German petty-bourgeois socialist Ferdinand Lassalle, members of the General Association of German Workers founded at the Congress of Workers' Organizations, held in Leipzig in 1863, to counterbalance the bourgeois progressists who were trying to gain influence over the working class. The first President of the Association was Lassalle, who formulated its program and the fundamentals of its tactics. The Association's political program was declared to be the struggle for universal suffrage, and its economic program, the struggle for workers' production associations, to be subsidized by the state. In their practical activities, Lassalle and his followers adapted themselves to the hegemony of Prussia and supported the Great Power policy of Bismarck. "Objectively," wrote

themselves Social Democrats. "... For Marx and myself," continued Engels, "it was therefore absolutely impossible to use such a loose term to characterize our special point of view. Today things are different, and the word ["Social Democrat"] may perhaps pass muster [mag passieren], inexact [*unpassend*, unsuitable] though it still is for a party whose economic program is not merely socialist in general, but downright communist, and whose ultimate political aim is to overcome the whole state and, consequently, democracy as well. The names of *real* political parties, however, are never wholly appropriate; the party develops while the name stays."[33]

The dialectician Engels remained true to dialectics to the end of his days. Marx and I, he said, had a splendid, scientifically exact name for the party, but there was no real party, i.e., no mass proletarian party. Now (at the end of the nineteenth century) there was a real party, but its name was scientifically wrong. Never mind, it would "pass muster," so long as the party *developed*, so long as the scientific in accuracy of the name was not hidden from it and did not hinder its development in the right direction!

Perhaps some wit would console us Bolsheviks in the manner of Engels: we have a real party, it is developing splendidly; even such a meaningless and ugly term as "Bolshevik" will "pass muster," although it expresses nothing whatever but the purely accidental fact that at the Brussels-London Congress of 1903 we were in the majority. Perhaps now that the persecution of our Party by republicans and "revolutionary" petty-bourgeois democrats in July and August has earned the name "Bolshevik" such universal respect, now that, in addition, this persecution marks the tremendous historical progress our Party has made in its real development—perhaps now even I might hesitate to insist on the suggestion I made in April to change the name of our Party. Perhaps I would propose a "compromise" to my comrades, namely, to call ourselves the Communist Party, but to retain the word "Bolshevik" in brackets.

But the question of the name of the Party is incomparably less Engels to Marx on January 27, 1865, "this was a base action and a betrayal of the whole working-class movement to the Prussians." Marx and Engels frequently and sharply criticized the theory, tactics, and organizational principles of the Lassalleans as an opportunist trend in the German working-class movement.

33   See Frederick Engels, "Vorwort zur Broschüre *Internationales aus dem 'Volksstaat' (1871-1875)*", Marx-Engels, *Werke,* Bd. 22, Berlin, 1963, S. 417-18.

important than the question of the attitude of the revolutionary proletariat to the state.

In the usual argument about the state, the mistake is constantly made against which Engels warned and which we have in passing indicated above, namely, it is constantly forgotten that the abolition of the state means also the abolition of democracy; that the withering away of the state means the withering away of democracy.

At first sight this assertion seems exceedingly strange and incomprehensible; indeed, someone may even suspect us of expecting the advent of a system of society in which the principle of subordination of the minority to the majority will not be observed—for democracy means the recognition of this very principle.

No, democracy is *not* identical with the subordination of the minority to the majority. Democracy is a *state* which recognizes the subordination of the minority to the majority, i.e., an organization for the systematic use of *force* by one class against another, by one section of the population against another.

We set ourselves the ultimate aim of abolishing the state, i.e., all organized and systematic violence, all use of violence against people in general. We do not expect the advent of a system of society in which the principle of subordination of the minority to the majority will not be observed. In striving for socialism, however, we are convinced that it will develop into communism and, therefore, that the need for violence against people in general, for the *subordination* of one man to another, and of one section of the population to another, will vanish altogether since people will *become accustomed* to observing the elementary conditions of social life *without violence* and *without subordination.*

In order to emphasize this element of habit, Engels speaks of a new *generation,* "reared in new, free social conditions," which will "be able to discard the entire lumber of the state"—of any state, including the democratic-republican state.

In order to explain this, it is necessary to analyze the economic basis of the withering away of the state.

# V
# The Economic Basis of the Withering Away of the State

Marx explains this question most thoroughly in his *Critique of the Gotha Programme* (letter to Bracke, May 5, 1875, which was not published until 1891 when it was printed in *Neue Zeit*, vol. IX, 1, and which has appeared in Russian in a special edition). The polemical part of this remarkable work, which contains a criticism of Lassalleanism, has, so to speak, overshadowed its positive part, namely, the analysis of the connection between the development of communism and the withering away of the state.

## 1. Presentation of the Question by Marx

From a superficial comparison of Marx's letter to Bracke of May 5, 1875, with Engels's letter to Bebel of March 28, 1875, which we examined above, it might appear that Marx was much more of a "champion of the state" than Engels, and that the difference of opinion between the two writers on the question of the state was very considerable.

Engels suggested to Bebel that all chatter about the state be dropped altogether, that the word "state" be eliminated from the program altogether and the word "community" substituted for it. Engels even declared that the Commune was no longer a state in the proper sense of the word. Yet Marx even spoke of the "future state in communist society," i.e., he would seem to recognize the need for the state even under communism.

But such a view would be fundamentally wrong. A closer examination shows that Marx's and Engels's views on the state and its withering away were completely identical, and that Marx's expression quoted above refers to the state in the process of *withering away*.

Clearly, there can be no question of specifying the moment of the *future* "withering away," the more so since it will obviously be a lengthy process. The apparent difference between Marx and Engels is due to the fact that they dealt with different subjects and pursued different aims. Engels set out to show Bebel graphically, sharply, and in broad outline the utter absurdity of the current prejudices concerning the state (shared to no small degree by Lassalle). Marx only touched upon *this* question in passing, being interested in another subject, namely, the *development* of communist society.

The whole theory of Marx is the application of the theory of development—in its most consistent, complete, considered and pithy form—to modern capitalism. Naturally, Marx was faced with the problem of applying this theory both to the *forthcoming* collapse of capitalism and to the future development of *future* communism.

On the basis of what *facts*, then, can the question of the future development of future communism be dealt with?

On the basis of the fact that it *has its origin* in capitalism, that it develops historically from capitalism, that it is the result of the action of a social force to which capitalism *gave birth*. There is no trace of an attempt on Marx's part to make up a utopia, to indulge in idle guesswork about what cannot be known. Marx treated the question of communism in the same way as a naturalist would treat the question of the development of, say, a new biological variety, once he knew that it had originated in such and such a way and was changing in such and such a definite direction.

To begin with, Marx brushed aside the confusion the Gotha Program brought into the question of the relationship between state and society. He wrote:

> "Present-day society" is capitalist society, which exists in all civilized countries, being more or less free from medieval admixture, more or less modified by the particular historical development of each country, more or less developed. On the other hand, the "present-day state" changes with a country's frontier. It is different in the Prusso-German Empire from what it is in Switzerland, and different in England from what it is in the United States. "The present-day state" is, therefore, a fiction.
>
> Nevertheless, the different states of the different civilized countries, in spite of their motley diversity of form, all have this in common, that they are based on modern bourgeois society, only one more or less capitalistically developed. The have, therefore, also certain essential characteristics in common. In this sense it is possible to speak of the "present-day state," in contrast with the future, in which its present root, bourgeois society, will have died off.
>
> The question then arises: what transformation will the state undergo in communist society? In other words, what social functions will remain in existence there that are analogous to present state functions? This question can only be answered scientifically, and one does not get

a flea-hop nearer to the problem by a thousandfold combination of the word people with the word state.[34]

After thus ridiculing all talk about a "people's state," Marx formulated the question and gave warning, as it were, that those seeking a scientific answer to it should use only firmly-established scientific data.

The first fact that has been established most accurately by the whole theory of development, by science as a whole—a fact that was ignored by the utopians, and is ignored by the present-day opportunists, who are afraid of the socialist revolution—is that, historically, there must undoubtedly be a special stage, or a special phase, of transition from capitalism to communism.

## 2. The Transition from Capitalism to Communism

Marx continued:

> Between capitalist and communist society lies the period of the revolutionary transformation of the one into the other. Corresponding to this is also a political transition period in which the state can be nothing but *the revolutionary dictatorship of the proletariat.*

Marx bases this conclusion on an analysis of the role played by the proletariat in modern capitalist society, on the data concerning the development of this society, and on the irreconcilability of the antagonistic interests of the proletariat and the bourgeoisie.

Previously the question was put as follows: to achieve its emancipation, the proletariat must overthrow the bourgeoisie, win political power and establish its revolutionary dictatorship.

Now the question is put somewhat differently: the transition from capitalist society—which is developing towards communism—to communist society is impossible without a "political transition period", and the state in this period can only be the revolutionary dictatorship of the proletariat.

What, then, is the relation of this dictatorship to democracy?

We have seen that the *Communist Manifesto* simply places side by

---

34    See Karl Marx, *Critique of the Gotha Programme* (Karl Marx and Frederick Engels, *Selected Works*, Vol. 3, Moscow, 1973, 26).

On pp. 154, 156–59 of this volume, Lenin is quoting from the same work by Marx (op. cit., 26, 17, 19).

side the two concepts: "to raise the proletariat to the position of the ruling class" and "to win the battle of democracy." On the basis of all that has been said above, it is possible to determine more precisely how democracy changes in the transition from capitalism to communism.

In capitalist society, providing it develops under the most favorable conditions, we have a more or less complete democracy in the democratic republic. But this democracy is always hemmed in by the narrow limits set by capitalist exploitation, and consequently always remains, in effect, a democracy for the minority, only for the propertied classes, only for the rich. Freedom in capitalist society always remains about the same as it was in the ancient Greek republics: freedom for the slave-owners. Owing to the conditions of capitalist exploitation, the modern wage slaves are so crushed by want and poverty that "they cannot be bothered with democracy," "cannot be bothered with politics"; in the ordinary, peaceful course of events, the majority of the population is debarred from participation in public and political life.

The correctness of this statement is perhaps most clearly confirmed by Germany, because constitutional legality steadily endured there for a remarkably long time—nearly half a century (1871–1914)—and during this period the Social Democrats were able to achieve far more than in other countries in the way of "utilizing legality," and organized a larger proportion of the workers into a political party than anywhere else in the world.

What is this largest proportion of politically conscious and active wage slaves that has so far been recorded in capitalist society? One million members of the Social Democratic Party—out of fifteen million wageworkers! Three million organized in trade unions—out of fifteen million!

Democracy for an insignificant minority, democracy for the rich— that is the democracy of capitalist society. If we look more closely into the machinery of capitalist democracy, we see everywhere, in the "petty"—supposedly petty—details of the suffrage (residential qualifications, exclusion of women, etc.), in the technique of the representative institutions, in the actual obstacles to the right of assembly (public buildings are not for "paupers"!), in the purely capitalist organization of the daily press, etc., etc.,—we see restriction after restriction upon democracy. These restrictions, exceptions, exclusions, obstacles for the poor seem slight, especially in the eyes of one who has never known want himself and has never been in close contact with the oppressed classes in their mass life (and nine out of ten, if not ninety-nine out of a hundred, bourgeois publicists and politicians come under this category); but in their sum total these restrictions exclude and squeeze out the poor from politics, from active participation in democracy.

Marx grasped this *essence* of capitalist democracy splendidly when, in analyzing the experience of the Commune, he said that the oppressed are allowed once every few years to decide which particular representatives of the oppressing class shall represent and repress them in parliament!

But from this capitalist democracy—that is inevitably narrow and stealthily pushes aside the poor, and is therefore hypocritical and false through and through—forward development does not proceed simply, directly and smoothly, towards "greater and greater democracy," as the liberal professors and petty-bourgeois opportunists would have us believe. No, forward development, i.e., development towards communism, proceeds through the dictatorship of the proletariat, and cannot do otherwise, for the *resistance* of the capitalist exploiters cannot be *broken* by anyone else or in any other way.

And the dictatorship of the proletariat, i.e., the organization of the vanguard of the oppressed as the ruling class for the purpose of suppressing the oppressors, cannot result merely in an expansion of democracy. *Simultaneously* with an immense expansion of democracy, which *for the first time* becomes democracy for the poor, democracy for the people, and not democracy for the money-bags, the dictatorship of the proletariat imposes a series of restrictions on the freedom of the oppressors, the exploiters, the capitalists. We must suppress them in order to free humanity from wage slavery, their resistance must be crushed by force; it is clear that there is no freedom and no democracy where there is suppression and where there is violence.

Engels expressed this splendidly in his letter to Bebel when he said, as the reader will remember, that

> the proletariat needs the state, not in the interests of freedom but in order to hold down its adversaries, and as soon as it becomes possible to speak of freedom the state as such ceases to exist.

Democracy for the vast majority of the people, and suppression by force, i.e., exclusion from democracy, of the exploiters and oppressors of the people—this is the change democracy undergoes during the transition from capitalism to communism.

Only in communist society, when the resistance of the capitalists have disappeared, when there are no classes (i.e., when there is no distinction between the members of society as regards their relation to the social means of production), *only* then "the state... ceases to exist", and "*it becomes possible to speak of freedom.*" Only then will a truly complete democracy become possible and be realized, a democracy without any exceptions whatever. And only then will democracy begin to *wither away*, owing to the simple fact that, freed from capitalist slavery, from the untold horrors, savagery, absurdities, and infamies of capitalist exploitation, people will gradually *become accustomed* to observing the elementary rules of social intercourse that have been known for centuries and repeated for thousands of years in all copy-book maxims. They will become accustomed to observing them without force, without coercion, without subordination, *without the special apparatus* for coercion called the state.

The expression "the state *withers away*" is very well chosen, for it indicates both the gradual and the spontaneous nature of the process. Only habit can, and undoubtedly will, have such an effect; for we see around us on millions of occasions how readily people become accustomed to observing the necessary rules of social intercourse when there is no exploitation, when there is nothing that arouses indignation, evokes protest and revolt, and creates the need for *suppression*.

And so in capitalist society we have a democracy that is curtailed, wretched, false, a democracy only for the rich, for the minority. The dictatorship of the proletariat, the period of transition to communism, will for the first time create democracy for the people, for the majority, along with the necessary suppression of the exploiters, of the minority. Communism alone is capable of providing really complete democracy, and the more complete it is, the sooner it will become unnecessary and wither away of its own accord.

In other words, under capitalism we have the state in the proper sense of the word, that is, a special machine for the suppression of one class by another, and, what is more, of the majority by the minority. Naturally, to be successful, such an undertaking as the systematic suppression of the exploited majority by the exploiting minority calls for the utmost ferocity and savagery in the matter of suppressing, it calls for seas of blood, through which mankind is actually wading its way in slavery, serfdom and wage labor.

Furthermore, during the *transition* from capitalism to communism suppression is *still* necessary, but it is now the suppression of the exploiting minority by the exploited majority. A special apparatus, a special machine for suppression, the "state," is *still* necessary, but this is now a transitional state. It is no longer a state in the proper sense of the word; for the suppression of the minority of exploiters by the majority of the wage slaves of *yesterday* is comparatively so easy, simple and natural a task that it will entail far less bloodshed than the suppression of the risings of slaves, serfs or wage-laborers, and it will cost mankind far less. And it is compatible with the extension of democracy to such an overwhelming majority of the population that the need for a *special machine* of suppression will begin to disappear. Naturally, the exploiters are unable to suppress the people without a highly complex machine for performing this task, but *the people* can suppress the exploiters even with a very simple "machine," almost without a "machine," without a special apparatus, by the simple *organization of the armed people* (such as the Soviets of Workers' and Soldiers' Deputies, we would remark, running ahead).

Lastly, only communism makes the state absolutely unnecessary, for there is *nobody* to be suppressed—"nobody" in the sense of a *class*, of a systematic struggle against a definite section of the population. We are not utopians, and do not in the least deny the possibility and inevitability of excesses on the part of *individual persons*, or the need to stop such excesses. In the first place, however, no special machine, no special apparatus of suppression, is needed for this: this will be done by the armed people themselves, as simply and as readily as any crowd of civilized people, even in modern society, interferes to put a stop to a scuffle or to prevent a woman from being assaulted. And, secondly, we know that the fundamental social cause of excesses, which consist in the violation of the rules of social intercourse, is the exploitation of the people, their want and their poverty. With the removal of this chief cause, excesses will inevitably begin to "*wither away.*" We do not know how quickly and in what succession, but we do know they will wither away. With their withering away the state will also *wither away.*

Without building utopias, Marx defined more fully what can be defined *now* regarding this future, namely, the differences between the lower and higher phases (levels, stages) of communist society.

## 3. The First Phase of Communist Society

In the *Critique of the Gotha Programme*, Marx goes into detail to disprove Lassalle's idea that under socialism the worker will receive the "undiminished" or "full product of his labor." Marx shows that from the whole of the social labor of society there must be deducted a reserve fund, a fund for the expansion of production, a fund for the replacement of the "wear and tear" of machinery, and so on. Then, from the means of consumption must be deducted a fund for administrative expenses, for schools, hospitals, old people's homes, and so on.

Instead of Lassalle's hazy, obscure, general phrase ("the full product of his labor to the worker"), Marx makes a sober estimate of exactly how socialist society will have to manage its affairs. Marx proceeds to make a *concrete* analysis of the conditions of life of a society in which there will be no capitalism, and says:

> What we have to deal with here [in analyzing the program of the workers' party] is a communist society, not as it has *developed* on its own foundations, but, on the contrary, just as it *emerges* from capitalist society; which is thus in every respect, economically, morally, and intellectually, still stamped with the birthmarks of the old society from whose womb it comes.

It is this communist society, which has just emerged into the light of day out of the womb of capitalism and which is in every respect stamped with the birthmarks of the old society, that Marx terms the "first," or lower, phase of communist society.

The means of production are no longer the private property of individuals. The means of production belong to the whole of society. Every member of society, performing a certain part of the socially-necessary work, receives a certificate from society to the effect that he has done a certain amount of work. And with this certificate he receives from the public store of consumer goods a corresponding quantity of products. After a deduction is made of the amount of labor which goes to the public fund, every worker, therefore, receives from society as much as he has given to it.

"Equality" apparently reigns supreme.

But when Lassalle, having in view such a social order (usually called socialism, but termed by Marx the first phase of communism), says that this is "equitable distribution," that this is "the equal right of all to an equal product of labor," Lassalle is mistaken and Marx exposes the mistake.

"Hence, the equal right," says Marx, in this case *still* certainly conforms to "bourgeois law," which, like all law, *implies inequality*. All law is an application of an *equal* measure to *different* people who in fact are not alike, are not equal to one another. That is why the "equal right" is violation of equality and an injustice. In fact, everyone, having performed as much social labor as another, receives an equal share of the social product (after the above-mentioned deductions).

But people are not alike: one is strong, another is weak; one is married, another is not; one has more children, another has less, and so on. And the conclusion Marx draws is:

> ... With an equal performance of labor, and hence an equal share in the social consumption fund, one will in fact receive more than another, one will be richer than another, and so on. To avoid all these defects, the right instead of being equal would have to be unequal.

The first phase of communism, therefore, cannot yet provide justice and equality; differences, and unjust differences, in wealth will still persist, but the *exploitation* of man by man will have become impossible because it will be impossible to seize the *means of production*—the factories, machines, land, etc.—and make them private property. In smashing Lassalle's petty-bourgeois, vague phrases about "equality" and "justice" *in general*, Marx shows the *course of development* of communist society, which is *compelled* to abolish at first *only* the "injustice" of the means of production seized by individuals, and which is *unable* at once to eliminate the other injustice, which consists in the distribution of consumer goods "according to the amount of labor performed" (and not according to needs).

The vulgar economists, including the bourgeois professors and "our" Tugan, constantly reproach the socialists with forgetting the inequality of people and with "dreaming" of eliminating this inequality. Such a reproach, as we see, only proves the extreme ignorance of the bourgeois ideologists.

Marx not only most scrupulously takes account of the inevitable inequality of men, but he also takes into account the fact that the mere conversion of the means of production into the common property of the whole society (commonly called "socialism") *does not remove* the defects of distribution and the inequality of "bourgeois law," which *continues to prevail* so long as products are divided "according to the amount of labor performed." Continuing, Marx says:

> But these defects are inevitable in the first phase of communist society

as it is when it has just emerged, after prolonged birth pangs, from capitalist society. Law can never be higher than the economic structure of society and its cultural development conditioned thereby.

And so, in the first phase of communist society (usually called socialism) "bourgeois law" is *not* abolished in its entirety, but only in part, only in proportion to the economic revolution so far attained, i.e., only in respect of the means of production. "Bourgeois law" recognizes them as the private property of individuals. Socialism converts them into *common* property. *To that extent*—and to that extent alone—"bourgeois law" disappears.

However, it persists as far as its other part is concerned; it persists in the capacity of regulator (determining factor) in the distribution of products and the allotment of labor among the members of society. The socialist principle, "He who does not work shall not eat," is *already* realized; the other socialist principle, "An equal amount of products for an equal amount of labor," is also *already* realized. But this is not yet communism, and it does not yet abolish "bourgeois law," which gives unequal individuals, in return for unequal (really unequal) amounts of labor, equal amounts of products.

This is a "defect," says Marx, but it is unavoidable in the first phase of communism; for if we are not to indulge in utopianism, we must not think that having overthrown capitalism people will at once learn to work for society *without any rules of law*. Besides, the abolition of capitalism *does not immediately create* the economic prerequisites for *such* a change.

Now, there are no other rules than those of "bourgeois law." To this extent, therefore, there still remains the need for a state, which, while safeguarding the common ownership of the means of production, would safeguard equality in labor and in the distribution of products.

The state withers away insofar as there are no longer any capitalists, any classes, and, consequently, no *class* can be *suppressed*.

But the state has not yet completely withered away, since there still remains the safeguarding of "bourgeois law," which sanctifies actual inequality. For the state to wither away completely, complete communism is necessary.

## 4. The Higher Phase of Communist Society

Marx continues:

> In a higher phase of communist society, after the enslaving subor-
> dination of the individual to the division of labor, and with it also
> the antithesis between mental and physical labor, has vanished, after
> labor has become not only a livelihood but life's prime want, after the
> productive forces have increased with the all-round development of
> the individual, and all the springs of cooperative wealth flow more
> abundantly—only then can the narrow horizon of bourgeois law be left
> behind in its entirety and society inscribe on its banners: From each
> according to his ability, to each according to his needs!

Only now can we fully appreciate the correctness of Engels' remarks
mercilessly ridiculing the absurdity of combining the words "freedom"
and "state." So long as the state exists there is no freedom. When there
is freedom, there will be no state.

The economic basis for the complete withering away of the state
is such a high state of development of communism at which the
antithesis between mental and physical labor disappears, at which
there consequently disappears one of the principal sources of modern
*social* inequality—a source, moreover, which cannot on any account be
removed immediately by the mere conversion of the means of production into public property, by the mere expropriation of the capitalists.

This expropriation will make it *possible* for the productive forces
to develop to a tremendous extent. And when we see how incredibly
capitalism is already *retarding* this development, when we see how
much progress could be achieved on the basis of the level of technique
already attained, we are entitled to say with the fullest confidence that
the expropriation of the capitalists will inevitably result in an enormous development of the productive forces of human society. But how
rapidly this development will proceed, how soon it will reach the point
of breaking away from the division of labor, of doing away with the
antithesis between mental and physical labor, of transforming labor
into "life's prime want"—we do not and *cannot* know.

That is why we are entitled to speak only of the inevitable withering
away of the state, emphasizing the protracted nature of this process
and its dependence upon the rapidity of development of the *higher
phase* of communism, and leaving the question of the time required
for, or the concrete forms of, the withering away quite open, because
there is no material for answering these questions.

The state will be able to wither away completely when society adopts the rule: "From each according to his ability, to each according to his needs", i.e., when people have become so accustomed to observing the fundamental rules of social intercourse and when their labor has become so productive that they will voluntarily work *according to their ability*. "The narrow horizon of bourgeois law," which compels one to calculate with the heartlessness of a Shylock whether one has not worked half an hour more than anybody else—this narrow horizon will then be left behind. There will then be no need for society, in distributing the products, to regulate the quantity to be received by each; each will take freely "according to his needs."

From the bourgeois point of view, it is easy to declare that such a social order is "sheer utopia" and to sneer at the socialists for promising everyone the right to receive from society, without any control over the labor of the individual citizen, any quantity of truffles, cars, pianos, etc. Even to this day, most bourgeois "savants" confine themselves to sneering in this way, thereby betraying both their ignorance and their selfish defense of capitalism.

Ignorance—for it has never entered the head of any socialist to "promise" that the higher phase of the development of communism will arrive; as for the greatest socialists' *forecast* that it will arrive, it presupposes not the present productivity of labor and not the present ordinary run of people, who, like the seminary students in Pomyalovsky's stories,[35] are capable of damaging the stocks of public wealth "just for fun," and of demanding the impossible.

Until the "higher" phase of communism arrives, the socialists demand the *strictest* control by society *and by the state* over the measure of labor and the measure of consumption; but this control must *start* with the expropriation of the capitalists, with the establishment of workers' control over the capitalists, and must be exercised not by a state of bureaucrats, but by a state of *armed workers*.

The selfish defense of capitalism by the bourgeois ideologists (and their hangers-on, like the Tseretelis, Chernovs, and Co.) consists in that they *substitute* arguing and talk about the distant future for the vital and burning question of *present-day* politics, namely, the expropriation of the capitalists, the conversion of *all* citizens into workers and other employees of *one* huge "syndicate"—the whole state—and the complete subordination of the entire work of this syndicate to a genuinely democratic state, *the state of the Soviets of Workers' and*

---

35 Reference is to the pupils of a seminary who won notoriety by their extreme ignorance and barbarous customs. They were portrayed by N. G. Pomyalovsky, a Russian author.

*Soldiers' Deputies.*

In fact, when a learned professor, followed by the philistine, followed in turn by the Tseretelis and Chernovs, talks of wild utopias, of the demagogic promises of the Bolsheviks, of the impossibility of "introducing" socialism, it is the higher stage, or phase, of communism he has in mind, which no one has ever promised or even thought to "introduce," because, generally speaking, it cannot be "introduced."

And this brings us to the question of the scientific distinction between socialism and communism which Engels touched on in his above-quoted argument about the incorrectness of the name "Social Democrat." Politically, the distinction between the first, or lower, and the higher phase of communism will in time, probably, be tremendous. But it would be ridiculous to recognize this distinction now, under capitalism, and only individual anarchists, perhaps, could invest it with primary importance (if there still are people among the anarchists who have learned nothing from the "Plekhanov" conversion of the Kropotkins, of Grave, Cornelissen, and other "stars" of anarchism into social-chauvinists or "anarcho-trenchists," as Ghe, one of the few anarchists who have still preserved a sense of humor and a conscience, has put it).

But the scientific distinction between socialism and communism is clear. What is usually called socialism was termed by Marx the "first," or lower, phase of communist society. Insofar as the means of production becomes *common* property, the word "communism" is also applicable here, providing we do not forget that this is *not* complete communism. The great significance of Marx's explanations is that here, too, he consistently applies materialist dialectics, the theory of development, and regards communism as something which develops *out of* capitalism. Instead of scholastically invented, "concocted" definitions and fruitless disputes over words (What is socialism? What is communism?), Marx gives an analysis of what might be called the stages of the economic maturity of communism.

In its first phase, or first stage, communism *cannot* as yet be fully mature economically and entirely free from traditions or vestiges of capitalism. Hence the interesting phenomenon that communism in its first phase retains "the narrow horizon of bourgeois law." Of course, bourgeois law in regard to the distribution of *consumer* goods inevitably presupposes the existence of the *bourgeois state*, for law is nothing without an apparatus capable of *enforcing* the observance of the rules of law.

It follows that under communism there remains for a time not only bourgeois law, but even the bourgeois state, without the bourgeoisie!

This may sound like a paradox or simply a dialectical conundrum of which Marxism is often accused by people who have not taken the slightest trouble to study its extraordinarily profound content.

But in fact, remnants of the old, surviving in the new, confront us in life at every step, both in nature and in society. And Marx did not arbitrarily insert a scrap of "bourgeois" law into communism, but indicated what is economically and politically inevitable in a society emerging *out of the womb* of capitalism.

Democracy is of enormous importance to the working class in its struggle against the capitalists for its emancipation. But democracy is by no means a boundary not to be overstepped; it is only one of the stages on the road from feudalism to capitalism, and from capitalism to communism.

Democracy means equality. The great significance of the proletariat's struggle for equality and of equality as a slogan will be clear if we correctly interpret it as meaning the abolition of *classes*. But democracy means only *formal* equality. And as soon as equality is achieved for all members of society *in relation* to ownership of the means of production, that is, equality of labor and wages, humanity will inevitably be confronted with the question of advancing father, from formal equality to actual equality, i.e., to the operation of the rule "from each according to his ability, to each according to his needs." By what stages, by means of what practical measures humanity will proceed to this supreme aim we do not and cannot know. But it is important to realize how infinitely mendacious is the ordinary bourgeois conception of socialism as something lifeless, rigid, fixed once and for all, whereas in reality *only* socialism will be the beginning of a rapid, genuine, truly mass forward movement, embracing first the *majority* and then the whole of the population, in all spheres of public and private life.

Democracy is a form of the state, one of its varieties. Consequently, like every other state, it represents, on the one hand, the organized, systematic use of force against persons; but, on the other hand, it signifies the formal recognition of equality of citizens, the equal right of all to determine the structure of, and to administer, the state. This, in turn, results in the fact that, at a certain stage in the development of democracy, it first welds together the class that wages a revolutionary struggle against capitalism—the proletariat, and enables it to crush, smash to atoms, wipe off the face of the earth the bourgeois, even the republican-bourgeois, state machine, the standing army, the police and the bureaucracy and to substitute for them a *more* democratic state machine, but a state machine nevertheless, in the shape of armed workers who proceed to form a militia involving the entire population.

Here "quantity turns into quality": *such* a degree of democracy implies overstepping the boundaries of bourgeois society and beginning its socialist reorganization. If really *all* take part in the administration of the state, capitalism cannot retain its hold. The development of capitalism, in turn, creates the *preconditions* that *enable* really "all" to take part in the administration of the state. Some of these preconditions are: universal literacy, which has already been achieved in a number of the most advanced capitalist countries, then the "training and disciplining" of millions of workers by the huge, complex, socialized apparatus of the postal service, railways, big factories, large-scale commerce, banking, etc., etc.

Given these *economic* preconditions, it is quite possible, after the overthrow of the capitalists and the bureaucrats, to proceed immediately, overnight, to replace them in the *control* over production and distribution, in the work of *keeping account* of labor and products, by the armed workers, by the whole of the armed population. (The question of control and accounting should not be confused with the question of the scientifically trained staff of engineers, agronomists, and so on. These gentlemen are working today in obedience to the wishes of the capitalists and will work even better tomorrow in obedience to the wishes of the armed workers.)

Accounting and control—that is *mainly* what is needed for the "smooth working," for the proper functioning, of the *first phase* of communist society. *All* citizens are transformed into hired employees of the state, which consists of the armed workers. *All* citizens become employees and workers of a *single* countrywide state "syndicate." All that is required is that they should work equally, do their proper share of work, and get equal pay. The accounting and control necessary for this have been *simplified* by capitalism to the utmost and reduced to the extraordinarily simple operations—which any literate person can perform—of supervising and recording, knowledge of the four rules of arithmetic, and issuing appropriate receipts.[36]

When the *majority* of the people begin independently and everywhere to keep such accounts and exercise such control over the capi-

---

36   When the more important functions of the state are reduced to such accounting and control by the workers themselves, it will cease to be a "political state" and "public functions will lose their political character and become mere administrative functions" (cf. above, Chapter IV, 2, Engels's controversy with the anarchists).

talists (now converted into employees) and over the intellectual gentry who preserve their capitalist habits, this control will really become universal, general, and popular; and there will be no getting away from it, there will be "nowhere to go."

The whole of society will have become a single office and a single factory, with equality of labor and pay.

But this "factory" discipline, which the proletariat, after defeating the capitalists, after overthrowing the exploiters, will extend to the whole of society, is by no means our ideal, or our ultimate goal. It is only a necessary *step* for thoroughly cleansing society of all the infamies and abominations of capitalist exploitation, *and for further* progress.

From the moment all members of society, or at least the vast majority, have learned to administer the state *themselves*, have taken this work into their own hands, have organized control over the insignificant capitalist minority, over the gentry who wish to preserve their capitalist habits and over the workers who have been thoroughly corrupted by capitalism—from this moment the need for government of any kind begins to disappear altogether. The more complete the democracy, the nearer the moment when it becomes unnecessary. The more democratic the "state" which consists of the armed workers, and which is "no longer a state in the proper sense of the word," the more rapidly *every form* of state begins to wither away.

For when *all* have learned to administer and actually to independently administer social production, independently keep accounts and exercise control over the parasites, the sons of the wealthy, the swindlers and other "guardians of capitalist traditions," the escape from this popular accounting and control will inevitably become so incredibly difficult, such a rare exception, and will probably be accompanied by such swift and severe punishment (for the armed workers are practical men and not sentimental intellectuals, and they scarcely allow anyone to trifle with them), that the *necessity* of observing the simple, fundamental rules of the community will very soon become a *habit*.

Then the door will be thrown wide open for the transition from the first phase of communist society to its higher phase, and with it to the complete withering away of the state.

# VI
# The Vulgarization of Marxism by the Opportunists

The question of the relation of the state to the social revolution, and of the social revolution to the state, like the question of revolution generally, was given very little attention by the leading theoreticians and publicists of the Second International (1889–1914). But the most characteristic thing about the process of the gradual growth of opportunism that led to the collapse of the Second International in 1914 is the fact that even when these people were squarely faced with this question they *tried to evade* it or ignored it.

In general, it may be said that *evasiveness* over the question of the relation of the proletarian revolution to the state—an evasiveness which benefited and fostered opportunism—resulted in the *distortion* of Marxism and in its complete vulgarization.

To characterize this lamentable process, if only briefly, we shall take the most prominent theoreticians of Marxism: Plekhanov and Kautsky.

## 1. Plekhanov's Controversy with the Anarchists

Plekhanov wrote a special pamphlet on the relation of anarchism to socialism, entitled *Anarchism and Socialism*, which was published in German in 1894.

In treating this subject, Plekhanov contrived completely to evade the most urgent, burning, and most politically essential issue in the struggle against anarchism, namely, the relation of the revolution to the state, and the question of the state in general! His pamphlet falls into two distinct parts: one of them is historical and literary, and contains valuable material on the history of the ideas of Stirner, Proudhon, and others; the other is philistine, and contains a clumsy dissertation on the theme that an anarchist cannot be distinguished from a bandit.

It is a most amusing combination of subjects and most characteristic of Plekhanov's whole activity on the eve of the revolution and during the revolutionary period in Russia. In fact, in the years 1905 to 1917,

Plekhanov revealed himself as a semi-doctrinaire and semi-philistine who, in politics, trailed in the wake of the bourgeoisie.

We have now seen how, in their controversy with the anarchists, Marx and Engels with the utmost thoroughness explained their views on the relation of revolution to the state. In 1891, in his foreword to Marx's *Critique of the Gotha Programme*, Engels wrote that "we"—that is, Engels and Marx—"were at that time, hardly two years after the Hague Congress of the [First] International,[37] engaged in the most violent struggle against Bakunin and his anarchists."

The anarchists had tried to claim the Paris Commune as their "own," so to say, as a collaboration of their doctrine; and they completely misunderstood its lessons and Marx's analysis of these lessons. Anarchism has given nothing even approximating true answers to the concrete political questions: Must the old state machine be *smashed?* And *what* should be put in its place?

But to speak of "anarchism and socialism" while completely evading the question of the state, and *disregarding* the whole development of Marxism before and after the Commune, meant inevitably slipping into opportunism. For what opportunism needs most of all is that the two questions just mentioned should *not* be raised at all. That *in itself* is a victory for opportunism.

## 2. Kautsky's Controversy with the Opportunists

Undoubtedly, an immeasurably larger number of Kautsky's works have been translated into Russian than into any other language. It is not without reason that some German Social Democrats say in jest that Kautsky is read more in Russia than in Germany (let us say, in parenthesis, that this jest has a far deeper historical meaning

---

37  *The Hague Congress of the First international* sat from September 2–7, 1872. It was attended by 65 delegates, among whom were Marx and Engels. The powers of the General Council and the political activity of the proletariat were among the items on the agenda. The Congress deliberations were marked throughout by a sharp struggle against the Bakuninists. The Congress passed a resolution extending the General Council's powers. Its resolution "On the Political Activity of the Proletariat" stated that the proletariat should organize a political party of its own to ensure the triumph of the social revolution and that the winning of political power was becoming its great task. The Congress expelled Bakunin and Guillaume from the International as disorganizers and founders of a new, anti-proletarian party.

than those who first made it suspect. The Russian workers, by making in 1905 an unusually great and unprecedented demand for the best works of the best Social Democratic literature in the world, and by receiving translations and editions of these works in quantities unheard of in other countries, rapidly transplanted, so to speak, the enormous experience of a neighboring, more advanced country to the young soil of our proletarian movement).

Besides his popularization of Marxism, Kautsky is particularly known in our country for his controversy with the opportunists, with Bernstein at their head. One fact, however, is almost unknown, one which cannot be ignored if we set out to investigate how Kautsky drifted into the morass of unbelievably disgraceful confusion and defense of social-chauvinism during the supreme crisis of 1914–15. This fact is as follows: shortly before he came out against the most prominent representatives of opportunism in France (Millerand and Jaurès) and in Germany (Bernstein), Kautsky betrayed very considerable vacillation. The Marxist *Zarya*,[38] which was published in Stuttgart in 1901–02, and advocated revolutionary proletarian views, was forced to *enter into controversy* with Kautsky and describe as "elastic" the half-hearted, evasive resolution, conciliatory towards the opportunists, that he proposed at the International Socialist Congress in Paris in 1900.[39] Kautsky's letters published in Germany reveal no

---

38   *Zarya* (Dawn)—a Marxist scientific and political journal published in Stuttgart in 1901–02 by the editors of *Iskra*. Four issues appeared in three installments.

39   Reference is to the *Fifth World Congress of the Second international*, which met in Paris from September 23 to 27, 1900. On the fundamental issue, "The Winning of Political Power, and Alliances with Bourgeois Parties," whose discussion was prompted by A. Millerand becoming a member of the Valdeck-Rousseau counterrevolutionary government, the Congress carried a motion tabled by Kautsky. The resolution said that "the entry of a single Socialist into a bourgeois Ministry cannot be considered as the normal beginning for winning political power: it can never be anything but a temporary and exceptional makeshift in an emergency situation." Afterwards opportunists frequently referred to this point to justify their collaboration with the bourgeoisie.

   *Zarya* published (No. 1, April 1901) an article by Plekhanov entitled "A Few Words About the Latest World Socialist Congress in Paris. An Open Letter to the Comrades Who Have Empowered Me," which sharply criticized Kautsky's resolution.

less hesitancy on his part before he took the field against Bernstein.

Of immeasurably greater significance, however, is the fact that, in his very controversy with the opportunists, in his formulation of the question and his manner of treating it, we can now see, as we study the *history* of Kautsky's latest betrayal of Marxism, his systematic deviation towards opportunism precisely on the question of the state.

Let us take Kautsky's first important work against opportunism, *Bernstein and the Social-Democratic Programme*. Kautsky refutes Bernstein in detail, but here is a characteristic thing:

Bernstein, in his *Premises of Socialism*, of Herostratean fame, accuses Marxism of "*Blanquism*" (an accusation since repeated thousands of times by the opportunists and liberal bourgeoisie in Russia against the revolutionary Marxists, the Bolsheviks). In this connection Bernstein dwells particularly on Marx's *The Civil War in France*, and tries, quite unsuccessfully, as we have seen, to identify Marx's views on the lessons of the Commune with those of Proudhon. Bernstein pays particular attention to the conclusion which Marx emphasized in his 1872 preface to the *Communist Manifesto*, namely, that "the working class cannot simply lay hold of the ready-made state machinery and wield it for its own purposes."

This statement "pleased" Bernstein so much that he used it no less than three times in his book, interpreting it in the most distorted, opportunist way.

As we have seen, Marx meant that the working class must *smash, break, shatter* (*Sprengung*, explosion—the expression used by Engels) the whole state machine. But according to Bernstein it would appear as though Marx in these words warned the working class *against* excessive revolutionary zeal when seizing power.

A cruder and more hideous distortion of Marx's idea cannot be imagined.

How, then, did Kautsky proceed in his most detailed refutation of Bernsteinism?

He refrained from analyzing the utter distortion of Marxism by opportunism on this point. He cited the above-quoted passage from Engels's preface to Marx's *Civil War* and said that according to Marx the working class cannot *simply* take over the *ready-made* state machinery, but that, generally speaking, it *can* take it over—and that was all. Kautsky did not say a word about the fact that Bernstein attributed to Marx the *very opposite* of Marx's real idea, that since

1852 Marx had formulated the task of the proletarian revolution as being to "smash" the state machine.

The result was that the most essential distinction between Marxism and opportunism on the subject of the tasks of the proletarian revolution was slurred over by Kautsky!

"We can quite safely leave the solution of the problem of the proletarian dictatorship to the future," said Kautsky, writing *"against"* Bernstein. (p.172, German edition)

This is not a polemic *against* Bernstein, but, in essence, a *concession* to him, a surrender to opportunism; for at present the opportunists ask nothing better than to "quite safely leave to the future" all fundamental questions of the tasks of the proletarian revolution.

From 1852 to 1891, or for forty years, Marx and Engels taught the proletariat that it must smash the state machine. Yet, in 1899, Kautsky, confronted with the complete betrayal of Marxism by the opportunists on this point, fraudulently *substituted* for the question whether it is necessary to smash this machine the question for the concrete forms in which it is to be smashed, and then sought refuge behind the "indisputable" (and barren) philistine truth that concrete forms cannot be known in advance!!

A gulf separates Marx and Kautsky over their attitude towards the proletarian party's task of training the working class for revolution.

Let us take the next, more mature, work by Kautsky, which was also largely devoted to a refutation of opportunist errors. It is his pamphlet, *The Social Revolution*. In this pamphlet, the author chose as his special theme the question of "the proletarian revolution" and "the proletarian regime." He gave much that was exceedingly valuable, but he *avoided* the question of the state. Throughout the pamphlet the author speaks of the winning of state power—and no more; that is, he has chosen a formula which makes a concession to the opportunists, inasmuch as it *admits* the possibility of seizing power *without* destroying the state machine. The very thing, which Marx in 1872 declared to be "obsolete" in the program of the *Communist Manifesto*, is revived by Kautsky in 1902.

A special section in the pamphlet is devoted to the "forms and weapons of the social revolution." Here Kautsky speaks of the mass political strike, of civil war, and of the "instruments of the might of the modern large state, its bureaucracy and the army"; but he does not say a word about what the Commune has already taught the workers.

Evidently, it was not without reason that Engels issued a warning, particularly to the German socialists against "superstitious reverence" for the state.

Kautsky treats the matter as follows: the victorious proletariat "will carry out the democratic program," and he goes on to formulate its clauses. But he does not say a word about the new material provided in 1871 on the subject of the replacement of bourgeois democracy by proletarian democracy. Kautsky disposes of the question by using such "impressive-sounding" banalities as:

> Still, it goes without saying that we shall not achieve supremacy under the present conditions. Revolution itself presupposes long and deep-going struggles, which, in themselves, will change our present political and social structure.

Undoubtedly, this "goes without saying," just as the fact that horses eat oats or the Volga flows into the Caspian. Only it is a pity that an empty and bombastic phrase about "deep-going" struggles is used to *avoid* a question of vital importance to the revolutionary proletariat, namely, *what* makes *its* revolution "deep-going" in relation to the state, to democracy, as distinct from previous, non-proletarian revolutions.

By avoiding this question, Kautsky *in practice* makes a concession to opportunism on this most essential point, although *in words* he declares stern war against it and stresses the importance of the "idea of revolution" (how much is this "idea" worth when one is afraid to teach the workers the concrete lessons of revolution?), or says, "revolutionary idealism before everything else," or announces that the English workers are now "hardly more than petty bourgeois."

"The most varied form of enterprises—bureaucratic [??], trade unionist, co-operative, private... can exist side by side in socialist society," Kautsky writes.

> ... There are, for example, enterprises which cannot do without a bureaucratic [??] organization, such as the railways. Here the democratic organization may take the following shape: the workers elect delegates who form a sort of parliament, which establishes the working regulations and supervises the management of the bureaucratic apparatus. The management of other countries may be transferred to the trade unions, and still others may become co-operative enterprises.

This argument is erroneous; it is a step backward compared with the explanations Marx and Engels gave in the seventies, using the lessons of the Commune as an example.

As far as the supposedly necessary "bureaucratic" organization is concerned, there is no difference whatever between a railway and any other enterprise in large-scale machine industry, any factory, large shop, or large-scale capitalist agricultural enterprise. The technique of all these enterprises makes absolutely imperative the strictest discipline, the utmost precision on the part of everyone in carry out his allotted task, for otherwise the whole enterprise may come to a stop, or machinery or the finished product may be damaged. In all these enterprises the workers will, of course, "elect delegates who will form *a sort of parliament.*"

The whole point, however, is that this "sort of parliament" will *not* be a parliament in the sense of a bourgeois parliamentary institution. The whole point is that this "sort of parliament" will *not* merely "establish the working regulations and supervise the management" of the "apparatus," *but* this apparatus will *not* be "bureaucratic." The workers, after winning political power, will smash the old bureaucratic apparatus, shatter it to its very foundations, and raze it to the ground; they will replace it by a new one, consisting of the very same workers and other employees, *against* whose transformation into bureaucrats the measures will at once be taken which were specified in detail by Marx and Engels: (1) not only election, but also recall at any time; (2) pay not to exceed that of a workman; (3) immediate introduction of control and supervision by *all*, so that *all* may become "bureaucrats" for a time and that, therefore, *nobody* may be able to become a "bureaucrat."

Kautsky has not reflected at all on Marx's words: "The Commune was a working, not parliamentary, body, executive and legislative at the same time."

Kautsky has not understood at all the difference between bourgeois parliamentarism, which combines democracy (*not for the people*) with bureaucracy (*against the people*), and proletarian democracy, which will take immediate steps to cut bureaucracy down to the roots, and which will be able to carry these measures through to the end, to the complete abolition of bureaucracy, to the introduction of complete democracy for the people.

Kautsky here displays the same old "superstitious reverence" for the state, and "superstitious belief" in bureaucracy.

Let us now pass to the last and best of Kautsky's works against the opportunists, his pamphlet *The Road to Power* (which, I believe, has not been published in Russian, for it appeared in 1909, when reaction was at its height in our country). This pamphlet is a big step forward, since it does not deal with the revolutionary program in general, as the pamphlet of 1899 against Bernstein, or with the tasks of the social revolution irrespective of the time of its occurrence, as the 1902 pamphlet, *The Social Revolution*; it deals with the concrete conditions which compels us to recognize that the "era of revolutions" is *setting in*.

The author explicitly points to the aggravation of class antagonisms in general and to imperialism, which plays a particularly important part in this respect. After the "revolutionary period of 1789–1871" in Western Europe, he says, a similar period began in the East in 1905. A world war is approaching with menacing rapidity. "It [the proletariat] can no longer talk of premature revolution." "We have entered a revolutionary period." The "revolutionary era is beginning."

These statements are perfectly clear. This pamphlet of Kautsky's should serve as a measure of comparison of what the German Social Democrats *promised to be* before the imperialist war and the depth of degradation to which they, including Kautsky himself, sank when the war broke out.

"The present situation," Kautsky wrote in the pamphlet under survey, "is fraught with the danger that we [i.e., the German Social Democrats] may easily appear to be more 'moderate' than we really are."

It turned out that in reality the German Social Democratic Party was much more moderate and opportunist than it appeared to be!

It is all the more characteristic, therefore, that although Kautsky so explicitly declared that the era of revolutions had already begun, in the pamphlet which he himself said was devoted to an analysis of the "*political* revolution," he again completely avoided the question of the state.

These evasions of the question, these omissions and equivocations, inevitably added up to that complete swing-over to opportunism with which we shall now have to deal.

Kautsky, the German Social Democrats' spokesman, seems to have declared: I abide by revolutionary views (1899), I recognize, above all, the inevitability of the social revolution of the proletariat (1902), I recognize the advent of a new era of revolutions (1909). Still, I am going back on what Marx said as early as 1852, since the question of the tasks of the proletarian revolution in relation to the state is being raised (1912).

It was in this point-blank form that the question was put in Kautsky's controversy with Pannekoek.

## 3. Kautsky's Controversy with Pannekoek

In opposing Kautsky, Pannekoek came out as one of the representatives of the "Left radical" trend which included Rosa Luxemburg, Karl Radek, and others. Advocating revolutionary tactics, they were united in the conviction that Kautsky was going over to the "Center," which wavered in an unprincipled manner between Marxism and opportunism. This view was proved perfectly correct by the war, when this "Centrist" (wrongly called Marxist) trend, or Kautskyism, revealed itself in all its repulsive wretchedness.

In an article touching on the question of the state, entitled "Mass Action and Revolution" (*Neue Zeit*, 1912, Vol.XXX, 2), Pannekoek described Kautsky's attitude as one of "passive radicalism", as "a theory of inactive expectancy." "Kautsky refuses to see the process of revolution," wrote Pannekoek (p.616). In presenting the matter in this way, Pannekoek approached the subject which interests us, namely, the tasks of the proletarian revolution in relation to the state.

"The struggle of the proletariat," he wrote, "is not merely a struggle against the bourgeoisie *for* state power, but a struggle *against* state power.... The content of this [the proletarian] revolution is the destruction and dissolution [Auflösung] of the instruments of power of the state with the aid of the instruments of power of the proletariat. (p.544) "The struggle will cease only when, as the result of it, the state organization is completely destroyed. The organization of the majority will then have demonstrated its superiority by destroying the organization of the ruling minority." (p.548)

The formulation in which Pannekoek presented his ideas suffers from serious defects. But its meaning is clear nonetheless, and it is interesting to note *how* Kautsky combated it.

"Up to now," he wrote, "the antithesis between the Social Democrats and the anarchists has been that the former wished to win the state power while the latter wished to destroy it. Pannekoek wants to do both." (p.724)

Although Pannekoek's exposition lacks precision and concreteness—not to speak of other shortcomings of his article which have no bearing on the present subject—Kautsky seized precisely on the point of *principle* raised by Pannekoek; and *on this fundamental* point of *principle* Kautsky completely abandoned the Marxist position and went over wholly to opportunism. His definition of the distinction between the Social Democrats and the anarchists is absolutely wrong; he completely vulgarizes and distorts Marxism.

The distinction between Marxists and the anarchists is this: (1) The former, while aiming at the complete abolition of the state, recognize that this aim can only be achieved after classes have been abolished by the socialist revolution, as the result of the establishment of social-ism, which leads to the withering away of the state. The latter want to abolish the state completely overnight, not understanding the conditions under which the state can be abolished. (2) The former recognize that after the proletariat has won political power it must completely destroy the old state machine and replace it by a new one consisting of an organization of the armed workers, after the type of the Commune. The latter, while insisting on the destruction of the state machine, have a very vague idea of *what* the proletariat will put in its place and *how* it will use its revolutionary power. The anarchists even deny that the revolutionary proletariat should use the state power, they reject its revolutionary dictatorship. (3) The former demand that the proletariat be trained for revolution by utilizing the present state. The anarchists reject this.

In this controversy, it is not Kautsky but Pannekoek who represents Marxism, for it was Marx who taught that the proletariat cannot simply win state power in the sense that the old state apparatus passes into new hands, but must smash this apparatus, must break it and replace it by a new one.

Kautsky abandons Marxism for the opportunist camp, for this destruction of the state machine, which is utterly unacceptable to the opportunists, completely disappears from his argument, and he leaves a loophole for them in that "conquest" may be interpreted as the simple acquisition of a majority.

To cover up his distortion of Marxism, Kautsky behaves like a doc-trinaire: he puts forward a "quotation" from Marx himself. In 1850, Marx wrote that a "resolute centralization of power in the hands of the state authority" was necessary, and Kautsky triumphantly asks: does Pannekoek want to destroy "Centralism"?

This is simply a trick, like Bernstein's identification of the views of Marxism and Proudhonism on the subject of federalism as against centralism.

Kautsky's "quotation" is neither here nor there. Centralism is possible with both the old and the new state machine. If the workers voluntarily unite their armed forces, this will be centralism, but it will be based on the "complete destruction" of the centralized state apparatus—the standing army, the police, and the bureaucracy. Kautsky acts like an outright swindler by evading the perfectly well-known arguments of Marx and Engels on the Commune and plucking out a quotation which has nothing to do with the point at issue.

"Perhaps he [Pannekoek]," Kautsky continues, "wants to abolish the state functions of the officials? But we cannot do without officials even in the party and trade unions, let alone in the state administration. And our program does not demand the abolition of state officials, but that they be elected by the people.... We are discussing here not the form the administrative apparatus of the 'future state' will assume, but whether our political struggle abolishes [literally *dissolves*—auflöst] the state power *before we have captured it*. [Kautsky's italics] Which ministry with its officials could be abolished?"

Then follows an enumeration of the ministries of education, justice, finance, and war.

> No, not one of the present ministries will be removed by our political struggle against the government.... I repeat, in order to prevent misunderstanding: we are not discussing here the form the 'future state' will be given by the victorious Social Democrats, but how the present state is changed by our opposition. (p.725)

This is an obvious trick. Pannekoek raised the question of *revolution*. Both the title of his article and the passages quoted above clearly indicate this. By skipping to the question of "opposition," Kautsky substitutes the opportunist for the revolutionary point of view. What he says means: at present we are an opposition; what we shall be *after* we have captured power, that we shall see. *Revolution has vanished!* And that is exactly what the opportunists wanted.

The point at issue is neither opposition nor political struggle in general, but *revolution*. Revolution consists in the proletariat destroying the "administrative apparatus" and the *whole* state machine, replacing it by a new one, made up of the armed workers. Kautsky displays a "superstitious reverence" for "ministries"; but why can they not be replaced, say, by committees of specialists working under sovereign, all-powerful Soviets of Workers' and Soldiers' Deputies?

The point is not at all whether the "ministries" will remain, or whether "committees of specialists" or some other bodies will be set up; that is quite immaterial. The point is whether the old state machine (bound by thousands of threads to the bourgeoisie and permeated through and through with routine and inertia) shall remain, or be *destroyed* and replaced by a *new* one. Revolution consists not in the new class commanding, governing with the aid of the *old* state machine, but in this class *smashing* this machine and commanding, governing with the aid of a *new* machine. Kautsky slurs over this *basic* idea of Marxism, or he does not understand it at all.

His question about officials clearly shows that he does not understand the lessons of the Commune or the teachings of Marx. "We cannot to without officials even in the party and the trade unions...."

We cannot do without officials *under capitalism*, under *the rule of the bourgeoisie*. The proletariat is oppressed, the working people are enslaved by capitalism. Under capitalism, democracy is restricted, cramped, curtailed, mutilated by all the conditions of wage slavery, and the poverty and misery of the people. This and this alone is the reason why the functionaries of our political organizations and trade unions are corrupted—or rather tend to be corrupted—by the conditions of capitalism and betray a tendency to become bureaucrats, i.e., privileged persons divorced from the people and standing *above* the people.

That is the essence of bureaucracy; and until the capitalists have been expropriated and the bourgeoisie overthrown, *even* proletarian functionaries will inevitably be "bureaucratized" to a certain extent.

According to Kautsky, since elected functionaries will remain under socialism, so will officials, so will the bureaucracy! This is exactly where he is wrong. Marx, referring to the example of the Commune, showed that under socialism functionaries will cease to be "bureaucrats," to be "officials," they will cease to be so *in proportion as*—in addition to the principle of election of officials—the principle of recall at any time is *also* introduced, as salaries are reduced to the level of the wages of the average workman, *and* as parliamentary institutions are replaced by "working bodies, executive and legislative at the same time."

As a matter of fact, the whole of Kautsky's argument against Pannekoek, and particularly the former's wonderful point that we cannot do without officials even in our party and trade union organizations, is merely a repetition of Bernstein's old "arguments" against Marxism in general. In his renegade book, *The Premises of Socialism,*

Bernstein combats the ideas of "primitive" democracy, combats what he calls "doctrinaire democracy": binding mandates, unpaid officials, impotent central representative bodies, etc. To prove that this "primitive" democracy is unsound, Bernstein refers to the experience of the British trade unions, as interpreted by the Webbs.[40] Seventy years of development "in absolute freedom," he says (p.137, German edition), convinced the trade unions that primitive democracy was useless, and they replaced it by ordinary democracy, i.e., parliamentarism combined with bureaucracy.

In reality, the trade unions did not develop "in absolute freedom" *but in absolute capitalist slavery*, under which, it goes without saying, a number of concessions to the prevailing evil, violence, falsehood, exclusion of the poor from the affairs of "higher" administration, "cannot be done without." Under socialism much of "primitive" democracy will inevitably be revived, since, for the first time in the history of civilized society, the *mass* of the population will rise to taking an *independent* part, not only in voting and elections, *but also in the everyday administration of the state*. Under socialism *all* will govern in turn and will soon become accustomed to no one governing.

Marx's critico-analytical genius saw in the practical measures of the Commune the *turning point* which the opportunists fear and do not want to recognize because of their cowardice, because they do not want to break irrevocably with the bourgeoisie, and which the anarchists do not want to see, either because they are in a hurry or because they do not understand at all the conditions of great social changes. "We must not even think of destroying the old state machine; how can we do without ministries and officials?" argues the opportunist, who is completely saturated with philistinism and who, at bottom, not only does not believe in revolution, in the creative power of revolution, but lives in mortal dread of it (like our Mensheviks and Socialist Revolutionaries).

"We must think *only* of destroying the old state machine; it is no use probing into the *concrete* lessons of earlier proletarian revolutions and analyzing *what* to put in the place of what has been destroyed, and *how*," argues the anarchist (the best of the anarchists, of course, and not those who, following the Kropotkins and Co., trail behind the bourgeoisie). Consequently, the tactics of the anarchist become the tactics of *despair* instead of a ruthlessly bold revolutionary effort

40   This refers to Sydney and Beatrice Webb, *Industrial Democracy*.

to solve concrete problems while taking into account the practical conditions of the mass movement.

Marx teaches us to avoid both errors; he teaches us to act with supreme boldness in destroying the entire old state machine, and at the same time he teaches us to put the question concretely: the Commune was able in the space of a few weeks to *start* building a *new*, proletarian state machine by introducing such-and-such measures to provide wider democracy and to uproot bureaucracy. Let us learn revolutionary boldness from the Communards; let us see in their practical measures the *outline* of really urgent and immediately possible measures, and then, *following this road*, we shall achieve the complete destruction of bureaucracy.

The possibility of this destruction is guaranteed by the fact that socialism will shorten the working day, will raise the *people* to a new life, will create such conditions for the *majority* of the population as will enable *everybody*, without exception, to perform "state functions," and this will lead to the *complete withering away* of every form of state in general.

"Its object [the object of the mass strike]," Kautsky continues, "cannot be to *destroy* the state power; its only object can be to make the government compliant on some specific question, or to replace a government hostile to the proletariat by one willing to meet it halfway [*entgegenkommende*]... But never, under no circumstances can it [that is, the proletarian victory over a hostile government] lead to the *destruction* of the state power; it can lead only to a certain *shifting* [*verschiebung*] of the balance of forces *within the state power*.... The aim of our political struggle remains, as in the past, the conquest of state power by winning a majority in parliament and by raising parliament to the ranks of master of the government." (pp.726, 727, 732)

This is nothing but the purest and most vulgar opportunism: repudiating revolution in deeds, while accepting it in words. Kautsky's thoughts go no further than a "government... willing to meet the proletariat halfway"—a step backward to philistinism compared with 1847, when the *Communist Manifesto* proclaimed "the organization of the proletariat as the ruling class."

Kautsky will have to achieve his beloved "unity" with the Scheidemanns, Plekhanovs and Vanderveldes, all of whom agree to fight for a government "willing to meet the proletariat halfway."

We, however, shall break with these traitors to socialism, and we shall fight for the complete destruction of the old state machine, in order that the armed proletariat itself *may become the government.* These are two vastly different things.

Kautsky will have to enjoy the pleasant company of the Legiens and Davids, Plekhanovs, Potresovs, Tseretelis, and Chernovs, who are quite willing to work for the "shifting of the balance of forces within the state power," for "winning a majority in parliament," and "raising parliament to the ranks of master of the government." A most worthy object, which is wholly acceptable to the opportunists and which keeps everything within the bounds of the bourgeois parliamentary republic.

We, however, shall break with the opportunists; and the entire class-conscious proletariat will be with us in the fight—not to "shift the balance of forces," but to *overthrow the bourgeoisie,* to *destroy* bourgeois parliamentarism, for a democratic republic after the type of the Commune, or a republic of Soviets of Workers' and Soldiers' Deputies, for the revolutionary dictatorship of the proletariat.

\*       \*       \*

To the right of Kautsky in international socialism there are trends such as *Socialist Monthly*[41] in Germany (Legien, David, Kolb, and many others, including the Scandinavian Stauning and Branting), Jaurès's followers and Vandervelde in France and Belgium; Turait, Treves, and other Right-wingers of the Italian Party; the Fabians and "Independents" (the Independent labor Party, which, in fact, has always been dependent on the Liberals) in Britain; and the like. All these gentry, who play a tremendous, very often a predominant role in the parliamentary work and the press of their parties, repudiate outright the dictatorship of the proletariat and pursue a policy of undisguised opportunism. In the eyes of these gentry, the "dictatorship" of the proletariat "contradicts" democracy!! There is really no essential distinction between them and the petty-bourgeois democrats.

Taking this circumstance into consideration, we are justified in drawing the conclusion that the Second International, that is, the overwhelming majority of its official representatives, has completely

41   *Socialist Monthly* (Sozialistische Monatshefte)—the principal journal of the opportunists among the German Social Democrats, a periodical of international opportunism. It was published in Berlin from 1897 to 1933. During the world imperialist war of 1914–18 it took a social-chauvinist stand.

sunk into opportunism. The experience of the Commune has been not only ignored, but distorted. Far from inculcating in the workers' minds the idea that the time is nearing when they must act to smash the old state machine, replace it by a new one, and in this way make their political rule the foundation for the socialist reorganization of society, they have actually preached to the masses the very opposite and have depicted the "conquest of power" in a way that has left thousands of loopholes for opportunism.

The distortion and hushing up of the question of the relation of the proletarian revolution to the state could not but play an immense role at a time when states, which possess a military apparatus expanded as a consequence of imperialist rivalry, have become military monsters which are exterminating millions of people in order to settle the issue as to whether Britain or Germany—this or that finance capital—is to rule the world.

# VII
# The Experience of the
# Russian Revolutions of 1905 and 1917

The subject indicated in the title of this chapter is so vast that volumes could be written about it. In the present pamphlet we shall have to confine ourselves, naturally, to the most important lessons provided by experience, those bearing directly upon the tasks of the proletariat in the revolution with regard to state power. [Here the manuscript breaks off—*Ed.*]

## PostScript to the First Edition

This pamphlet was written in August and September 1917. I had already drawn up the plan for the next, the seventh chapter, "The Experience of the Russian Revolutions of 1905 and 1917." Apart from the title, however, I had no time to write a single line of the chapter; I was "interrupted" by a political crisis—the eve of the October revolution of 1917. Such an "interruption" can only be welcomed; but the writing of the second part of this pamphlet ("The Experience of the Russian Revolutions of 1905 and 1917") will probably have to be put off for a long time. It is more pleasant and useful to go through the "experience of revolution" than to write about it.

*The Author*
Petrograd
November 30, 1917

Leon Trotsky in 1938

# The Transitional Program:

## The Death Agony of Capitalism and the Tasks of the Fourth International

**Leon Trotsky**

*This program was adopted by the first congress of the newly formed Fourth International in 1938. In it Trotsky clearly lays out the need for "transitional demands" that will allow the workers to draw the necessary conclusions about the need for the socialist revolution. A transitional program is a bridge between what the Social Democratic parties referred to as the minimum program (basic reforms) and the maximum program (social revolution).*

I

## The Objective Prerequisites for a Socialist Revolution

The world political situation as a whole is chiefly characterized by a historical crisis of the leadership of the proletariat.

The economic prerequisite for the proletarian revolution has already in general achieved the highest point of fruition that can be reached under capitalism. Mankind's productive forces stagnate. Already new inventions and improvements fail to raise the level of material wealth. Conjunctural crises under the conditions of the social crisis of the whole capitalist system inflict ever heavier deprivations and sufferings upon the masses. Growing unemployment, in its turn, deepens the financial crisis of the state and undermines the unstable monetary systems. Democratic regimes, as well as fascist, stagger on from one bankruptcy to another.

The bourgeoisie itself sees no way out. In countries where it has already been forced to stake its last upon the card of fascism, it now toboggans with closed eyes toward an economic and military catastrophe. In the historically privileged countries, i.e., in those where the bourgeoisie can still for a certain period permit itself the luxury of democracy at the expense of national accumulations (Great Britain, France, United States, etc.), all of capital's traditional parties are in a state of perplexity bordering on a paralysis of will.

The "New Deal," despite its first period of pretentious resoluteness, represents but a special form of political perplexity, possible only in a country where the bourgeoisie succeeded in accumulating incalculable wealth. The present crisis, far from having run its full course, has already succeeded in showing that "New Deal" politics, like Popular Front politics in France, opens no new exit from the economic blind alley.

International relations present no better picture. Under the increasing tension of capitalist disintegration, imperialist antagonisms reach an impasse at the height of which separate clashes and bloody local disturbances (Ethiopia, Spain, the Far East, Central Europe) must inevitably coalesce into a conflagration of world dimensions. The bourgeoisie, of course, is aware of the mortal danger to its domination represented by a new war. But that class is now immeasurably less capable of averting war than on the eve of 1914.

All talk to the effect that historical conditions have not yet "ripened" for socialism is the product of ignorance or conscious deception. The objective prerequisites for the proletarian revolution have not only "ripened"; they have begun to get somewhat rotten. Without a socialist revolution, in the next historical period at that, a catastrophe threatens the whole culture of mankind. The turn is now to the proletariat, i.e., chiefly to its revolutionary vanguard. The historical crisis of mankind is reduced to the crisis of the revolutionary leadership.

## The Proletariat and its Leadership

The economy, the state, the politics of the bourgeoisie and its international relations are completely blighted by a social crisis, characteristic of a prerevolutionary state of society. The chief obstacle in the path of transforming the prerevolutionary into a revolutionary state is the opportunist character of proletarian leadership: its petty bourgeois cowardice before the big bourgeoisie and its perfidious connection with it, even in its death agony.

In all countries the proletariat is racked by a deep disquiet. The multimillioned masses again and again enter the road of revolution. But each time they are blocked by their own conservative bureaucratic machines.

The Spanish proletariat has made a series of heroic attempts since April 1931 to take power in its hands and guide the fate of society. However, its own parties (Social Democrats, Stalinists, Anarchists, POUMists)—each in its own way—acted as a brake and thus prepared Franco's triumphs.

In France, the great wave of "sit-down" strikes, particularly during June 1936, revealed the wholehearted readiness of the proletariat to overthrow the capitalist system. However, the leading organizations (Socialists, Stalinists, Syndicalists) under the label of the Popular Front succeeded in canalizing and damming, at least temporarily, the revolutionary stream.

The unprecedented wave of sit-down strikes and the amazingly rapid growth of industrial unionism in the United States (the CIO) is the most indisputable expression of the instinctive striving of the American workers to raise themselves to the level of the tasks imposed on them by history. But here, too, the leading political organizations, including the newly created CIO, do everything possible to keep in check and paralyze the revolutionary pressure of the masses.

The definite passing over of the Comintern to the side of bourgeois order, its cynically counterrevolutionary role throughout the world, particularly in Spain, France, the United States and other "democratic" countries, created exceptional supplementary difficulties for the world proletariat. Under the banner of the October Revolution, the conciliatory politics practiced by the "People's Front" doom the working class to impotence and clear the road for fascism.

"People's Fronts" on the one hand—fascism on the other: these are the last political resources of imperialism in the struggle against the proletarian revolution. From the historical point of view, however, both these resources are stopgaps. The decay of capitalism continues under the sign of the Phrygian cap in France as under the sign of the swastika in Germany. Nothing short of the overthrow of the bourgeoisie can open a road out.

The orientation of the masses is determined first by the objective conditions of decaying capitalism, and second, by the treacherous politics of the old workers' organizations. Of these factors, the first, of course, is the decisive one: the laws of history are stronger than the bureaucratic apparatus. No matter how the methods of the social betrayers differ—from the "social" legislation of Blum to the judicial frame-ups of Stalin—they will never succeed in breaking the revolutionary will of the proletariat. As time goes on, their desperate efforts to hold back the wheel of history will demonstrate more clearly to the masses that the crisis of the proletarian leadership, having become the crisis in mankind's culture, can be resolved only by the Fourth International.

## The Minimum Program and the Transitional Program

The strategic task of the next period—prerevolutionary period of agitation, propaganda and organization—consists in overcoming the contradiction between the maturity of the objective revolutionary conditions and the immaturity of the proletariat and its vanguard (the confusion and disappointment of the older generation, the inexperience of the younger generation). It is necessary to help the masses in the process of the daily struggle to find the bridge between present demands and the socialist program of the revolution. This bridge should include a system of *transitional demands*, stemming from today's conditions and from today's consciousness of wide layers of the working class and unalterably leading to one final conclusion: the conquest of power by the proletariat.

Classical Social Democracy, functioning in an epoch of progressive capitalism, divided its program into two parts independent of each other: the *minimum program,* which limited itself to reforms within the framework of bourgeois society, and the *maximum program,* which promised substitution of socialism for capitalism in the indefinite future. Between the minimum and the maximum program, no bridge existed. And indeed Social Democracy has no need of such a bridge, since the word *socialism* is used only for holiday speechifying. The Comintern has set out to follow the path of Social Democracy in an epoch of decaying capitalism: when, in general, there can be no discussion of systematic social reforms and the raising of the masses' living standards; when every serious demand of the proletariat and even every serious demand of the petty bourgeoisie, inevitably reaches beyond the limits of capitalist property relations and of the bourgeois state.

The strategic task of the Fourth International lies not in reforming capitalism but in its overthrow. Its political aim is the conquest of power by the proletariat for the purpose of expropriating the bourgeoisie. However, the achievement of this strategic task is unthinkable without the most considered attention to all, even small and partial, questions of tactics. All sections of the proletariat, all its layers, occupations and groups should be drawn into the revolutionary movement. The present epoch is distinguished not for the fact that it frees the revolutionary party from day-to-day work but because it permits this work to be carried on indissolubly with the actual tasks of the revolution.

The Fourth International does not discard the program of the old "minimal" demands to the degree to which these have preserved at least part of their vital forcefulness. Indefatigably, it defends the democratic rights and social conquests of the workers. But it carries on this day-to-day work within the framework of the correct actual, that is, revolutionary perspective. Insofar as the old, partial, "minimal" demands of the masses clash with the destructive and degrading tendencies of decadent capitalism—and this occurs at each step—the Fourth International advances a system of *transitional demands,* the essence of which is contained in the fact that ever more openly and decisively they will be directed against the very bases of the bourgeois regime. The old "minimal program" is superseded by the *transitional program*, the task of which lies in systematic mobilization of the masses for the proletarian revolution.

## Sliding Scale of Wages and Sliding Scale of Hours

Under the conditions of disintegrating capitalism, the masses continue to live the meagerized life of the oppressed, threatened now more than at any other time with the danger of being cast into the pit of pauperism. They must defend their mouthful of bread, if they cannot increase or better it. There is neither the need nor the opportunity to enumerate here those separate, partial demands which time and again arise on the basis of concrete circumstances—national, local, trade union. But two basic economic afflictions, in which is summarized the increasing absurdity of the capitalist system, that is, *unemployment* and *high prices*, demand generalized slogans and methods of struggle.

The Fourth International declares uncompromising war on the politics of the capitalists which, to a considerable degree, like the politics of their agents, the reformists, aims to place the whole burden of militarism, the crises, the disorganization of the monetary system, and all other scourges stemming from capitalism's death agony upon the backs of the toilers. The Fourth International demands *employment* and *decent living conditions* for all.

Neither monetary inflation nor stabilization can serve as slogans for the proletariat because these are but two ends of the same stick. Against a bounding rise in prices, which with the approach of war will assume an ever more unbridled character, one can fight only under the slogan of a *sliding scale of wages*. This means that collective agreements should assure an automatic rise in wages in relation to the increase in price of consumer goods.

Under the menace of its own disintegration, the proletariat cannot permit the transformation of an increasing section of the workers into chronically unemployed paupers, living off the slops of a crumbling society. The *right to employment* is the only serious right left to the worker in a society based upon exploitation. This right today is being shorn from him at every step. Against unemployment, "structural" as well as "conjunctural," the time is ripe to advance, along with the slogan of public works, the slogan of a *sliding scale of working hours*. Trade unions and other mass organizations should bind the workers and the unemployed together in the solidarity of mutual responsibility. On this basis all the work on hand would then be divided among all existing workers in accordance with how the extent of the working week is defined. The average wage of every worker remains the same as it was under the old working week. Wages, under a strictly guaranteed *minimum*, would follow the movement of prices. It is impossible to accept any other program for the present catastrophic period.

Property owners and their lawyers will prove the "unrealizability" of these demands. Smaller, especially ruined capitalists, in addition will refer to their account ledgers. The workers categorically denounce such conclusions and references. The question is not one of a "normal" collision between opposing material interests. The question is one of guarding the proletariat from decay, demoralization and ruin. The question is one of life or death of the only creative and progressive class, and by that token of the future of mankind. If capitalism is incapable of satisfying the demands inevitably arising from the calamities generated by itself, then let it perish. "Realizability" or "unrealizability" is in the given instance a question of the relationship of forces, which can be decided only by the struggle. By means of this struggle, no matter what its immediate practical successes may be, the workers will best come to understand the necessity of liquidating capitalist slavery.

## Trade Unions in the Transitional Epoch

In the struggle for partial and transitional demands, the workers now more than ever before need mass organizations, principally trade unions. The powerful growth of trade unionism in France and the United States is the best refutation of the preachments of those ultraleft doctrinaires who have been teaching that trade unions have "outlived their usefulness."

The Bolshevik-Leninist stands in the front-line trenches of all kinds of struggles, even when they involve only the most modest material interests or democratic rights of the working class. He takes active part in mass trade unions for the purpose of strengthening them and raising their spirit of militancy. He fights uncompromisingly against any attempt to subordinate the unions to the bourgeois state and bind the proletariat to "compulsory arbitration" and every other form of police guardianship—not only fascist but also "democratic." Only on the basis of such work within the trade unions is successful struggle possible against the reformists, including those of the Stalinist bureaucracy. Sectarian attempts to build or preserve small "revolutionary" unions, as a second edition of the party, signify in actuality the renouncing of the struggle for leadership of the working class. It is necessary to establish this firm rule: self-isolation of the capitulationist variety from mass trade unions, which is tantamount to a betrayal of the revolution, is incompatible with membership in the Fourth International.

At the same time, the Fourth International resolutely rejects and condemns trade union fetishism, equally characteristic of trade union-ists and syndicalists.

a.  Trade unions do not offer, and in line with their task, compo-sition and manner of recruiting membership, cannot offer a finished revolutionary program; in consequence, they cannot replace the *party*. The building of national revolutionary parties as sections of the Fourth International is the central task of the transitional epoch.

b.  Trade unions, even the most powerful, embrace no more than 20 to 25 percent of the working class, and at that, predominant-ly the more skilled and better-paid layers. The more oppressed majority of the working class is drawn only episodically into the struggle, during a period of exceptional upsurges in the labor movement. During such moments it is necessary to cre-ate organizations *ad hoc*, embracing the whole fighting mass: strike committees, factory committees, and finally, soviets.

c.  As organizations expressive of the top layers of the proletariat, trade unions, as witnessed by all past historical experience, including the fresh experience of the anarcho-syndicalist unions in Spain, developed powerful tendencies toward com-promise with the bourgeois-democratic regime. In periods of acute class struggle, the leading bodies of the trade unions aim to become masters of the mass movement in order to render it harmless. This is already occurring during the period of simple strikes, especially in the case of the mass sit-down strikes which shake the principle of bourgeois property. In time of war or revolution, when the bourgeoisie is plunged into exceptional difficulties, trade union leaders usually become bourgeois ministers.

Therefore, the sections of the Fourth International should always strive not only to renew the top leadership of the trade unions, boldly and resolutely in critical moments advancing new militant leaders in place of routine functionaries and careerists, but also to create in all possible instances independent militant organizations corresponding more closely to the tasks of mass struggle against bourgeois society; and, if necessary, not flinching even in the face of a direct break with the conservative apparatus of the trade unions. If it be criminal to turn one's back on mass organizations for the sake of fostering sectarian fictions, it is no less so to passively tolerate subordination of the revolutionary mass movement to the control of openly reactionary or disguised conservative ("progressive") bureaucratic cliques. Trade unions are not ends in themselves; they are but means along the road to proletarian revolution.

## Factory Committees

During a transitional epoch, the workers' movement does not have a systematic and well-balanced, but a feverish and explosive character. Slogans as well as organizational forms should be subordinated to the indices of the movement. On guard against routine handling of a situation as against a plague, the leadership should respond sensitively to the initiative of the masses.

*Sit-down strikes*, the latest expression of this kind of initiative, go beyond the limits of "normal" capitalist procedure. Independently of the demands of the strikers, the temporary seizure of factories deals a blow to the idol, capitalist property. Every sit-down strike poses in a practical manner the question of who is boss of the factory: the capitalist or the workers?

If the sit-down strike raises this question episodically, the *factory committee* gives it organized expression. Elected by all the factory employees, the factory committee immediately creates a counterweight to the will of the administration.

To the reformist criticism of bosses of the so-called "economic royalist" type like Ford in contradistinction to "good," "democratic" exploiters, we counterpose the slogan of factory committees as centers of struggle against both the first and the second.

Trade union bureaucrats will, as a general rule, resist the creation of factory committees, just as they resist every bold step along the road of mobilizing the masses.

However, the wider the sweep of the movement, the easier will it be to break this resistance. Where the closed shop has already been instituted in "peaceful" times, the committee will formally coincide with the usual organ of the trade union, but will renew its personnel and widen its functions. The prime significance of the committee, however, lies in the fact that it becomes the militant staff for such working class layers, as the trade union is usually incapable of moving to action. It is precisely from these more oppressed layers that the most self-sacrificing battalions of the revolution will come.

From the moment that the committee makes its appearance, a *de facto* dual power is established in the factory. By its very essence it represents the transitional state, because it includes in itself two irreconcilable regimes: the capitalist and the proletarian. The fundamental significance of factory committees is precisely contained in the fact that they open the doors, if not to a direct revolutionary, then to a prerevolutionary period—between the bourgeois and the proletarian regimes. That the propagation of the factory committee idea is neither premature nor artificial is amply attested to by the waves of sit-down strikes spreading through several countries. New waves of this type will be inevitable in the immediate future. It is necessary to begin a timely campaign in favor of factory committees in order not to be caught unawares.

## "Business Secrets" and Workers' Control of Industry

Liberal capitalism, based upon competition and free trade, has completely receded into the past. Its successor, monopolistic capitalism, not only does not mitigate the anarchy of the market, but on the contrary imparts to it a particularly convulsive character. The necessity of "controlling" economy, of placing state "guidance" over industry and of "planning" is today recognized—at least in words—by almost all current bourgeois and petty-bourgeois tendencies, from fascist to Social Democratic. With the fascists, it is mainly a question of "planned" plundering of the people for military purposes. The Social Democrats prepare to drain the ocean of anarchy with spoonfuls of bureaucratic "planning." Engineers and professors write articles about "technocracy." In their cowardly experiments in "regulation," democratic governments run head-on into the invincible sabotage of big capital.

The actual relationship existing between the exploiters and the democratic "controllers" is best characterized by the fact that the gentlemen "reformers" stop short in pious trepidation before the threshold of the trusts and their business "secrets." Here the principle of "non-interference" with business dominates. The accounts kept between the individual capitalist and society remain the secret of the capitalist: they are not the concern of society. The motivation offered for the principle of business "secrets" is ostensibly, as in the epoch of liberal capitalism, that of free "competition." In reality, the trusts keep no secrets from one another. The business secrets of the present epoch are part of a persistent plot of monopoly capitalism against the interests of society. Projects for limiting the autocracy of "economic royalists" will continue to be pathetic farces as long as private owners of the social means of production can hide from producers and consumers the machinations of exploitation, robbery and fraud. The abolition of "business secrets" is the first step toward actual control of industry.

Workers no less than capitalists have the right to know the "secrets" of the factory, of the trust, of the whole branch of industry, of the national economy as a whole. First and foremost, banks, heavy industry, and centralized transport should be placed under a magnifying glass.

The immediate tasks of workers' control should be to explain the debits and credits of society, beginning with individual business undertakings; to determine the actual share of the national income appropriated by individual capitalists and by the exploiters as a whole; to expose the behind-the-scenes deals and swindles of banks and trusts; finally, to reveal to all members of society that unconscionable squandering of human labor which is the result of capitalist anarchy and the naked pursuit of profits.

No office holder of the bourgeois state is in a position to carry out this work, no matter with how great authority one would wish to endow him. All the world was witness to the impotence of President Roosevelt and Premier Blum against the plottings of the "60" or "200 Families" of their respective nations. To break the resistance of the exploiters, the mass pressure of the proletariat is necessary. Only factory committees can bring about real control of production, calling in—as consultants but not as "technocrats"—specialists sincerely devoted to the people: accountants, statisticians, engineers, scientists, etc.

The struggle against unemployment is not to be considered without the calling for a broad and bold organization of *public works*. But public works can have a continuous and progressive significance for society, as for the unemployed themselves, only when they are made part of a general plan worked out to cover a considerable number of years. Within the framework of this plan, the workers would demand resumption, as public utilities, of work in private businesses closed as a result of the crisis. Workers' control in such cases would be replaced by direct workers' management.

The working out of even the most elementary economic plan—from the point of view of the exploited, not the exploiters—is impossible without workers' control, that is, without the penetration of the workers' eyes into all the open and concealed mechanisms of capitalist economy. Committees representing individual business enterprises should meet at conferences to choose corresponding committees of trusts, whole branches of industry, economic regions, and, finally, of national industry as a whole. Thus, workers' control becomes a *school for planned economy*. On the basis of the experience of control, the proletariat will prepare itself for direct management of nationalized industry when the hour for that eventuality strikes.

To those capitalists, mainly of the lower and middle strata, who of their own accord sometimes offer to throw open their books to the workers—usually to demonstrate the necessity of lowering wages—the workers answer that they are not interested in the bookkeeping of individual bankrupts or semibankrupts but in the account ledgers of all exploiters as a whole. The workers cannot and do not wish to accommodate the level of their living conditions to the exigencies of individual capitalists, themselves victims of their own regime. The task is one of reorganizing the whole system of production and distribution on a more dignified and workable basis. If the abolition of business secrets be a necessary condition to workers' control, then control is the first step along the road to the socialist guidance of economy.

## Expropriation of Separate Groups of Capitalists

The socialist program of expropriation, i.e., of political overthrow of the bourgeoisie and liquidation of its economic domination, should in no case during the present transitional period hinder us from advancing, when the occasion warrants, the demand for the expropriation of several key branches of industry vital for national existence or of the most parasitic group of the bourgeoisie.

Thus, in answer to the pathetic jeremiads of the gentlemen democrats about the dictatorship of the "60 Families" of the United States or the "200 Families" of France, we counterpose the demand for the expropriation of those 60 or 200 feudalistic capitalist overlords.

In precisely the same way, we demand the expropriation of the corporations holding monopolies on war industries, railroads, the most important sources of raw materials, etc.

The difference between these demands and the muddleheaded reformist slogan of "nationalization" lies in the following: (1) we reject indemnification; (2) we warn the masses against demagogues of the People's Front who, giving lip service to nationalization, remain in reality agents of capital; (3) we call upon the masses to rely only upon their own revolutionary strength; (4) we link up the question of expropriation with that of seizure of power by the workers and farmers.

The necessity of advancing the slogan of expropriation in the course of daily *agitation* in partial form, and not only in our propaganda in its more comprehensive aspects, is dictated by the fact that different branches of industry are on different levels of development, occupy a different place in the life of society, and pass through different stages of the class struggle. Only a general revolutionary upsurge of the proletariat can place the complete expropriation of the bourgeoisie on the order of the day. The task of transitional demands is to prepare the proletariat to solve this problem.

## Expropriation of the Private Banks and State-ization of the Credit System

Imperialism means the domination of *finance capital*. Side by side with the trusts and syndicates, and very frequently rising above them, the *banks* concentrate in their hands the actual command over the economy. In their structure the banks express in a concentrated form the entire structure of modern capital: they combine tendencies of *monopoly* with tendencies of *anarchy*. They organize the miracles of technology, giant enterprises, mighty trusts; and they also organize high prices, crises and unemployment. It is impossible to take a single serious step in the struggle against monopolistic despotism and capitalistic anarchy—which supplement one another in their work of destruction—if the commanding posts of banks are left in the hands of predatory capitalists. In order to create a unified system of investments and credits, along a rational plan corresponding to the interests of the entire people, it is necessary to merge all the banks into a single national institution. Only the expropriation of the private banks and the concentration of the entire credit system in the hands of the state will provide the latter with the necessary actual, i.e., material resources—and not merely paper and bureaucratic resources—for economic planning.

The expropriation of the banks in no case implies the expropriation of bank deposits. On the contrary, the single *state bank* will be able to create much more favorable conditions for the small depositors than could the private banks. In the same way, only the state bank can establish for farmers, tradesmen and small merchants conditions of favorable, that is, cheap credit. Even more important, however, is the circumstance that the entire economy—first and foremost large-scale industry and transport—directed by a single financial staff, will serve the vital interests of the workers and all other toilers.

However, the *state-ization of the banks* will produce these favorable results only if the state power itself passes completely from the hands of the exploiters into the hands of the toilers.

## The Picket Line, Defense Guards/Workers' Militia and the Arming of the Proletariat

Sit-down strikes are a serious warning from the masses addressed not only to the bourgeoisie but also to the organizations of the workers, including the Fourth International. In 1919–20, the Italian workers seized factories on their own initiative, thus signaling the news to their "leaders" of the coming of the social revolution. The "leaders" paid no heed to the signal. The victory of fascism was the result.

Sit-down strikes do not yet mean the seizure of factories in the Italian manner, but they are a decisive step toward such seizures. The present crisis can sharpen the class struggle to an extreme point and bring nearer the moment of denouement. But that does not mean that a revolutionary situation comes on at one stroke. Actually, its approach is signalized by a continuous series of convulsions. One of these is the wave of sit-down strikes. The problem of the sections of the Fourth International is to help the proletarian vanguard understand the general character and tempo of our epoch and to fructify in time the struggle of the masses with ever more resolute and militant organizational measures.

The sharpening of the proletariat's struggle means the sharpening of the methods of counterattack on the part of capital. New waves of sit-down strikes can call forth and undoubtedly will call forth resolute countermeasures on the part of the bourgeoisie. Preparatory work is already being done by the confidential staffs of big trusts. Woe to the revolutionary organizations, woe to the proletariat if it is again caught unawares!

The bourgeoisie is nowhere satisfied with the official police and army. In the United States, even during "peaceful" times the bourgeoisie maintains militarized battalions of scabs and privately armed thugs in factories. To this must now be added the various groups of American Nazis. The French bourgeoisie at the first approach of danger mobilized semilegal and illegal fascist detachments, including such as are in the army. No sooner does the pressure of the English workers once again become stronger than immediately the fascist bands are doubled, trebled, increased tenfold to come out in bloody march against the workers. The bourgeoisie keeps itself most accurately informed about the fact that in the present epoch the class struggle irresistibly tends to transform itself into civil war. The examples of Italy, Germany, Austria, Spain and other countries taught considerably more to the magnates and lackeys of capital than to the official leaders of the proletariat.

The politicians of the Second and Third Internationals as well as the bureaucrats of the trade unions, consciously close their eyes to the bourgeoisie's private army; otherwise they could not preserve their alliance with it for even twenty-four hours. The reformists systematically implant in the minds of the workers the notion that the sacredness of democracy is best guaranteed when the bourgeoisie is armed to the teeth and the workers are unarmed.

The duty of the Fourth International is to put an end to such slavish polices once and for all. The petty bourgeois democrats—including Social Democrats, Stalinists and Anarchists—yell louder about the struggle against fascism the more cravenly they capitulate to it in actuality. Only armed workers' detachments, who feel the support of tens of millions of toilers behind them, can successfully prevail against the fascist bands. The struggle against fascism does not start in the liberal editorial office but in the factory—and ends in the street. Scabs and private gunmen in factory plants are the basic nuclei of the fascist army. *Strike pickets* are the basic nuclei of the proletarian army. This is our point of departure. In connection with every strike and street demonstration, it is imperative to propagate the necessity of creating *workers' groups for self-defense*. It is necessary to write this slogan into the program of the revolutionary wing of the trade unions. It is imperative wherever possible, beginning with the youth groups, to organize groups for self-defense, to drill and acquaint them with the use of arms.

A new upsurge of the mass movement should serve not only to increase the number of these units but also to unite them according to neighborhoods, cities, regions. It is necessary to give organized expression to the valid hatred of the workers toward scabs and bands of gangsters and fascists. It is necessary to advance the slogan of a *workers' militia* as the one serious guarantee for the inviolability of workers' organizations, meetings and press.

Only with the help of such systematic, persistent, indefatigable, courageous agitational and organizational work, always on the basis of the experience of the masses themselves, is it possible to root out from their consciousness the traditions of submissiveness and passivity; to train detachments of heroic fighters capable of setting an example to all toilers; to inflict a series of tactical defeats upon the armed thugs of counterrevolution; to raise the self-confidence of the exploited and oppressed; to compromise fascism in the eyes of the petty bourgeoisie and pave the road for the conquest of power by the proletariat.

Engels defined the state as "bodies of armed men." *The arming of the proletariat* is an imperative concomitant element to its struggle for liberation. When the proletariat wills it, it will find the road and the means to arming. In this field, also, else leadership falls naturally to the sections of the Fourth International.

## The Alliance of the Workers and Farmers

The brother-in-arms and counterpart of the worker in the country is the agricultural laborer. They are two parts of one and the same class. Their interests are inseparable. The industrial workers' program of transitional demands, with changes here and there, is likewise the program of the agricultural proletariat.

The peasants (farmers) represent another class: they are the petty bourgeoisie of the village. The petty bourgeoisie is made up of various layers, from the semiproletarian to the exploiter elements. In accordance with this, the political task of the industrial proletariat is to carry the class struggle into the country. Only thus will it be able to draw a dividing line between its allies and its enemies.

The peculiarities of national development of each country find their queerest expression in the status of farmers and, to some extent, of the urban petty bourgeoisie (artisans and shopkeepers). These classes, no matter how numerically strong they may be, essentially are representative survivals of pre-capitalist forms of production. The sections of the Fourth International should work out with all possible concreteness a program of transitional demands concerning the peasants (farmers) and urban petty bourgeoisie, in conformity with the conditions of each country. The advanced workers should learn to give clear and concrete answers to the questions put by their future allies.

While the farmer remains an "independent" petty producer, he is in need of cheap credit, of agricultural machines and fertilizer at prices he can afford to pay, favorable conditions of transport, and conscientious organization of the market for his agricultural products. But the banks, the trusts, the merchants rob the farmer from every side. Only the farmers themselves, with the help of the workers, can curb this robbery. *Committees elected by small farmers* should make their appearance on the national scene and, jointly with the workers' committees and committees of bank employees, take into their hands control of transport, credit, and mercantile operations affecting agriculture.

By falsely citing the "excessive" demands of the workers the big bourgeoisie skillfully transforms the question of *commodity prices* into a wedge to be driven between the workers and farmers and between the workers and the petty bourgeoisie of the cities. The peasant, artisan, small merchant, unlike the industrial worker, office and civil service employee, cannot demand a wage increase corresponding to the increase in prices. The official struggle of the government with high prices is only a deception of the masses. But the farmers, artisans, and merchants, in their capacity of consumers, can step into the politics of price-fixing shoulder to shoulder with the workers. To the capitalist's lamentations about costs of production, of transport and trade, the consumers answer: "Show us your books; we demand control over the fixing of prices." The organs of this control should be the *committees on prices*, made up of delegates from the factories, trade unions, cooperatives, farmers' organizations, the "little man" of the city, housewives, etc. By this means the workers will be able to prove to the farmers that the real reason for high prices is not high wages but the exorbitant profits of the capitalists and the overhead expenses of capitalist anarchy.

The program for the *nationalization of the land and collectivization of agriculture* should be so drawn that from its very basis it should exclude the possibility of expropriation of small farmers and their compulsory collectivization. The farmer will remain owner of his plot of land as long as he himself believes it possible or necessary. In order to rehabilitate the program of socialism in the eyes of the farmer, it is necessary to expose mercilessly the Stalinist methods of collectivization, which are dictated not by the interests of the farmers or workers but by the interests of the bureaucracy.

The expropriation of the expropriators likewise does not signify forcible confiscation of the property of artisans and shopkeepers. On the contrary, workers' control of banks and trusts—even more, the nationalization of these concerns—can create for the urban petty bourgeoisie incomparably more favorable conditions of credit purchase, and sale than is possible under the unchecked domination of the monopolies. Dependence upon private capital will be replaced by dependence upon the state, which will be the more attentive to the needs of its small co-workers and agents the more firmly the toilers themselves keep the state in their own hands.

The practical participation of the exploited farmers in the control of different fields of economy will allow them to decide for themselves whether or not it would be profitable for them to go over to collective working of the land—at what date and on what scale. Industrial workers should consider themselves duty-bound to show farmers every cooperation in traveling this road: through the trade unions, factory committees, and, above all, through a workers' and farmers' government.

The alliance proposed by the proletariat—not to the "middle classes" in general but to the exploited layers of the urban and rural petty bourgeoisie, against all exploiters, including those of the "middle classes"—can be based not on compulsion but only on free consent, which should be consolidated in a special "contract." This "contract" is the program of transitional demands voluntarily accepted by both sides.

## The Struggle Against Imperialism and War

The whole world outlook, and consequently also the inner political life of individual countries, is overcast by the threat of world war. Already the imminent catastrophe sends violent ripples of apprehension through the very broadest masses of mankind.

The Second International repeats its infamous politics of 1914 with all the greater assurance since today it is the Comintern which plays first fiddle in chauvinism. As quickly as the danger of war assumed concrete outline, the Stalinists, outstripping the bourgeois and petty-bourgeois pacifists by far, became blatant haranguers for so-called "national defense." The revolutionary struggle against war thus rests fully on the shoulders of the Fourth International.

The Bolshevik-Leninist policy regarding this question, formulated in the thesis of the International Secretariat (*War and the Fourth International*, 1934), preserves all of its force today.

In the next period a revolutionary party will depend for success primarily on its policy on the question of war. A correct policy is composed of two elements: an uncompromising attitude on imperialism and its wars, and the ability to base one's program on the experience of the masses themselves.

The bourgeoisie and its agents use the war question, more than any other, to deceive the people by means of abstractions, general formulas, lame phraseology: "neutrality," "collective defense," "arming for the defense of peace," "struggle against fascism," and so on. All such formulas reduce themselves in the end to the fact that the war question, i.e., the fate of the people, is left in the hands of the imperialists, their governing staffs, their diplomacy, their generals, with all their intrigues and plots against the people.

The Fourth International rejects with abhorrence all such abstractions which play the same role in the democratic camp as in the fascist: "honor," "blood," "race." But abhorrence is not enough. It is imperative to help the masses discern, by means of verifying criteria, slogans and demands, the concrete essence of fraudulent abstractions.

"*Disarmament*"?—But the entire question revolves around who will disarm whom. The only disarmament which can avert or end war is the disarmament of the bourgeoisie by the workers. But to disarm the bourgeoisie, the workers must arm themselves.

"*Neutrality*"?—But the proletariat is nothing like neutral in the war between Japan and China, or a war between Germany and the USSR. "Then what is meant is the defense of China and the USSR?" Of course! But not by the imperialists who will strangle both China and the USSR.

"*Defense of the Fatherland*"?—But by this abstraction, the bourgeoisie understands the defense of its profits and plunder. We stand ready to defend the fatherland from foreign capitalists, if we first bind our own (capitalists) hand and foot and hinder them from attacking foreign fatherlands; if the workers and the farmers of our country become its real masters; if the wealth of the country be transferred from the hands of a tiny minority to the hands of the people; if the army becomes a weapon of the exploited instead of the exploiters.

It is necessary to interpret these fundamental ideas by breaking them up into more concrete and partial ones, dependent upon the course of events and the orientation of thought of the masses. In addition, it is necessary to differentiate strictly between the pacifism of the diplomat, professor, journalist, and the pacifism of the carpenter, agricultural worker, and the charwoman. In one case, pacifism is a screen for imperialism; in the other, it is the confused expression of distrust in imperialism. When the small farmer or worker speaks about the defense of the fatherland, he means defense of his home, his family and other similar families from invasion, bombs and poison gas. The capitalist and his journalist understand by the defense of the fatherland the seizure of colonies and markets, the predatory increase of the "national" share of world income. Bourgeois pacifism and patriotism are shot through with deceit. In the pacifism and even patriotism of the oppressed, there are elements which reflect on the one hand a hatred of destructive war, and on the other a clinging to what they believe to be their own good—elements which we must know how to seize upon in order to draw the requisite conclusions.

Using these considerations as its point of departure, the Fourth International supports every, even if insufficient, demand, if it can draw the masses to a certain extent into active politics, awaken their criticism and strengthen their control over the machinations of the bourgeoisie.

From this point of view, our American section, for example, critically supports the proposal for establishing a referendum on the question of declaring war. No democratic reform, it is understood, can by itself prevent the rulers from provoking war when they wish it. It is necessary to give frank warning of this. But not withstanding the illusions of the masses in regard to the proposed referendum, their support of it reflects the distrust felt by workers and farmers for the bourgeois government and Congress. Without supporting and without sparing illusions, it is necessary to support with all possible strength the progressive distrust of the exploited toward the exploiters. The more widespread the movement for the referendum becomes, the sooner will the bourgeois pacifists move away from it; the more completely will the betrayers of the Comintern be compromised; the more acute will distrust of the imperialists become.

From this viewpoint, it is necessary to advance the demand: electoral rights for men and women beginning with age of eighteen. Those who will be called upon to die for the fatherland tomorrow should have the right to vote today. The struggle against war must first of all begin with the *revolutionary mobilization of the youth.*

Light must be shed upon the problem of war from all angles, hinging upon the side from which it will confront the masses at a given moment.

War is a gigantic commercial enterprise, especially for the war industry. The "60 Families" are therefore first-line patriots and the chief provocateurs of war. *Workers' control of war industries* is the first step in the struggle against the "manufacturers" of war.

To the slogan of the reformists: *a tax on military profits*, we counterpose the slogans: *confiscation of military profits* and *expropriation of the traffickers in war industries.* Where military industry is "nationalized," as in France, the slogan of *workers' control* preserves its full strength. The proletariat has as little confidence in the government of the bourgeoisie as in an individual capitalist.

*Not one man and not one penny for the bourgeois government.*

*Not an armaments program but a program of useful public works!*

*Complete independence of workers' organizations from military-police control!*

Once and for all we must tear from the hands of the greedy and merciless imperialist clique, scheming behind the backs of the people, the disposition of the people's fate. In accordance with this, we demand:

*Complete abolition of secret diplomacy;*

*All treaties and agreements to be made accessible to all workers and farmers;*

*Military training and arming of workers and farmers under direct control of workers' and farmers' committees;*

*Creation of military schools for the training of commanders among the toilers, chosen by workers' organizations;*

*Substitution for the standing army of a people's militia, indissolubly linked up with factories, mines, farms, etc.*

Imperialist war is the continuation and sharpening of the predatory politics of the bourgeoisie. The struggle of the proletariat against war is the continuation and sharpening of its class struggle. The beginning of war alters the situation and partially the means of struggle between the classes, but not the aim and basic course. The imperialist bourgeoisie dominates the world. In its basic character the approaching war will therefore be an imperialist war. The fundamental content of the politics of the international proletariat will consequently be a struggle against imperialism and its war. In this struggle the basic principle is: "the chief enemy is in *your own* country" or "the defeat of *your own* (imperialist) government is the lesser evil."

But not all countries of the world are imperialist countries. On the contrary, the majority are victims of imperialism. Some of the colonial or semi colonial countries will undoubtedly attempt to utilize the war in order to east off the yoke of slavery. Their war will be not imperialist but liberating. It will be the duty of the international proletariat to aid the oppressed countries in their war against oppressors. The same duty applies in regard to aiding the USSR, or whatever other workers' government might arise before the war or during the war. The defeat of *every* imperialist government in the struggle with the workers' state or with a colonial country is the lesser evil.

The workers of imperialist countries, however, cannot help an anti-imperialist country through their own government, no matter what might be the diplomatic and military relations between the two countries at a given moment. If the governments find themselves in a temporary and, by the very essence of the matter, unreliable alliance, then the proletariat of the imperialist country continues to remain in class opposition to its own government and supports the non-imperialist "ally" through its *own* methods, i.e., through the methods of the international class struggle (agitation not only against their perfidious allies, but also in favor of a workers' state in a colonial country; boycott, strikes, in one case; rejection of boycott and strikes in another case, etc.)

In supporting the colonial country or the USSR in a war, the proletariat does not in the slightest degree solidarize either with the bourgeois government of the colonial country or with the Thermidorian bureaucracy of the USSR. On the contrary, it maintains full political independence from the one as from the other. Giving aid in a just and progressive war, the revolutionary proletariat wins the sympathy of the workers in the colonies and in the USSR, strengthens there the authority and influence of the Fourth International, and increases its ability to help overthrow the bourgeois government in the colonial country, the reactionary bureaucracy in the USSR.

At the beginning of the war the sections of the Fourth International will inevitably feel themselves isolated: every war takes the national masses unawares and impels them to the side of the government apparatus. The internationalists will have to swim against the stream. However, the devastation and misery brought about by the new war, which in the first months will far outstrip the bloody horrors of 1914–18, will quickly prove sobering. The discontents of the masses and their revolt will grow by leaps and bounds. The sections of the Fourth International will be found at the head of the revolutionary tide. The program of transitional demands will gain burning actuality. The problem of the conquest of power by the proletariat will loom in full stature.

Before exhausting or drowning mankind in blood, capitalism befouls the world atmosphere with the poisonous vapors of national and race hatred. *Anti-Semitism* today is one of the most malignant convulsions of capitalism's death agony.

An uncompromising disclosure of the roots of race prejudice and all forms and shades of national arrogance and chauvinism, particularly anti-Semitism, should become part of the daily work of all sections of the Fourth International, as the most important part of the struggle against imperialism and war. Our basic slogan remains: Workers of the World Unite!

# II

## Workers' and Farmers' Government

This formula, "workers' and farmers' government," first appeared in the agitation of the Bolsheviks in 1917 and was definitely accepted after the October Revolution. In the final instance it represented nothing more than the popular designation for the already established dictatorship of the proletariat. The significance of this designation comes mainly from the fact that it underscored the idea of an *alliance between the proletariat and the peasantry* upon which the Soviet power rests.

When the Comintern of the epigones tried to revive the formula buried by history of the "democratic dictatorship of the proletariat and peasantry," it gave to the formula of the "workers' and peasants' government" a completely different, purely "democratic," i.e., bourgeois content, *counterposing* it to the dictatorship of the proletariat. The Bolshevik-Leninists resolutely rejected the slogan of the "workers' and peasants' government" in the bourgeois-democratic version. They affirmed then and affirm now that. when the party of the proletariat refuses to step beyond bourgeois democratic limits, its alliance with the peasantry is simply turned into a support for capital, as was the case with the Mensheviks and the Social Revolutionaries in 1917, with the Chinese Communist Party in 1925–27, and as is now the case with the "People's Front" in Spain, France and other countries.

From April to September 1917, the Bolsheviks demanded that the SRs and Mensheviks break with the liberal bourgeoisie and take power into their own hands. Under this provision the Bolshevik Party promised the Mensheviks and the SRs, as the petty-bourgeois representatives of the workers and peasants, its revolutionary aid against the bourgeoisie, categorically refusing, however, either to enter into the government of the Mensheviks and SRs or to carry political responsibility for it. If the Mensheviks and SRs had actually broken with the Cadets (liberals) and with foreign imperialism, then the "workers' and peasants' government" created by them could only have hastened and facilitated the establishment of the dictatorship of the proletariat. But it was exactly because of this that the leadership of petty-bourgeois democracy resisted with all possible strength the establishment of its own government. The experience of Russia demonstrated, and the experience of Spain and France once again confirms, that even under very favorable conditions the parties of petty-bourgeois democracy (SRs, Social Democrats, Stalinists, Anarchists) are incapable of creating a government of workers and peasants, that is, a government independent of the bourgeoisie.

Nevertheless, the demand of the Bolsheviks, addressed to the Mensheviks and the SRs: "Break with the bourgeoisie, take the power into your own hands!" had for the masses tremendous educational significance. The obstinate unwillingness of the Mensheviks and SRs to take power, so dramatically exposed during the July Days, definitely doomed them before mass opinion and prepared the victory of the Bolsheviks.

The central task of the Fourth International consists in freeing the proletariat from the old leadership, whose conservatism is in complete contradiction to the catastrophic eruptions of disintegrating capitalism and represents the chief obstacle to historical progress. The chief accusation which the Fourth International advances against the traditional organizations of the proletariat is the fact that they do not wish to tear themselves away from the political semicorpse of the bourgeoisie. Under these conditions the demand, systematically addressed to the old leadership: "Break with the bourgeoisie, take the power!" is an extremely important weapon for exposing the treacherous character of the parties and organizations of the Second, Third and Amsterdam Internationals. The slogan, "workers' and farmers' government," is thus acceptable to us only in the sense that it had in 1917 with the Bolsheviks, i.e., as an antibourgeois and anticapitalist slogan, but in no case in that "democratic" sense which later the epigones gave it, transforming it from a bridge to Socialist revolution into the chief barrier upon its path.

Of all parties and organizations which base themselves on the workers and peasants and speak in their name, we demand that they break politically from the bourgeoisie and enter upon the road of struggle for the workers' and farmers' government. On this road we promise them full support against capitalist reaction. At the same time, we indefatigably develop agitation around those transitional demands which should in our opinion form the program of the workers' and farmers' government.

Is the creation of such a government by the traditional workers' organizations possible? Past experience shows, as has already been stated, that this is, to say the least, highly improbable. However, one cannot categorically deny in advance the theoretical possibility that, under the influence of completely exceptional circumstances (war, defeat, financial crash, mass revolutionary pressure, etc.), the petty-bourgeois parties, including the Stalinists, may go further than they wish along the road to a break with the bourgeoisie. In any case one thing is not to be doubted: even if this highly improbable variant somewhere, at some time, becomes a reality and the "workers' and farmers' government" in the above-mentioned sense is established in fact, it would represent merely a short episode on the road to the actual dictatorship of the proletariat.

However, there is no need to indulge in guesswork. The agitation around the slogan of a workers' and farmers' government preserves under all conditions a tremendous educational value. And not accidentally. This generalized slogan proceeds entirely along the line of the political development of our epoch (the bankruptcy and decomposition of the old bourgeois parties, the downfall of democracy, the growth of fascism, the accelerated drive of the workers toward more active and aggressive politics). Each of the transitional demands should, therefore, lead to one and the same political conclusion: the workers need to break with all traditional parties of the bourgeoisie in order, jointly with the farmers, to establish their own power.

It is impossible in advance to foresee what will be the concrete stages of the revolutionary mobilization of the masses. The sections of the Fourth International should critically orient themselves at each new stage and advance such slogans as will aid the striving of the workers for independent politics, deepen the class character of these politics, destroy reformist and pacifist illusions, strengthen the connection of the vanguard with the masses, and prepare the revolutionary conquest of power.

## Soviets

*Factory committees*, as already stated, are elements of dual power inside the factory. Consequently, their existence is possible only under conditions of increasing pressure by the masses. This is likewise true of special mass groupings for the struggle *against war*, of the *committees on prices*, and all other new centers of the movement, the very appearance of which bears witness to the fact that the class struggle has overflowed the limits of the traditional organizations of the proletariat.

These new organs and centers, however, will soon begin to feel their lack of cohesion and their insufficiency. Not one of the transitional demands can be fully met under the conditions of preserving the bourgeois regime. At the same time, the deepening of the social crisis will increase not only the sufferings of the masses but also their impatience, persistence and pressure. Ever new layers of the oppressed will raise their heads and come forward with their demands. Millions of toilworn "little men," to whom the reformist leaders never gave a thought, will begin to pound insistently on the doors of the workers' organizations. The unemployed will join the movement. The agricultural workers, the ruined and semiruined farmers, the oppressed of the cities, the women workers, housewives, proletarianized layers of the intelligentsia—all of these will seek unity and leadership.

How are the different demands and forms of struggle to be harmonized, even if only within the limits of one city? History has already answered this question: through *soviets*. These will unite the representatives of all the fighting groups. For this purpose, no one has yet proposed a different form of organization; indeed, it would hardly be possible to think up a better one. Soviets are not limited to an *a priori* party program. They throw open their doors to all the exploited. Through these doors pass representatives of all strata, drawn into the general current of the struggle. The organization, broadening out together with the movement, is renewed again and again in its womb. All political currents of the proletariat can struggle for leadership of the soviets on the basis of the widest democracy. The slogan of *soviets*, therefore, crowns the program of transitional demands.

Soviets can arise only at the time when the mass movement enters into an openly revolutionary stage. From the first moment of their appearance, the soviets, acting as a pivot around which millions of toilers are united in their struggle against the exploiters, become competitors and opponents of local authorities and then of the central government. If the factory committee creates a dual power in the factory, then the soviets initiate a period of dual power in the country.

Dual power in its turn is the culminating point of the transitional period. Two regimes, the bourgeois and the proletarian, are irreconcilably opposed to each other. Conflict between them is inevitable. The fate of society depends on the outcome. Should the revolution be defeated, the fascist dictatorship of the bourgeoisie will follow. In the case of victory, the power of the soviets, that is, the dictatorship of the proletariat and the socialist reconstruction of society, will arise.

## Backward Countries and the Program of Transitional Demands

Colonial and semicolonial countries are backward countries by their very essence. But backward countries are part of a world dominated by imperialism. Their development, therefore, has a *combined* character: the most primitive economic forms are combined with the last word in capitalist technique and culture. In like manner are defined the political strivings of the proletariat of backward countries: the struggle for the most elementary achievements of national independence and bourgeois democracy is combined with the socialist struggle against world imperialism. Democratic slogans, transitional demands and the problems of the socialist revolution are not divided into separate historical epochs in this struggle, but stem directly from one another. The Chinese proletariat had barely begun to organize trade unions before it had to provide for soviets. In this sense, the present program is completely applicable to colonial and semi-colonial countries, at least to those where the proletariat has become capable of carrying on independent politics.

The central task of the colonial and semicolonial countries is the *agrarian revolution*, i.e., liquidation of feudal heritages, and *national independence*, i.e., the overthrow of the imperialist yoke. Both tasks are closely linked with each other.

It is impossible merely to reject the democratic program; it is imperative that in the struggle the masses outgrow it. The slogan for a national (or constituent) assembly preserves its full force for such countries as China or India. This slogan must be indissolubly tied up with the problem of national liberation and agrarian reform. As a primary step, the workers must be armed with this democratic program. Only they will be able to summon and unite the farmers. On the basis of the revolutionary democratic program, it is necessary to oppose the workers to the "national" bourgeoisie. Then, at a certain stage in the mobilization of the masses under the slogans of revolutionary democracy, soviets can and should arise. Their historical role in each given period, particularly their relation to the national assembly, will be determined by the political level of the proletariat, the bond between them and the peasantry, and the character of the proletarian party policies. Sooner or later, the soviets should overthrow bourgeois democracy. Only they are capable of bringing the democratic revolution to a conclusion and likewise opening an era of socialist revolution.

The relative weight of the individual democratic and transitional demands in the proletariat's struggle, their mutual ties and their order of presentation, is determined by the peculiarities and specific conditions of each backward country and to a considerable extent by the *degree* of its backwardness. Nevertheless, the general trend of revolutionary development in all backward countries can be determined by the formula of the *permanent revolution* in the sense definitely imparted to it by the three revolutions in Russia (1905, February 1917, October 1917).

The Comintern has provided backward countries with a classic example of how it is possible to ruin a powerful and promising revolution. During the stormy mass upsurge in China in 1925–27, the Comintern failed to advance the slogan for a national assembly, and at the same time forbade the creation of soviets. (The bourgeois party, the Kuomintang, was to replace, according to Stalin's plan, both the national assembly and soviets.) After the masses had been smashed by the Kuomintang, the Comintern organized a caricature of a soviet in Canton. Following the inevitable collapse of the Canton uprising, the Comintern took the road of guerrilla warfare, of peasant soviets, with complete passivity on the part of the industrial proletariat. Landing thus in a blind alley, the Comintern took advantage of the Sino-Japanese War to liquidate "Soviet China" with a stroke of the pen, subordinating not only the peasant "Red Army" but also the so-called "Communist" Party to the identical Kuomintang, i.e., the bourgeoisie.

Having betrayed the international proletarian revolution for the sake of friendship with the "democratic" slavemasters, the Comintern could not help betraying simultaneously also the struggle for liberation of the colonial masses, and, indeed, with even greater cynicism than did the Second International before it. One of the tasks of People's Front and "national defense" politics is to turn hundreds of millions of the colonial population into cannon fodder for "democratic" imperialism. The banner on which is emblazoned the struggle for the liberation of the colonial and semicolonial peoples, i.e., a good half of mankind, has definitely passed into the hands of the Fourth International.

## The Program of Transitional Demands in Fascist Countries

It is a far cry today from the time when the strategists of the Comintern announced the victory of Hitler as being merely a step toward the victory of Thälmann. Thälmann has been in Hitler's prisons now for more than five years. Mussolini has held Italy enchained by fascism for more than sixteen years. Throughout this time, the parties of the Second and Third Internationals have been impotent, not only to conduct a mass movement, but even to create a serious illegal organization, even to some extent comparable to the Russian revolutionary parties during the epoch of tsarism.

Not the least reason exists for explaining these failures by reference to the power of fascist ideology. (Essentially, Mussolini never advanced any sort of ideology.) Hitler's "ideology" never seriously gripped the workers. Those layers of the population which at one time were intoxicated with fascism, i.e., chiefly the middle classes, have had enough time in which to sober up. The fact that a somewhat perceptible opposition is limited to Protestant and Catholic church circles is not explained by the might of the semidelirious and semicharlatan theories of "race" and "blood," but by the terrific collapse of the ideologies of democracy, Social Democracy and the Comintern.

After the massacre of the Paris Commune, black reaction reigned for nearly eight years. After the defeat of the 1905 Russian revolution, the toiling masses remained in a stupor for almost as long a period. But in both instances the phenomenon was only one of physical defeat, conditioned by the relationship of forces. In Russia, in addition, it concerned an almost virgin proletariat. The Bolshevik faction had at that time not celebrated even its third birthday. It is completely otherwise in Germany where the leadership came from powerful parties, one of which had existed for seventy years, the other almost fifteen. Both these parties, with millions of voters behind them, were morally paralyzed before the battle and capitulated without a battle. History has recorded no parallel catastrophe. The German proletariat was not smashed by the enemy in battle. It was crushed by the cowardice, baseness, and perfidy of its own parties. Small wonder then that it has lost faith in everything in which it had been accustomed to believe for almost three generations. Hitler's victory in turn strengthened Mussolini.

The protracted failure of revolutionary work in Spain or Germany is but the reward for the criminal politics of the Social Democracy and the Comintern. Illegal work needs not only the sympathy of the masses but the conscious enthusiasm of its advanced strata. But can enthusiasm possibly be expected for historically bankrupt organizations? The majority of those who come forth as émigré leaders are either demoralized to the very marrow of their bones, agents of the Kremlin and the GPU, or Social Democratic ex-ministers, who dream that the workers by some sort of miracle, will return them to their lost posts. Is it possible to imagine even for a minute these gentlemen in the role of future leaders of the "anti-fascist" revolution?

And events on the world arena—the smashing of the Austrian workers, the defeat of the Spanish Revolution, the degeneration of the Soviet state—could not give aid to a revolutionary upsurge in Italy and Germany. Since for political information the German and Italian workers depend in great measure upon the radio, it is possible to say with assurance that the Moscow radio station, combining Thermidorian lies with stupidity and insolence, has become the most powerful factor in the demoralization of the workers in the totalitarian states. In this respect as in others, Stalin acts merely as Goebbels's assistant.

At the same time, the class antagonisms which brought about the victory of fascism, continuing their work under fascism too, are gradually undermining it. The masses are more dissatisfied than ever. Hundreds and thousands of self-sacrificing workers, in spite of everything, continue to carry on revolutionary mole-work. A new generation, which has not directly experienced the shattering of old traditions and high hopes, has come to the fore. Irresistibly, the molecular preparation of the proletarian revolution proceeds beneath the heavy totalitarian tombstone. But, for concealed energy to flare into open revolt, it is necessary that the vanguard of the proletariat find new perspectives, a new program, and a new, unblemished banner.

Herein lies the chief handicap. It is extremely difficult for workers in fascist countries to make a choice of a new program. A program is verified by experience. And it is precisely experience in mass movements which is lacking in countries of totalitarian despotism. It is very likely that a genuine proletarian success in one of the "democratic" countries will be necessary to give impetus to the revolutionary movement on fascist territory. A similar effect is possible by means of a financial or military catastrophe. At present, it is imperative that primarily propagandistic, preparatory work be carried on which will yield large-scale results only in the future. One thing can be stated with conviction even at this point: once it breaks through, the revolutionary wave in fascist countries will immediately be a grandiose sweep and under no circumstances will stop short at the experiment of resuscitating some sort of Weimar corpse.

It is from this point onward that an uncompromising divergence begins between the Fourth International and the old parties, which outlive their bankruptcy. The émigré "People's Front" is the most malignant and perfidious variety of all possible People's Fronts. Essentially, it signifies the impotent longing for coalition with a nonexistent liberal bourgeoisie. Had it met with success, it would simply have prepared a series of new defeats of the Spanish type for the proletariat. A merciless exposure of the theory and practice of the "People's Front" is therefore the first condition for a revolutionary struggle against fascism.

Of course, this does not mean that the Fourth International rejects democratic slogans as a means of mobilizing the masses against fascism. On the contrary, such slogans at certain moments can play a serious role. But the formulae of democracy (freedom of press, the right to unionize, etc.) mean for us only incidental or episodic slogans in the independent movement of the proletariat and not a democratic noose fastened to the neck of the proletariat by the bourgeoisie's agents (Spain!). As soon as the movement assumes something of a mass character, the democratic slogans will be intertwined with the transitional ones; factory committees, it may be supposed, will appear before the old routinists rush from their chancelleries to organize trade unions; soviets will cover Germany before a new Constituent Assembly will gather in Weimar. The same applies to Italy and the rest of the totalitarian and semitotalitarian countries.

Fascism plunged these countries into political barbarism. But it did not change their social structure. Fascism is a tool in the hands of finance capital and not of feudal landowners. A revolutionary program should base itself on the dialectics of the class struggle, obligatory also to fascist countries, and not on the psychology of terrified bankrupts. The Fourth International rejects with disgust the ways of political masquerade which impelled the Stalinists, the former heroes of the "Third Period," to appear in turn behind the masks of Catholics, Protestants, Jews, German nationalists, liberals—only in order to hide their own unattractive faces. The Fourth International always and everywhere appears under its own banner. It proposes its own program openly to the proletariat in fascist countries. The advanced workers of all the world are already firmly convinced that the overthrow of Mussolini, Hitler and their agents and imitators will occur only under the leadership of the Fourth International.

## The USSR and Problems of the Transitional Epoch

The Soviet Union emerged from the October Revolution as a workers' state. State ownership of the means of production, a necessary prerequisite to socialist development, opened up the possibility of rapid growth of the productive forces. But the apparatus of the workers' state underwent a complete degeneration at the same time: it was transformed from a weapon of the working class into a weapon of bureaucratic violence against the working class, and more and more a weapon for the sabotage of the country's economy. The bureaucratization of a backward and isolated workers' state and the transformation of the bureaucracy into an all-powerful privileged caste constitute the most convincing refutation—not only theoretically, but this time practically—of the theory of socialism in one country.

The USSR thus embodies terrific contradictions. But it still remains a *degenerated workers' state*. Such is the social diagnosis. The political prognosis has an alternative character: either the bureaucracy, becoming ever more the organ of the world bourgeoisie in the workers' state, will overthrow the new forms of property and plunge the country back to capitalism; or the working class will crush the bureaucracy and open the way to socialism.

To the sections of the Fourth International, the Moscow Trials came not as a surprise and not as a result of the personal madness of the Kremlin dictator, but as the legitimate offspring of the Thermidor. They grew out of the unbearable conflicts within the Soviet bureaucracy itself, which in turn mirror the contradictions between the bureaucracy and the people, as well as the deepening antagonisms among the "people" themselves. The bloody "fantastic" nature of the trials gives the measure of the intensity of the contradictions and, by the same token, predicts the approach of the denouement.

The public utterances of former foreign representatives of the Kremlin, who refused to return to Moscow, irrefutably confirm in their own way that all shades of political thought are to be found among the bureaucracy: from genuine Bolshevism (Ignace Reiss) to complete fascism (F. Butenko). The revolutionary elements within the bureaucracy, only a small minority, reflect, passively it is true, the socialist interests of the proletariat. The fascist, counterrevolutionary elements, growing uninterruptedly, express with even greater consistency the interests of world imperialism. These candidates for the role of compradors consider, not without reason, that the new ruling layer can insure their positions of privilege only through rejection of nationalization, collectivization and monopoly of foreign trade in the name of the assimilation of "Western civilization," i.e., capitalism. Between these two poles, there are intermediate, diffused Menshevik-SR-liberal tendencies which gravitate toward bourgeois democracy.

Within the very ranks of that so-called "classless" society, there unquestionably exist groupings exactly similar to those in the bureaucracy, only less sharply expressed and in inverse proportions: conscious capitalist tendencies distinguish mainly the prosperous part of the collective farms (*kolkhozi*) and are characteristic of only a small minority of the population. But this layer provides itself with a wide base for petty-bourgeois tendencies of accumulating personal wealth at the expense of general poverty, and are consciously encouraged by the bureaucracy.

Atop this system of mounting antagonisms, trespassing ever more on the social equilibrium, the Thermidorian oligarchy, today reduced mainly to Stalin's Bonapartist clique, hangs on by terroristic methods. The latest judicial frame-ups were aimed as a blow *against the left*. This is true also of the mopping up of the leaders of the Right Opposition, because the Right group of the old Bolshevik Party, seen from the viewpoint of the bureaucracy's interests and tendencies, represented a *left* danger. The fact that the Bonapartist clique, likewise in fear of its own right allies of the type of Butenko, is forced in the interests of self-preservation to execute the generation of Old Bolsheviks almost to a man, offers indisputable testimony of the vitality of revolutionary traditions among the masses as well as of their growing discontent.

Petty-bourgeois democrats of the West, having but yesterday assayed the Moscow Trials as unalloyed gold, today repeat insistently that there is "neither Trotskyism nor Trotskyists within the USSR." They fail to explain, however, why all the purges are conducted under the banner of a struggle with precisely this danger. If we are to examine "Trotskyism" as a finished program, and, even more to the point, as an organization, then unquestionably "Trotskyism" is extremely weak in the USSR. However, its indestructible force stems from the fact that it expresses not only revolutionary tradition, but also today's actual opposition of the Russian working class. The social hatred stored up by the workers against the bureaucracy—this is precisely what from the viewpoint of the Kremlin clique constitutes "Trotskyism." It fears with a deathly and thoroughly well-grounded fear the bond between the deep but inarticulate indignation of the workers and the organization of the Fourth International.

The extermination of the generation of Old Bolsheviks and of the revolutionary representatives of the middle and young generations has acted to disrupt the political equilibrium still more in favor of the right, bourgeois wing of the bureaucracy and of its allies throughout the land. From them, i.e., from the right, we can expect ever more determined attempts in the next period to revise the socialist character of the USSR and bring it closer in pattern to "Western civilization" in its fascist form.

From this perspective, impelling concreteness is imparted to the question of the "defense of the USSR." If tomorrow the bourgeois-fascist grouping, the "faction of Butenko," so to speak, should attempt the conquest of power, the "faction of Reiss" inevitably would align itself on the opposite side of the barricades. Although it would find itself temporarily the ally of Stalin, it would nevertheless defend not the Bonapartist clique but the social base of the USSR, i.e., the property wrenched away from the capitalists and transformed into state property. Should the "faction of Butenko" prove to be in alliance with Hitler, then the "faction of Reiss" would defend the USSR from military intervention, inside the country as well as on the world arena. Any other course would be a betrayal.

Although it is thus impermissible to deny in advance the possibility, in strictly defined instances, of a "united front" with the Thermidorian section of the bureaucracy against open attack by capitalist counter-revolution, the chief political task in the USSR still remains the *overthrow of this same Thermidorian bureaucracy*. Each day added to its domination helps rot the foundations of the socialist elements of the economy and increases the chances for capitalist restoration. It is in precisely this direction that the Comintern moves as the agent and accomplice of the Stalinist clique in strangling the Spanish Revolution and demoralizing the international proletariat.

As in fascist countries, the chief strength of the bureaucracy lies not in itself but in the disillusionment of the masses, in their lack of a new perspective. As in fascist countries, from which Stalin's *political* apparatus does not differ, save in more unbridled savagery, only preparatory propagandistic work is possible today in the USSR. As in fascist countries, the impetus to the Soviet workers' revolutionary upsurge will probably be given by events outside the country. The struggle against the Comintern on the world arena is the most important part today of the struggle against the Stalinist dictatorship. There are many signs that the Comintern's downfall, because it does not have a *direct* base in the GPU, will precede the downfall of the Bonapartist clique and the Thermidorian bureaucracy as a whole.

A fresh upsurge of the revolution in the USSR will undoubtedly begin under the banner of the struggle against *social inequality* and *political oppression*. Down with the privileges of the bureaucracy! Down with Stakhanovism! Down with the Soviet aristocracy and its ranks and orders! Greater equality of wages for all forms of labor!

The struggle for the freedom of the trade unions and the factory committees, for the right of assembly and freedom of the press, will unfold in the struggle for the regeneration and development of *Soviet democracy*.

The bureaucracy replaced the soviets as class organs with the fiction of universal electoral rights—in the style of Hitler-Goebbels. It is necessary to return to the soviets not only their free democratic form but also their class content. As once the bourgeoisie and kulaks were not permitted to enter the soviets, so now *it is necessary to drive the bureaucracy and the new aristocracy out of the soviets*. In the soviets there is room only for representatives of the workers, rank-and-file collective farmers, peasants, and Red Army men.

Democratization of the soviets is impossible without the *legalization of soviet parties*. The workers and peasants themselves by their own free vote will indicate what parties they recognize as soviet parties.

A revision of *planned economy* from top to bottom in the interests of producers and consumers! Factory committees should be returned the right to control production. A democratically organized consumers' cooperative should control the quality and price of products.

Reorganization of the *collective farms* in accordance with the will and in the interests of the workers there engaged!

The reactionary *international policy* of the bureaucracy should be replaced by the policy of proletarian internationalism. The complete diplomatic correspondence of the Kremlin to be published. *Down with secret diplomacy!*

All political trials, staged by the Thermidorian bureaucracy, to be reviewed in the light of complete publicity and controversial openness and integrity. Only the victorious revolutionary uprising of the oppressed masses can revive the Soviet regime and guarantee its further development toward socialism. There is but one party capable of leading the Soviet masses to insurrection—the party of the Fourth International!

*Down with the bureaucratic gang of Cain-Stalin!*
*Long live Soviet democracy!*
*Long live the international socialist revolution!*


## Against Opportunism and Unprincipled Revisionism

The politics of Léon Blum's party in France demonstrate anew that reformists are incapable of learning anything from even the most tragic lessons of history. French Social Democracy slavishly copies the politics of German Social Democracy and goes to meet the same end. Within a few decades the Second International intertwined itself with the bourgeois democratic regime, became, in fact, a part of it, and is rotting away together with it.

The Third International has taken to the road of reformism at a time when the crisis of capitalism definitely placed the proletarian revolution on the order of the day. The Comintern's policy in Spain and China today—the policy of cringing before the "democratic" and "national" bourgeoisie—demonstrates that the Comintern is likewise incapable of learning anything further or of changing. The bureaucracy which became a reactionary force in the USSR cannot play a revolutionary role on the world arena.

Anarcho-syndicalism in general has passed through the same kind of evolution. In France, the syndicalist bureaucracy of Léon Jouhaux has long since become a bourgeois agency in the working class. In Spain, anarcho-syndicalism shook off its ostensible revolutionism and became the fifth wheel in the chariot of bourgeois democracy.

Intermediate centrist organizations centered about the London Bureau represent merely "left" appendages of the Social Democracy or of the Comintern. They have displayed a complete inability to make head or tail of the political situation and draw revolutionary conclusions from it. Their highest point was the Spanish POUM, which under revolutionary conditions proved completely incapable of following a revolutionary line.

The tragic defeats suffered by the world proletariat over a long period of years doomed the official organizations to yet greater conservatism and simultaneously sent disillusioned petty-bourgeois "revolutionists" in pursuit of "new ways." As always during epochs of reaction and decay, quacks and charlatans appear on all sides, desirous of revising the whole course of revolutionary thought. Instead of learning from the past, they "reject" it. Some discover the inconsistency of Marxism, others announce the downfall of Bolshevism. There are those who put responsibility upon revolutionary doctrine for the mistakes and crimes of those who betrayed it; others who curse the medicine because it does not guarantee an instantaneous and miraculous cure. The more daring promise to discover a panacea and, in anticipation, recommend the halting of the class struggle. A good many prophets of "new morals" are preparing to regenerate the labor movement with the help of ethical homeopathy. The majority of these apostles have succeeded in becoming themselves moral invalids before arriving on the field of battle. Thus, under the guise of "new ways," old recipes, long since buried in the archives of pre-Marxian socialism, are offered to the proletariat.

The Fourth International declares uncompromising war on the bureaucracies of the Second, Third, Amsterdam and Anarchosyndicalist Internationals, as on their centrist satellites; on reformism without reforms; on democracy in alliance with the GPU; on pacifism without peace; on anarchism in the service of the bourgeoisie; on "revolutionists" who live in deathly fear of revolution. All of these organizations are not pledges for the future, but decayed survivals of the past. The epoch of wars and revolutions will raze them to the ground.

The Fourth International does not search after and does not invent panaceas. It takes its stand completely on Marxism as the only revolutionary doctrine that enables one to understand reality, unearth the cause behind the defeats and consciously prepare for victory. The Fourth International continues the tradition of Bolshevism which first showed the proletariat how to conquer power. The Fourth International sweeps away the quacks, charlatans and unsolicited teachers of morals. In a society based upon exploitation, the highest morality is that of the social revolution. All methods are good which raise the class consciousness of the workers, their trust in their own forces, their readiness for self-sacrifice in the struggle. The impermissible methods are those which implant fear and submissiveness in the oppressed before their oppressors, which crush the spirit of protest and indignation or substitute for the will of the masses—the will of the leaders; for conviction—compulsion; for an analysis of reality—demagogy and frame-up. That is why Social Democracy, prostituting Marxism, and Stalinism—the antithesis of Bolshevism—are both mortal enemies of the proletarian revolution and its morals.

To face reality squarely; not to seek the line of least resistance; to call things by their right names; to speak the truth to the masses, no matter how bitter it may be; not to fear obstacles; to be true in little things as in big ones; to base one's program on the logic of the class struggle; to be bold when the hour for action arrives—these are the rules of the Fourth International. It has shown that it could swim against the stream. The approaching historical wave will raise it on its crest.

## Against Sectarianism

Under the influence of the betrayal by the historical organizations of the proletariat, certain sectarian moods and groupings of various kinds arise or are regenerated at the periphery of the Fourth International. At their base lies a refusal to struggle for partial and transitional demands, i.e., for the elementary interests and needs of the working masses, as they are today. Preparing for the revolution means, to the sectarians, convincing themselves of the superiority of socialism. They propose turning their backs on the "old" trade unions, i.e., to tens of millions of organized workers—as if the masses could somehow live outside of the conditions of the actual class struggle!

They remain indifferent to the inner struggle within reformist organizations—as if one could win the masses without intervening in their daily strife! They refuse to draw a distinction between bourgeois democracy and fascism—as if the masses could help but feel the difference on every hand!

Sectarians are capable of differentiating between but two colors: red and black. So as not to tempt themselves, they simplify reality. They refuse to draw a distinction between the fighting camps in Spain for the reason that both camps have a bourgeois character. For the same reason they consider it necessary to preserve "neutrality" in the war between Japan and China. They deny the principled difference between the USSR and the imperialist countries, and because of the reactionary policies of the Soviet bureaucracy they reject defense of the new forms of property, created by the October Revolution, against the onslaughts of imperialism. Incapable of finding access to the masses, they therefore zealously accuse the masses of inability to raise themselves to revolutionary ideas.

These sterile politicians generally have no need of a bridge in the form of transitional demands because they do not intend to cross over to the other shore. They simply dawdle in one place, satisfying themselves with a repetition of the same meager abstractions. Political events are for them an occasion for comment but not for action. Since sectarians, as in general every kind of blunderer and miracle-man, are toppled by reality at each step, they live in a state of perpetual exasperation, complaining about the "regime" and the "methods" and ceaselessly wallowing in small intrigues. In their own circles they customarily carry on a regime of despotism. The political prostration of sectarianism serves to complement, shadow-like, the prostration of opportunism, revealing no revolutionary vistas. In practical politics, sectarians unite with opportunists, particularly with centrists, every time in the struggle against Marxism.

Most of the sectarian groups and cliques, nourished on accidental crumbs from the table of the Fourth International, lead an "independent" organizational existence, with great pretensions but without the least chance for success. Bolshevik-Leninists, without waste of time, calmly leave these groups to their own fate. However, sectarian tendencies are to be found also in our own ranks and display a ruinous influence on the work of the individual sections. It is impossible to make any further compromise with them even for a single day. A correct policy regarding trade unions is a basic condition for adherence to the Fourth International. He who does not seek and does not find the road to the masses is not a fighter but a dead weight to the party. A program is formulated not for the editorial board or for the leaders of discussion clubs, but for the revolutionary action of millions. The cleansing of the ranks of the Fourth International of sectarianism and incurable sectarians is a primary condition for revolutionary success.

## Open the Road to the Woman Worker! Open the Road to the Youth!

The defeat of the Spanish Revolution engineered by its "leaders," the shameful bankruptcy of the People's Front in France, and the exposure of the Moscow juridical swindles—these three facts in their aggregate deal an irreparable blow to the Comintern and, incidentally, grave wounds to its allies: the Social Democrats and Anarchosyndicalists. This does not mean, of course, that the members of these organizations will immediately turn to the Fourth International. The older generation, having suffered terrible defeats, will leave the movement in significant numbers. In addition, the Fourth International is certainly not striving to become an asylum for revolutionary invalids, disillusioned bureaucrats and careerists. On the contrary, against a possible influx into our party of petty bourgeois elements, now reigning in the apparatus of the old organizations, strict preventive measures are necessary: a prolonged probationary period for those candidates who are not workers, especially former party bureaucrats: prevention from holding any responsible post for the first three years, etc. There is not and there will not be any place for careerism, the ulcer of the old internationals, in the Fourth International. Only those who wish to live for the movement, and not at the expense of the movement, will find access to us. The revolutionary workers should feel themselves to be the masters. The doors of our organization are wide open to them.

Of course, even among the workers who had at one time risen to the first ranks, there are not a few tired and disillusioned ones. They will remain, at least for the next period as bystanders. When a program or an organization wears out, the generation which carried it on its shoulders wears out with it. The movement is revitalized by the youth who are free of responsibility for the past. The Fourth International pays particular attention to the young generation of the proletariat. All of its policies strive to inspire the youth with belief in its own strength and in the future. Only the fresh enthusiasm and aggressive spirit of the youth can guarantee the preliminary successes in the struggle; only these successes can return the best elements of the older generation to the road of revolution. Thus it was, thus it will be.

Opportunist organizations by their very nature concentrate their chief attention on the top layers of the working class and therefore ignore both the youth and the women workers. The decay of capitalism, however, deals its heaviest blows to the woman as a wage earner and as a housewife. The sections of the Fourth International should seek bases of support among the most exploited layers of the working class; consequently, among the women workers. Here they will find

inexhaustible stores of devotion, selflessness and readiness to sacrifice.
*Down with the bureaucracy and careerism! Open the road to the youth! Turn to the woman worker!* These slogans are emblazoned on the banner of the Fourth International.

## Under the Banner of the Fourth International!

Skeptics ask: But has the moment for the creation of the Fourth International yet arrived? It is impossible, they say, to create an International "artificially"; it can arise only out of great events, etc., etc. All of these objections merely show that skeptics are no good for the building of a new International. They are good for scarcely anything at all.

The Fourth International has already arisen out of great events: the greatest defeats of the proletariat in history. The cause for these defeats is to be found in the degeneration and perfidy of the old leadership. The class struggle does not tolerate an interruption. The Third International, following the Second, is dead for purposes of revolution. Long live the Fourth International!

But has the time yet arrived to proclaim its creation? ... the skeptics are not quieted down. The Fourth International, we answer, has no need of being "proclaimed." It exists and it fights. Is it weak? Yes, its ranks are not numerous because it is still young. They are as yet chiefly cadres. But these cadres are pledges for the future. Outside these cadres there does not exist a single revolutionary current on this planet really meriting the name. If our international be still weak in numbers, it is strong in doctrine, program, tradition, in the incomparable tempering of its cadres. Who does not perceive this today, let him in the meantime stand aside. Tomorrow it will become more evident.

The Fourth International, already today, is deservedly hated by the Stalinists, Social Democrats, bourgeois liberals and fascists. There is not and there cannot be a place for it in any of the People's Fronts. It uncompromisingly gives battle to all political groupings tied to the apron-strings of the bourgeoisie. Its task—the abolition of capitalism's domination. Its aim—socialism. Its method—the proletarian revolution.

Without inner democracy—no revolutionary education. Without discipline—no revolutionary action. The internal structure of the Fourth International is based on the principles of *democratic centralism*: full freedom in discussion, complete unity in action.

The present crisis in human culture is the crisis in the proletarian leadership. The advanced workers, united in the Fourth International, show their class the way out of the crisis. They offer a program based on international experience in the struggle of the proletariat and of all the oppressed of the world for liberation. They offer a spotless banner.

Workers—men and women—of all countries, place yourselves under the banner of the Fourth International. It is the banner of your approaching victory!

# *Also from Wellred Books*

## ➤*Dialectics of Nature*
By Frederick Engels

Price: £10.00

Pub. Date: 2012
Format: Paperback
No. Pages: 410
ISBN: 9781900007450

'Dialectics of Nature' is one of the classics of Marxist literature. Engels, analysing the advances of science, demonstrates how dialectical materialism, the philosophy of Marxism, corresponds to the very way in which nature unfolds.

## *Bolshevism: The Road to Revolution* ◄
By Alan Woods

Price: £10.00

Pub. Date: 1999
Format: Paperback
No. Pages: 636
ISBN: 9781900007054

Using a wealth of primary sources, Alan Woods uncovers the fascinating growth and development of Bolshevism in pre-revolutionary Russia up to the seizure of power in October 1917.

## ➤*Reformism or Revolution*
By Alan Woods

Price: £10.00

Pub. Date: 2008
Format: Paperback
No. Pages: 410
ISBN: 9781900007337

Reformism or Revolution deals with practically every aspect of Marxism. It is a reaffirmation of the fundamental ideas of scientific socialism and a timely refutation of the current attempts by the revisionists to "improve" it by turning it into its opposite.

**Order online at www.wellredbooks.net
or send orders to PO Box 50525, London, E14 6WG.
Add £2.25 postage per book. Cheques payable to Wellred.**